Carl A. Grant has held the positions of Assistant Professor of Education at the University of Wisconsin—Madison, and Director of Teacher Corps Associates. He was also a classroom teacher and administrator in the Chicago public school system. His areas of interest and research include the study of the active involvement of the community and other groups in decision-making areas of education, and multicultural education. A well-known speaker and consultant, Professor Grant is a member of a number of professional organizations and has been chairperson of ASCD's Multicultural Commission.

"This book will be an important and excellent contribution. Little of consequence on community control and community issues has been published in book form in the past few years. This volume provides an excellent summary of what has happened and an excellent discussion of the implications. People interested in this topic will be eager to see the book.

". . . (the book) provides excellent material on a wide range of issues involving community participation in education. It has a good balance between analytic and illustrative material, a number of varying viewpoints are represented, and the issues raised are of substantive importance."

PROFESSOR DANIEL U. LEVINE
School of Education
Center for the Study of Metropolitan
Problems in Education
University of Missouri at Kansas City
(from a pre-publication review)

"Community participation/community control is still a current issue and certainly an important factor in obtaining funding. The volume presents many important facets of the issue with some examples of problems faced, some resolved, others not."

PROFESSOR HARRIET TALMADGE
College of Education
University of Illinois at Chicago Circle

Community Participation
in Education

Community Participation in Education

Carl A. Grant
University of Wisconsin – Madison

Allyn and Bacon, Inc.
Boston, London, Sydney, Toronto

Library of Congress Cataloging in Publication Data

Main entry under title:

Community participation in education.

    Includes bibliographical references and index.
    1. Decision-making in school management.
I. Grant, Carl A.
LB2806.C562   379   78–9167
ISBN 0–205–06052–8

Printed in the United States of America

Contents

Preface

"Student rights," "busing," "multicultural education," "tracking," and "community participation"—all terms which denote critical issues for education today. These issues are crucial because of the varying degrees of ineffectiveness displayed by schools, historically as well as currently, in responding to the needs of all children. Consequently, many citizens are demanding radical structural and functional changes in our schools. As we tackle these specific issues, we must concomitantly address some difficult, soul-searching questions. Will schools change? How will they change? Who will determine the changes? Although these questions can only be answered by the combined efforts of many concerned parties, one group of citizens which must provide input in determining what changes will ensue in schools, and how they will come about, is, clearly, the community.

This book considers these questions, along with other relevant inquiries, and proposes possible solutions. The book evolved from a conference on Community Participation in Education sponsored by Teacher Corps Associates, which was held at the University of Wisconsin-Madison. Eight of the articles in this book are adaptations of papers which were presented and discussed at that conference.

The conference focused on community participation in three primary areas: school budget, school personnel, and school curriculum. While some articles discuss these issues in considerable detail, the special interests and backgrounds of the contributing authors raised further questions relevant to the area of community participation. Additional papers were then solicited to increase the diversification of viewpoints in the book. The result is, I feel, a mixture of articles as rich and diverse as American society itself.

The reader should keep in mind that the term "community participation" is subject to different interpretations. Community participation is an expression of political decentralization which entrusts to more than one group of citizens all or some portion of decision-making responsibilities formerly reserved for the professional administration. This is to be distinguished from administrative decentralization, which is a sharing of power among professionals.

There is also a difference between community control and community participation. Under community control, the community negotiates politically to become entrusted with *all or most* decision-making responsibilities. Viable community participation, however, is that in which citizens and social agencies affected by schools *are partners* in making important school policy decisions in areas such as budget, curriculum planning, selection of school personnel, and plans for racial integration.

As the reader progresses through this book, whether for casual information or for serious contemplation, certain themes or broad topic areas will emerge as pervasive elements. I would suggest several areas that have particularly concerned the authors of this book: historical perspectives of American education and of community participation; school budget, personnel, and curriculum in relation to community participation; problems of community participation, past, present, and those anticipated in the future; and proposals to effect viable community participation.

Half of the articles pay particular attention to the historical perspectives of American education and of community participation. More precisely, these articles consider the evolutionary development and the conceptual meaning of community participation. Barbara R. Hatton provides a review of past strategies for school-community relationships, focusing on characteristics of past action that may help to formulate future urban educational policy. She explores two relevant questions for policy making: (1) To what extent have past changes in the nature of school-community relationships provided instructive experiences for a reassessment of present policies for community participation in education? and (2) What evidence exists to support the nature of the school-community relationship as an important factor in the distribution of educational opportunity?

Continuing in this vein, Robert J. Havighurst considers the rise of the local community control movement from 1966 to 1970, and the parallel increase in concern for cultural pluralism after 1965. He points out the apparent weaknesses in forms of local community participation in school affairs and presents some positive functions of local control, including a twenty-point program for real community control of schools. He further explores the growing recognition and affirmation of different groups and cultures in American society.

David Selden presents a brief history of American education from its beginnings in the small towns of New England to the present. He emphasizes notable changes in American society and in the educational establishment since World War II, and their concurrent effects on the political structures of cities. The most notable change in American society has been in the racial and ethnic composition of populations of American cities. In the educational establishment, the most notable change has been the rise of teacher power. Unfortunately, these two elements of society are often in conflict with each other when their combined efforts might be redirected toward better education.

Patricia Locke discusses the historical background of American Indian educational policies and current federal policies and legislation in this area, focusing her discussion on four federal programs supportive of public school education for Indian children: (1) the Johnson-O'Malley Act of 1934; (2) Impact Aid Laws; (3) Title I—Elementary and Secondary Education Act (ESEA); and (4) Title IV—The Indian Education Act. She further discusses some contemporary efforts by various tribes and organizations to achieve control. Specific examples include the Rocky Boy School in Montana, a national model for Indian curriculum development, and the Rough Rock Demonstration School in Arizona, a bilingual school which stresses fluency in both Navajo and English.

Questions regarding the relationship between school and community have become more pervasive since the advent of federal funding of school programs for the poor, according to Manuel Montano. Historically, the middle class has taken a more active interest in schools than have the poor, and thus the middle class has been a partner with the school, often dominating it, while the poor have been used to support the schools. He views this relationship of school and community as one of dominance and subordination, that of boss-worker. He proposes instead the concept of school-community partnership as a joint exercise in communication and redistribution of power, responsibility, and money.

According to Michael W. Apple and Barry M. Franklin, schools have a history that links them to other powerful institutions in ways that are often hidden and complex. They suggest that we need to understand this history and these linkages in order to recognize possibilities for our actions in schools. Since the curriculum field has played a major part in this history of the relationship between school and community, it can serve as an excellent example to analyze the linkages schools have had with other institutions. They ask compelling questions: What did "community" mean for the educators and intellectuals who had the strongest influence on the early curriculum field? What social and ideological interests guided their work? They conclude that one of the primary legacies of the curriculum field has been a commitment to maintain a sense of community based on cultural homogeneity and valuative consensus, reflecting the cultural values of those who hold economic power.

To outline possible forms of community participation, Marilyn Gittell cites recent specific examples. In particular, she discusses New York City's attempts at community participation through the establishment of three demonstration districts in 1968 and decentralization in 1969. In terms of conceptual meaning, Gittell defines community participation as a direct community involvement in decision making. Accordingly, no aspect of educational decision making should be isolated from consumer or citizen input and accountability. A clearly developed governance structure is therefore essential to insure that educational policy setting is an ongoing, dynamic process. Community participation is intended to create an environment conducive to the development of more meaningful educational policies and a variety of alternate solutions and techniques.

A second general category of significance to some of the authors concerns school budget, personnel, and curriculum in relation to community participation. The often critical impact of this broad topic is acknowledged by James A. Harris, who emphasizes that the control of education is a public function, and professional teacher associations "must promote public understanding of education and encourage wide public and parental participation in solving education problems." In their respective articles Havighurst, Gittell, and Montano share Harris's concern with regard to these three areas of community participation.

The reader will also find a strong negative statement regarding the effectiveness of community participation in this area in Edison Uno's article. Concerned with just how realistic it is to expect community participation in the formulation of budget priorities, Uno compares community needs with those needs articulated by professional educators, making the reader aware of a discrepancy between the goals and objectives of each group. He feels that community participation has had little influence in changing school administration with regard to school personnel; and that in the area of curriculum, community participation has been relatively ineffective. Overall, he paints a dim, but to his way of thinking realistic, view for community participation.

A third general area concerns problems for community participation, past, present, and those anticipated in the future. Occasionally, they are addressed in the form of questions, such as those posed in Havighurst's article: How is the policy of local community participation in educational affairs working? What are its weaknesses and what are its strengths? How can it be made to work better?

Thomas Popkewitz's consideration of problems focuses on "symbolic" uses of community participation in education. He cites numerous examples, not only in education but in other areas, such as politics, where participation is projected as meaningful by those in power, but in reality poses no threat to the established power structure. He contends that participation sometimes serves conflicting purposes and is used as much to maintain existing institutional practices as to change them.

According to Alex Molnar, inhibition of progressive movement has occurred in education simply because many educators have become too removed from social issues which affect them. Molnar feels critical theorists only recently have begun to address the structural relationship between school practices and American political and economic organization, and they have not yet described the meaning of their analyses at the level of classroom practices. While Molnar perceives some considerable difficulties for meaningful alliances between educators and the community, he charges teachers to continually strive toward a recognition of the relationship classroom practices have to social organization, and to purposefully use this perspective to develop alternative teaching techniques and curriculum materials.

For those of us concerned with community participation, its sometimes inconsistent development, inherent problems, and uncertain future, the problems we have found, and those yet to be encountered, will inevitably prove to be of perpetual concern. I am not an exception. My article considers what I have labeled "practical constraints," specifically, lack of knowledge, representation, and financial resources. What I propose to combat these problems might well serve to introduce our final pervasive category, common to the articles in this book: the future. I have put forth some proposals that might move us more quickly toward the ultimate goals of community participation. The reader is offered a three-stage model for partnership as an effective means toward overcoming practical constraints in community participation: identifying the problem, organizing for action, and gaining independence.

Other identified problems modulate into more proposals for future successes. Patricia Locke presents several problems that native Americans must consider to achieve a quality education on their own terms. These include adequate and equitable funding, consolidation of educational programs under departments of tribal education, and development of teacher competencies and accreditation systems for Indian education. But most importantly, Indian education must be viewed as a right, not as a privilege.

Donald Tobias and Donna Hager, discussing "macro" and "micro" political systems, suggest that community education can become a vehicle for the development of a community political structure—a structure that would effect and maintain local influence in decision making and make resultant policies more truly representative.

Any consideration of the future requires specific attention to the role of parents, and Daniel Safran's article addresses the following questions within the area of parent involvement: (1) Why involve parents in the formal education of their children? (2) Why should teachers be trained to involve parents? (3) What competencies do teachers need for working with parents? (4) How can teachers achieve these competencies? (5) What can be done to enable schools of education to meet challenges of teacher preparation for parent involvement? Safran concludes that teachers must be "trained" to reach out to the community, and techniques must be developed to prepare teachers to work with parents.

As might be expected, problem areas for the future of community participation can be endless. However, many of the authors provide provocative examples for resolution of problems.

Selden and Hatton urge a coalition of teachers and leaders of new urban social power structures; Apple and Franklin forcefully argue for a new responsiveness of institutions to communities, at the same time preserving cultural identities; and Popkewitz suggests ways to make community participation in education more meaningful and less symbolic.

As these articles suggest, we have witnessed a renewed interest in the area of community citizen participation since the late 1960s—a renaissance caused and directed by those who have been denied first-class citizenship. These citizens have insisted that they must participate in the processes that ensure them fulfillment of the principles of the Declaration of Independence: "We hold these truths to be self-evident, that all men are created equal . . ." And one process most basic to life in our society is the educational process. For this reason, we need to seriously and systematically examine community participation in education. Like freedom of speech, community participation in education is a concept which most readers of this book will endorse. For in essence, the question is not, "Should there be community involvement?" but rather, "What should the scope of community participation entail?"

Acknowledgments

I wish to acknowledge my appreciation and gratitude to the Teacher Corps, under the direction of William Smith and with the active support of James Steffensen and Preston Royster, for the support which they gave this project.

Special thanks also go to Carol Willis for her support in helping to organize the conference and to Susan Melnick for her valuable comments on the manuscripts.

In addition, I wish to express my appreciation and indebtedness to several persons who assisted in completing this book: Rita Johnson and Gwen Woolever, who exercised patience and understanding while typing the manuscript; and Susan Clifford and Nadine Goff for their uncommonly valuable assistance in copy editing and proofreading the manuscript.

Community Participation
in Education

Community Control in Retrospect

A Review of Strategies for Community Participation in Education

Barbara R. Hatton
Stanford University

The current challenge to traditional forms of urban school government has been caused both by inadequacies of structure and performance in the schools and by broader social and political trends outside of the schools. Present-day centralized systems (professional bureaucracies) were developed by turn-of-the-century reformers. They sought centralization to "fix" responsibility and give power only to those "qualified" to run the school systems. It has been well documented that such centralization no longer fits the needs of this urban society.

For many concerned about the problems of urban education, decentralization of school systems has seemed a necessary step. Even recent variations on the call for decentralization have included calls for "community control," "empowerment of the poor," and "community participation." Yet metropolitanism, regional redistricting, and district mergers are increasingly the focus of reports and studies that seek alternatives to the present arrangements for providing quality educational services within the constraints of urban environments. At the same time, local school districts face declining enrollments, shrinking resources, and cost inflation, and they must consolidate resources by closing schools and regrouping educational programs to operate more cost-effectively. Educational planners and urban policy analysts seem to be concentrating on reorganizational approaches in the formulation of public policy to address what is termed the "urban crisis."

Such approaches ignore the fact that alternative organizational forms will not overcome the technological and institutional failure of the past which resulted in educational failure for black

3

and poor children, increased racial tensions, faculty discontent, student dissatisfaction, and political or economic inequities in the dispensation of educational resources. Such approaches seem to presume that biases and inequalities in the distribution and provision of educational opportunity are directly tied to the way in which school systems are financed and administered. Such an assumption precludes attention to questions of by whom and for whom educational decision making occurs.

The consideration of policies regarding the proper relationship between the school and its correspondent community seems relegated by current urban policy makers to secondary importance in the face of seemingly more pressing issues of urban economic crises. Yet the apparent move toward radically reorganized structures for education would seem to require a reassessment of how, in fact, schools can best relate to the communities they serve. When considering any educational change, the major influential constituencies will try to effect that change in such a way that incompatible notions of self-interest, public interest, and professional interest are brought into an arena of conflict. Particularly, those who have experienced feelings of despair and disillusionment as a result of their relatively low political power or economic status have almost invariably sought to control educational systems or processes. Recently, some black communities across the country have been identified with a demand for what has been termed community control. Now there appears to be an emerging trend among teachers' groups across the country to approximate teacher control of educational systems through their collective bargaining strength. Any current consideration of policies regarding school-community relationships will almost certainly occur in an atmosphere of personal and political conflict.

In light of such predictably political behavior, some evidence of which is already present, a comprehensive, albeit brief, overview of past strategies for school-community relationships would seem essential to an understanding of present dilemmas. Unless one appreciates what has happened, the mistakes of the past can persist in the present. The review of strategies for school-community relationships which is presented here attempts to look for certain characteristics of the past which may help to formulate perspectives for future action in addressing urban educational policy. The review focuses on two relevant issues in current policy formulation:

1. To what extent have past changes in the nature of the school-community relationship provided instructive experiences for a reassessment of present policies for community participation in education?
2. What evidence is there that the nature of the school-community relationship is an important factor in the distribution of educational opportunity?

Some Historical Perspectives

American public school systems were designed to be free, closely controlled by the public, operated for all, and of high quality. Early in the history of American schools, urban ward systems were developed to implement these basic ideals. However, such systems did not overcome the systemic denial of educational opportunity to significant groups of Americans. Consider the following excerpt from one statement addressed to their fellow citizens by a state convention of Ohio blacks in the mid-nineteenth century:

> ... *you framed a United States Constitution. This you claimed as supreme law, and in accordance with it in 1802 framed a constitution for this State. To the principles thus announced we heartily subscribed ... We believe they ought to be enforced as well for us as for you ...*
>
> *We believe in the fact, the "fixed and unalterable" fact "that to secure these rights governments are instituted among men deriving their just powers from the consent of the governed." This you have taught us. Ohio law is a violation of this principle ...*
> *... [the] State Constitution says that "no law shall be passed to prevent the poor in the several counties and townships within this state, from an equal participation in the schools ... which are endowed, in whole or in part, from the revenue arising from the donations made by the United States for support of schools ... and the doors of said schools ... shall be open for the reception of scholars, students and teachers of every grade, without distinction or preference whatever, contrary to the intent for which the donations were made." We hold that the actual exclusion of*

*colored inhabitants from benefit of the school fund is a violation
of the principles here announced.*

*. . . such a law encourages ignorance in your communities. To
encourage ignorance is to encourage vice. The vicious character of
uneducated communities, both in the direct and indirect influence, is seen the world over, and to prove it we need not cite you
all past history. Therefore, even if the colored people of Ohio
were aliens, your own interest would demand the extending of
educational privileges to them all; but here we are, born on your
soil, and unless your own professed principles be a lie, entitled to
all the rights and privileges of all others. Consequently, you are
doubly bound to act for us for yourselves . . .*

*We ask for school privileges in common with others, for we
pay school taxes in the same proportion.*

—Cleveland, January 1849 [1]

After the Civil War, freemen and freedmen joined to utilize whatever resources were at hand to acquire education. They
pooled pennies, searched for teachers, and organized schools.
Classes were held in abandoned freight cars, in barns and sheds,
even in open fields. If no proper teacher could be located, anyone
who knew something taught it to those who did not. Largely due
to their efforts and those of their northern allies, the concept of
state-supported public schools became established in the South
during the Reconstruction period.[2] Current efforts to establish
community schools which are more responsive to the specific needs
of that community's children (such as projects in New York City;
Washington, D.C.; Flint, Michigan; and the increasing use of
community aides in the classroom) have begun in much the same
way; communities are organizing and now calling upon the appropriate governments to support and fund their efforts.

By World War I, because of compulsory attendance laws,
most children—black and white, except in the South—were in
school until they were sixteen. The war, as well as new discoveries
and growing technology, awoke the nation to the need for more
intellectual and technical training. Great emphasis was placed on
teaching aids such as educational films, radio broadcasts, and other
mechanical means of bringing interest into classrooms.[3] And in
the larger picture, many of the concerns familiar to educators
today were raised in the period 1890–1920. Largely, these concerns
centered around the following issues: (1) accountability for edu-

cational quality, (2) adaptation to new conditions, (3) the cutting of "red tape," (4) the development of national networks for innovation and political support, (5) the concern for realism about class and power in the administration of education, and (6) the development of local leadership.[4] The watchwords of the reform movement, as interpreted by Professor David Tyack of Stanford University, became centralization, expertise, professionalization, nonpolitical control, and efficiency in the city schools. The most attractive models of organization were the large-scale industrial bureaucracies rapidly emerging in that age of consolidation. In city after city—Cleveland, New York, Boston, St. Louis, Baltimore, and others—leading business people and professionals spearheaded reform.[5]

Continued inequities, however, prevented most minority and poor citizens from full participation in this "new wave" of education. These were the years of the "melting pot" philosophy, during which the stated goals of education were to separate children from all that was different and un-American in their backgrounds and to mold them for participation in the great American middle class. And underlying much of the reform movement was an elitist assumption that prosperous, native born, Protestant, Anglo-Saxons were superior to other groups and thus should determine the curriculum and the allocation of jobs.[6] It was the mission of the schools to imbue children of the immigrants and the poor with uniformly white, middle-class ideals.[7] Consider this statement by Ellwood P. Cubberly, a prominent and powerful advocate of educational reform at the turn of the century:

> *These Southern and Eastern Europeans [in our cities are] of a very different type from the North and West Europeans who preceded them. Largely illiterate, docile, often lacking in initiative, and almost wholly without the Anglo-Saxon conception of righteousness, liberty, law, order, public decency, and government, their coming served to dilute tremendously our national stock and to weaken and corrupt our political life.*[8]

Of course, it followed that reformers at the turn of the century sought the "best people" to run the schools, assuming that the working class, immigrants, and poor could not be expected to understand or participate in the affairs of education. Thus today, we see the development of systems based on this decision about *who* should actually determine the goals and processes of education.

We now realize the negative effect of this rejection of the rich cultural heritages of the children of the immigrants. Yet, these children were white and many of them did achieve middle-class status and acceptance. Nonetheless, schools even today continue to impose a biased education upon minority children, with the accompanying rejection of any possible value in their unique heritage. If this was destructive to the children of *white* immigrants, it is many times more destructive to the self-realization and aspiration of children of color.

Another critical factor in the reform movement for urban education at the turn of the century, which has implications for reform movements underfoot today, was the development of close ties between school systems and the business community. David Tyack provides a most comprehensive analysis of the development of centralization in urban centers and the consequent reliance on the then current business techniques. He concludes:

> *Urban school reform in the period from 1890 to 1910 clearly fits the pattern of elite municipal change described by the historian Samuel P. Hays. Probing beneath the surface rhetoric which pitted the "corrupt politicians" v. "the good citizen," Hays finds that most of the prominent urban "progressives" were leaders in the financial and professional life of their cities. Their motives were more complicated than simple abhorrence of graft. They deplored the fact that under the decentralized ward system, political power belonged mostly to lower- and middle-class groups (many of them first or second generation immigrants). They wished to apply to urban government the same process of centralization and bureaucratization, the same delegation of power to professional experts, as they had developed in their own businesses and associations. Reformers wanted, says Hays, "not simply to replace bad men with good; they proposed to change the occupational and class origins of decision makers." When these innovators talked of selecting "the best people" as school board members they, like many schoolmen, tended to disqualify the working class.*[9]

In their development of the "nonpolitical" school board, these business-oriented reformers in emphasizing bureaucratic efficiency removed education from politics only in the sense of removing it from manipulation by political bosses. This development and other factors caused education to develop in isolation from other local government agencies which were more responsive to political party controls. The reformed educational structure also developed in isolation from the residents of respective districts; policies of the time failed to reflect the needs indicated by the distinctive characteristics of the several neighborhoods within a particular district.[10]

While some gains were made as a result of this isolation, they were made at certain costs. These gains included the more rapid advancement of education than would probably have occurred otherwise; the development of merit plans for appointment of teachers and administrators prior to such development in other governmental agencies; and the strengthening of administrators' responsibilities. On the other hand, this isolation led to a lack of responsibilities on the part of boards of education to the changing needs of the society, a concern on the part of teachers and administrators with classroom activity rather than with the total situation in which the children lived and which had a large impact on their education; an inability of educators and others engaged in public services, such as housing, public health, libraries, and social welfare, to work together with understanding; a belief that educational services were removed from politics (not recognizing the politics of the nonpolitical), a view which in the long run may have hindered rather than advanced the quality of educational services.[11]

This isolation indeed may have been justified in the late nineteenth and early twentieth centuries. In rural areas and small towns it was readily understandable because of the limited nature of local government services. However, the growing complexity of society, with its enormous concentrations of population and expanding programs of governmental services, called for a thorough reexamination of this question. These turn-of-the-century reformers succeeded so well in insulating school officials from popular demands that opponents of the centralized concept found it almost impossible to change school policies. And even in many cities with regular elections, there were widespread feelings that the school officials were not sensitive or accountable.[12] However, a modest step toward decentralization was made in the "community school" plan begun in Flint, Michigan with the help of the Mott Foundation in 1935.

In the Flint plan, the school is viewed as the center of an urban neighborhood, providing education and social services for adults as well as children. For this plan to work well, residents must be given some role in designing the program, but specific administrative delegations were not initially delineated. About fifty other cities also began to experiment with community schools over the next two decades. In the fifties, cities like Detroit and St. Louis went further and delegated limited powers to all field administrators in the system. In 1949, the Public Education Association, Teachers College, and the New York Board of Education began the Bronx Park Community Project as a step toward community control of schools. Elections to the local board were held regularly, but the board had no formal legal status, little actual power, and shortly thereafter was absorbed back into the system.[13]

The increasing incidence of decentralization or community control efforts paralleled the conversion of the nation to peacetime industry after World War II. Blacks and members of other ethnic minorities who had faced death in the war as equals (of a sort) with whites or who had worked side by side with whites in wartime plants were unwilling to reassume their old inferior posture at the war's end. They settled into cities where they had worked or been stationed and were joined by their relatives when automation changed the nature of the job market in the South. The rapid expansion of communication during this period, especially the growth of the television industry, reminded all of the growing postwar affluence. As the former poor immigrant city dweller became the middle-class suburbanite, the cities were increasingly left to the in-migrant black, the Puerto Rican, the Mexican-American, and the Oriental. All these factors contributed to a steady escalation of demands for equal participation in education and educational decisions.

Throughout these periods, equality of educational opportunity was generally interpreted as the provision of a free education, available to all children, and with no invidious distinctions in the facilities used to provide such education. This interpretation led to efforts to insure that all students, regardless of race or wealth, received equal educational resources. This seemed to mean equalization of per pupil expenditures or, to some others, giving all students the *same* educational resources. However, during the 1950s, what Moynihan has termed an "exponential growth of knowledge" occurred in economics, statistics, and throughout the social sciences, accompanied by a greatly expanded number of social science and service professionals—many of whom were interested in the particular problems of urban environments.[14]

The Ford Foundation's action-oriented research of the 1950s, aimed at attacking social problems of cities, included large grants to several city school systems to help them respond to community conditions. These efforts failed to determine whether schools could be a significant tool in urban reform for any group.[15] Significantly, in this period the United States Supreme Court handed down a series of decisions validating blacks' constitutional claims to equality under the law—the most visible of these being the 1954 decision (*Brown* v. *Board of Education*) repudiating the long-standing "separate but equal" doctrine in schools.

Over the next ten years, the factors listed above seemed to coalesce around the work of the President's Committee on Juvenile Delinquency, social upheavals, and the political environment surrounding the Kennedy administration. Intense drives were launched to develop programs to improve the environment of the poor, partially through new approaches to the education of the poor. The education projects resulting from this "new thrust" of the 1960s were large and supposedly comprehensive, i.e., having relevance to large numbers of the poor and attacking a wide variety of "causes"—ranging from inadequate resources to inadequate representation of the poor. The idea of decentralizing urban school systems continued to find support and acceptance. During the 1960s, an impressive series of officially sponsored reports on the reform of school systems (Chicago–Havighurst, Booz–Allen–Hamilton; District of Columbia–Passow; Louisville–Cunningham; Milwaukee–Stiles; New York–Gittell, Bundy; and Philadelphia–Odell) all concluded that some kind of decentralization was required. As of 1967, "pilot projects" such as the Adams-Morgan Community School Project approved by the District of Columbia Board of Education were still being launched.

Since the mid-1960s and the panacea era of "maximum feasible participation" of the poor, many federal programs have adopted a policy of community parity as an essential condition for the successful implementation of programs designed to serve the urban, the poor, the miseducated, and other targeted communities. Community parity as a strategy remains an important policy issue today precisely because the questions of equal educational opportunity and school-community relationships are still substantial concerns in American education. The elitist reform movement at the turn of the century systematically excluded the very basis for the development of public schools. In most cities today, school boards are not representative of the people who have children in schools. Where the systems are large—and most pupils attend school in large systems—even a truly representative board would find it impossible to be fully responsive to the often conflicting needs of the people they try to serve. The structures of our school systems, developed in an earlier period, tried to meet the needs of their times. In order to get back to the basic concept of the right and the responsibility of the community, as well as professionals, to participate in the educational process, it is only minimally necessary to restructure school districts. If such restructuring is to provide a vehicle for protecting educational opportunity for the black and poor, we must further consider the ways in which the school-community relationship affects educational opportunity. In the final analysis, questions of school district reorganization must be considered with a fundamental goal of ensuring equal educational opportunity.

The School-Community Relationship and Educational Opportunity

In their report, "Equal Educational Opportunity," James S. Coleman and his colleagues concluded that inequitable investment in educational resources was not the key variable in educational achievement (as measured by standardized tests).[16] Coleman went further in stating that "Equality of educational opportunity implies, not merely 'equal' schools, but equally effective schools, whose influences will overcome the differences in starting points of children from different social groups." [17] This view launched a new era of insistence that schools do whatever is necessary to free disabled children of their disabling origins.[18] Educational researchers have grappled with the enormous difficulties of conceptually defining the implications of such a policy with the necessary precision for educational programming: How shall equality of effectiveness be measured? What does it mean, opera-

tionally, that education be independent of family and social background and reflective only of the randomly distributed innate
capacities of children? How can one distinguish between disabling
social origins that are related to group membership and those that
are related to individual psychological or social disorientation? [19]
And most importantly, are the significant differences between
groups *disabling* or are educational standards overly narrow in
defining achievement?

Advocates of community control answer this last question
with mounting evidence from recent research. Equalizing educational resources would provide some small gains for blacks,[20] but
community control advocates argue that present structures are
incapable of equalization. The works of Berke and associates
("Federal Aid to Education: Who Benefits?" [21]), Berke and Kirst
(in their research documenting the inefficiency of federal and state
delivery systems[22]), and the now infamous NAACP documentation[23] of the failure of Title I programs to reach the poor all support this charge. Valentine and others have provided documentation that evaluations of educational progress are culture-bound,
reflecting the values of middle-class whites as the dominant group
that defines educational standards.[24] Community control advocates propose diversification of the definition of educational
achievement by broadening participation in the process of setting
standards, thereby arriving at a more eclectic definition of educational success.

Further support for community control advocates comes
from the widely held view that a major ingredient in academic
success is teacher expectations. Both Rosenthal and Jacobson
(*Pygmalion in the Classroom*[25]) and Coleman (EEO) document
this view. Community control would provide a kind of veto
power over particularly negatively oriented or pessimistic teachers. By the structure in which this power is exercised, it would
aid in defining the kind of teacher expectations that are productive for black students. Finally, the findings of Stodolsky and
Lesser[26] lend credence to the position taken by community control advocates that there is a black way of learning. The study
provides the most empirical evidence to date that social class may
be a leading determinant of the *level* of achievement, but the
pattern of achievement is more a function of ethnic group.[27] In
his discussion of the study Fein interprets its findings as follows:

If one accepts the Stodolsky-Lesser position that different ethnic learning patterns are both enduring and benign, it would appear to add a powerful argument in favor of community control. It is hard to imagine an ethnically integrated school sufficiently flexible to encourage each group in its own unique pattern; schools, having come to behave as organizations, are strongly biased towards uniformity and impersonal standards.[28]

This view certainly suggests community control as a *viable* alternative.

More studies report that the difficulty the school faces in developing active citizens among the poor and blacks is partially accounted for by the child's view of his or her parents as powerless and uninvolved, or what Dan Dodson has called the "power hypothesis." [29] The preponderance of evidence is compelling. Esther Battle and Julian Rotter found that the "interaction of social class and ethnic groups was highly related to internal-external control of attitudes. Lower class Negroes were significantly more external than middle-class Whites or Negroes." [30] This is the core of a rather significant group of factors affecting the schooling of blacks, which further research findings have shown to be disarmingly simple and yet at the same time overwhelming.

Dr. Robert Hess, in "Social Class and Ethnic Influences upon Socialization," says that, "a sense of power has much in common with a sense of efficacy." [31] He points out that the "extent to which an individual can exercise power" is a "significant dimension of social class structure in the United States." [32] "One of the consequences of lower-class life is a cluster of attitudes that express low self-esteem, a sense of inefficiency and passivity." [33] In their paper, "Maternal Attitudes toward the School and the Role of the Pupil: Some Social Class Comparisons," Hess and Virginia Shipman argue that "social class and cultural effects upon cognitive development of children can best be understood in terms of the specifics of interactional transactions between the mother and her young child." [34] Among several other factors, their research team measured a "feeling of powerlessness toward the school." They found that as the mother's social class standing went down, her feelings of powerlessness toward the school also decreased. In their summary they note that, *the mother's attitude toward the school as reflected in the Educational Attitude Survey is significantly related to the child's I.Q. and to the child's behavior on the Stanford-Binet Testing situation . . . Factor One (feeling of power or powerlessness) is particularly important. It is negatively related to the child's tendency to engage in initiatory behavior in the Stanford-Binest testing situation, to his quickness of response, social confidence, and comfortableness with an adult examiner.*[35]

Analyzing the causes of the low-income mother's feeling of powerlessness, Hess and Shipman maintain that

the mother's attitudes indicate that the problem is not due to a lack of respect for the school or to the belief that it is ineffective: it is due to the fact that the mothers regard it as a distant and formidable institution with which they have little interaction and over which they exercise very little control.[36]

Further, in the *Development of Political Attitudes in Children*, Hess and Judith Torney note that,

the relatively lower sense of effectiveness on the part of children from the working class is congruent with their judgment about their families' interest in political matters and with their opinions about the decisiveness and power of their fathers.[37]

This detailing of selected studies is borne out by many others: the Coleman report in its measurement of a sense of control over the child's environment, and the work of Greenstein in *Children and Politics* are most notable examples.[38] Still further, studies at the organizational level have indicated that organizational power structure does have some effect on behavioral orientations. One group of organizational level studies found that lowering the locus of power along the hierarchy leads to increases in members' motivation to produce, identify with, and get involved in the organization.[39] In another group, actual participation in consequential decision making has been found to effect such personality variables as self-discipline, initiative-taking, and efficiency.[40] The foregoing evidence shows that any form of school organization which permits both community and professional participation in educational decision making can be expected to enhance educational opportunity. Community participation, particularly the participation of parents, appears to be one essential ingredient in the behavioral orientations of minority and poor students toward schooling. It is also reasonable to assume that the participation of professionals (the actual members of the organization) in consequential decision making in the schools can affect their behavioral orientations toward their jobs and toward other participants in the organization. If community participation and professional participation in educational decision making permit some measure of power to accrue to participants, such participation can be expected to create an atmosphere in which new approaches to educational decision making can occur.

In Retrospect

The foregoing discussions do not constitute solid documentation that community participation or control leads to the kind of sweeping changes in schools necessary for the improvement of educational opportunity for minorities and the poor. But no matter what the evidence, one factor is clear from this brief historical review. Schools were bureaucratized by educational professionals and elite community influentials to be controlled by them. Since that time, teachers and other lower echelon educational professionals have been excluded from consequential educational decision making concerning the dispensation and the choice of educational resources. Since that time, it has been impossible for minority and poor community residents to pinpoint who is responsible or accountable for the treatment of their children.

Repeatedly, urban community groups have tried single-handedly to reform the public school system to enhance educational opportunity for minority groups and the poor by demanding greater community participation. Community groups have long organized, operated, and taught in schools themselves within and without the public school context. Government support to fund their efforts has been dependent upon the whims of contemporary political processes. As was described in the Flint plan, the community schools approach did not yield significant community power to affect educational opportunity and was in fact dependent on the good will and preferred approaches of funding sources. Decentralization of school districts with the accompanying community participation in the form of parent advisory boards, school-community councils, and the like has not effected the basic restructuring of school districts it purported to accomplish. The decentralization which has occurred has in fact occurred without significant changes in the organizational power structure of schools, despite the attempts by concerned academics or social science professionals to accomplish this goal. Now teacher groups, long occupying the relatively powerless bottom rung of the hierarchical ladder in highly centralized school districts, have begun to militantly demand changes. This collective activity may have some impact, but many observers of the urban educational scene have predicted that current teacher collective activity will not enhance educational opportunity or increase responsiveness of educational processes to community needs.

In no place has a coalition between powerless insiders, e.g., teachers and other lower echelon professionals, and powerless outsiders, e.g., black and other poor parent groups, been apparent in the many efforts to reform urban school systems over the years. Yet we have some cause to believe that such a coalition toward the end of increasing both professional and community participation is beneficial to both, in different but certainly effective ways. However, such a partnership is unlikely to occur in the absence of educational policies which increase the ability of low-power insiders and outsiders to affect educational decision making and which force collaboration of community participants and professional participants on essential educational matters.[41] A policy of genuine parent-teacher parity in consequential educational decision making seems the only way to interrupt daily erosion of educational opportunity for blacks and the poor in urban schools. At the very minimum, it seems possible to require full hearings of teacher negotiations by school-community groups who are now excluded entirely from such decisions.[42] Within the present structures of the school systems, we can utilize classroom formats that deploy interrelated roles among several available community adults as well as the classroom teacher. But the great need is to require whenever and wherever possible that schools be restructured to accomplish consequential changes in the power structure within which educational decisions are made, to require the joint participation of school and community at every level in the power structure, and to focus the urban educational system on the enhancement of educational opportunity.

NOTES

1. Herbert Aptheker, ed., *A Documentary History of the Negro People in the United States* (New York: Citadel Press, 1951), Vol. I, p. 283.

2. Dorothy A. Jones, "Community Control, Decentralization, and the Black Community," paper presented at the national conference of the National Urban League as resource document for the workshop on community control, Washington, D.C., July 1969, p. 6.

3. Ibid., p. 8.

4. David B. Tyack, "City Schools at the Turn of the Century: Centralization and Social Control" (unpublished essay), May 1970.

5. David B. Tyack, "Needed: The Reform of a Reform" (publication source unknown; portions included here excerpted from reprint obtained from the author), May 1970, p. 35. (Also see Tyack, *The One Best System*, 1974).

6. Tyack, "Needed," p. 35.

7. Ibid.

8. Ellwood P. Cubberly, *Changing Conceptions of Education* (Boston: Houghton Mifflin Co., 1909), p. 15.

9. David B. Tyack, "City Schools at the Turn of the Century: Centralization and Social Control," p. 37.

10. Edgar L. Morphet, Roe L. Johns, and Theodore Reller, *Educational Organization and Administration: Concepts, Practices, and Issues* (Englewood Cliffs, N.J.: Prentice-Hall, Inc., 1967), p. 177.

11. Ibid., p. 178.

12. Joseph Pois, *The School Board Crisis* (Chicago: Educational Methods, Inc., 1964).

13. George La Noue and Bruce Smith, "Decentralization of Schools" (unpublished article written for inclusion in the Macmillan Encyclopedia of Education, May 1970), p. 5.

14. Daniel P. Moynihan, *Maximum Feasible Misunderstanding* (New York: The Free Press, 1969), pp. 1–36.

15. P. Michael Timpane, "Educational Experimentation in National Social Policy," *Harvard Educational Review*, Vol. 40, No. 4 (November 1970), pp. 547–566.

16. James Coleman et al., *Equality of Educational Opportunity* (Washington, D.C.: U.S. Government Printing Office, 1966), pp. 21–22.

17. Ibid., p. 22.

18. An even further discussion and detailing of this era is conducted in: Peter Marris and Martin Rein, *Dilemmas of Social Reform* (New York: Atherton Press, 1969).

19. James A. Coleman points out these methodological difficulties subsequent to the publication of this report in, "The Concept of Equality of Educational Opportunity," *Harvard Educational Review*, Vol. 38, No. 1 (Winter 1968), pp. 7–22.

20. Henry S. Dyer, "School Factors," *Harvard Educational Review*, Vol. 38, No. 1 (Winter 1968), p. 55.

21. Joel S. Berke et al., "Federal Aid to Public Education: Who Benefits?" (The Policy Institute of Syracuse University Research Corp. and Maxwell Graduate School of Citizenship and Public Affairs, January 31, 1971), pp. 52–53.

22. Joel S. Berke and Michael W. Kirst, *Federal Aid to Education: Who Governs, Who Benefits* (Lexington, Mass.: D. C. Heath, 1972).

23. Report by Ruby Martin of the Washington Research Project and Phyllis McClure of the NAACP Legal Defense and Education Fund, Inc., *Title I of ESEA: Is It Helping Poor Children?*, 1969.

24. Charles A. Valentine, "Deficit, Difference, and Bicultural Models of Afro-American Behavior," *Harvard Educational Review*, Vol. 41, No. 2 (May 1971), pp. 137–157.

25. Robert Rosenthal and Lenore Jacobson, *Pygmalion in the Classroom: Teacher Expectations and Pupils' Intellectual Development* (New York: Holt, Rinehart and Winston, Inc., 1968).

26. Susan S. Stodolsky and Gerald Lesser, "Learning Patterns in the Disadvantaged," *Harvard Educational Review*, Reprint Series No. 5 (1971), pp. 137–157.

27. Ibid.

28. Leonard Fein, *The Ecology of Public Schools* (New York: Pegasus, 1971), p. 116.

29. Dan W. Dodson, "Education and the Powerless," in *Developing Programs for the Educationally Disadvantaged*, ed. A. Harry Passow (New York: Teachers College Press, 1968), p. 330.

30. Esther S. Battle and Julian B. Rotter, "Children's Feelings of Personal Control as Related to Social Class and Ethnic Groups," *Journal of Personality* 21 (1963), p. 490.

31. Robert D. Hess, "Social Class and Ethnic Influences Upon Socialization" (mimeographed), p. 15.

32. Ibid., p. 13.

33. Ibid., p. 19.

34. Robert D. Hess and Virginia Shipman, "Maternal Attitudes

Toward the School and the Role of the Pupil: Some Social Class Comparisons" (mimeographed), 1966, p. 3.

35. Ibid., p. 17.

36. Ibid.

37. Robert D. Hess and J. V. Torney, *The Development of Political Attitudes in Children* (Chicago: Adeline Publishing Co., 1967), p. 149.

38. Fred Greenstein, *Children and Politics* (New Haven: Yale University Press, 1965).

39. For examples from the group, see Nancy C. Morse and Everett Reimer, "Experimental Change of a Major Organizational Variable," *Journal of Abnormal and Social Psychology*, January 1956, pp. 120–129.

40. For an example from this group see R. Likert, *New Pattern of Management* (New York: McGraw-Hill, 1961).

41. Don Davies, *Citizen Action in Education* 2 (Institute for Responsive Education Newsletter, Fall 1974), p. 1.

42. Ibid.

Local Community Participation in Educational Policy Making and School Administration

Robert J. Havighurst

University of Chicago

Experimentation and experience with local community control of schools in big cities has been a frustrating experience for educators, for parents, and for those who wish to improve the city as a place for democratic living. After fifteen years of trial and error in this direction, it is now possible to review the situation and perhaps to draw some useful conclusions.

Legislation of the "War on Poverty" under President Johnson provided that poor people were to have a full share in determining how they should be served by those agencies which were funded to help eliminate or reduce poverty. Up to that time, poor people in America had things done *for* them and *to* them by well-meaning people who were not themselves poor. Even the Catholic clergy with their vow of poverty and the settlement-house workers of the Jane Addams' decades were assured of physical comfort and economic security, though they came much closer to the lives of poor people than did the middle-class population which paid for alleviation of poverty through charitable giving and tax payments.

The Economic Opportunity Act of 1964 and the Elementary and Secondary Education Act of 1965 required participation of the poor in making policies and decisions about the actual use of federal money under these laws. This policy has continued up to the present. For instance, the American Indian Education Act of 1972 requires participation of Indian parents in the planning and supervision of any project or program supported under this act.

Involving poor people and disadvantaged minority groups in the decision making and supervision of programs aimed at assisting them is desirable, as are the policies of encouraging *local* community participation in *local* school affairs, and of encouraging close interaction between parents and school personnel. In retrospect, the New England local school district organization of colonial and 19th century days seems ideal, as does its transplantation to the rural district schools of the middle west.

But these institutions arose in a rural and small town society, with the citizens relatively homogeneous in language, lifestyle, and values. Now we are an urbanized society, with a wide variety of ethnic and religious groups living in every city, with racial and economic residential segregation in our metropolitan areas. How is local community participation in educational affairs working? What are its weaknesses and what are its strengths? How can it be made to work better? This chapter will deal with these questions.

Distinction between Local Community Control and Administrative Decentralization

An important distinction should be made between two phenomena of the past ten years, which sometimes are treated as though they are closely related. One, administrative decentralization, is the reduction in size of the administrative unit of the big-city school system. Examples are the legislative actions which divided the city school systems of New York City and Detroit into a number of separate and relatively autonomous school districts. The other, local community control of the schools, is the allocation of power to make important choices and decisions about the operation of schools so as to give community members authority over their local schools.

The goal of local community control is to bring decision making and consequent responsible action on behalf of their children into the hands of disadvantaged adults. On the other hand, the goal of decentralization into autonomous districts of about fifty schools is to make educational operations more efficient, more flexible, and less bureaucratic. Since such a school district would have a total population of three or four hundred thousand, it would be much too big to serve as a unit in which the "little people" would naturally control their own schools.

There is some connection between the two phenomena.

Administrative decentralization may help to pave the way for local community control of schools, but this is not necessarily true. We shall deal primarily with the movement for local community participation and control of schools.

Rise of the Local Community Control Movement: 1966–1970

By 1966, the situation in big cities was ripe for local community participation and influence in local schools. The following factors had prepared this situation:

1. The 1954 Supreme Court Decision on racial segregation in public schools, followed by the Civil Rights Act and the Elementary and Secondary Education Act in the 1960s, supported the conviction by black citizens that they had the right to expect and demand educational facilities and programs as good as those which served whites.
2. The extent of racial and economic segregation in the public schools was increasing in the big cities.
3. Achievement test data were being published by city school systems, separately for black and white students.
4. The school achievement of children from low-income families was clearly below that of children from middle-income families, and was not improving.
5. There was widespread public opinion that school achievement was due mainly to the quality of teaching in the schools, and that equal quality of schooling would produce equal achievement, regardless of the socioeconomic status of the parents.
6. It was widely believed that schools were the major avenue of upward economic and social mobility for youth of poor families.
7. Some educational experts (not all of them) concluded that the teaching methods and the teachers' attitudes generally existing in the public schools were unfavorable to achievement by children of low-income and black families.

By 1966, it was becoming clear that:

a. The Head Start and Remedial Instruction programs of the Elementary and Secondary Education Act were not solving the problem of low school achievement by children of low-income families.

b. There would be no major reduction of racial and economic segregation in the public schools in the near future.

c. The federal government policy of placing poor people and minority representatives in decision and policy-making positions with respect to government programs was leading them to greater participation and responsibility for decision making in the educational systems of big cities.

At this time there emerged a separatist (black power) movement among blacks which argued for separate political, economic, and educational institutions for blacks (at least for a period of years) as the most effective means to improve the situation for black people. While a number of outstanding black leaders rejected this policy, some immediate gains were scored in the form of "black studies" programs in colleges and special college admissions programs for black students.

Local community participation in the conduct of schools was essentially a result of the dissatisfaction of poor people and disadvantaged minorities with the public schools. They believed that the schools were not serving their youth in a satisfactory way, and consequently they demanded a voice in the conduct of the schools.

Middle-class people did not object in principle to greater community participation in local school affairs, since they were accustomed to the informal but quite effective influence which middle-class parents had exerted during recent decades through the Parent-Teacher Association and through informal access to the school administration. A more formal system of local community participation in local school affairs was acceptable to them, and they saw no reason to oppose such a system in other parts of the city.

Rise of Cultural Pluralism

Not only blacks, but also other minority groups began to assert their separateness after 1965. Although the Anglo-Protestant group has been in the majority, American society has always contained many different nationality, racial, and religious groups. Relations between these groups have at times been tense, yet the general attitude of Americans has been to anticipate a reduction of group differences through various forms of common activity within a framework of a democratic society. Thus, it was common to speak of America as a "melting pot."

However, in recent years the attitude toward the continued existence of different groups and cultures in American society has become more approving and more appreciative. Educational systems now are expected to assist various groups to maintain their cultural differences and to achieve their cultural goals within a cooperative framework. Thus James E. Allen, Jr., former United States Commissioner of Education, in recommending support for ASPIRA, the Puerto Rican organization, wrote:

> *The day of the melting pot is over. No longer is it the ideal of each minority to become an indistinguishable part of the majority. Today, each strives to maintain its identity while seeking its rightful share of the social, economic, and political fruits of our system. Self-help and self-determination have become the rallying cries of all minorities.*

Separate and different group cultures and traditions are now regarded as healthy in a complex democratic society because they enrich the society. At the same time, the "mainstream" of the society is open to new recruits, and offers many rewards to members of minority groups who join the mainstream and who consequently reduce their participation and allegiance to a minority group. Thus, inherent tension exists between the societal forces which push for democratic cultural pluralism and those which work toward democratic social integration.

In the period from 1965 to 1974, the slogans of pluralism were popular, but integration continued to be an important social goal. Social integration means the mixing of various racial and cultural groups through association in business, education, government, and cultural affairs, and through some degree of intermarriage, with the goal being one common culture. Democratic cultural pluralism refers to the amicable coexistence of a variety of racial, ethnic, religious, and economic groups, with each group keeping its subculture fairly intact and intermarrying little or not at all with other groups. If equal respect and equal opportunities and privileges are accorded to all groups, a condition of democratic pluralism may be said to exist, as it does in Switzerland, with its French, German, and Italian cantons, and as in Holland where religious subcultures set themselves apart in political and civic as well as social and religious affairs.

Minority groups who wanted to keep their ethnic identity and to pass it on to their children saw the schools (whether public or private) as helps or hindrances, depending on the school program. Therefore they sought a degree of influence in the local schools, particularly if they wanted to preserve their native tongue. They could take advantage of the Bilingual Education Act to secure funds to help their children learn the ethnic language.

Michael Novak speaks eloquently on behalf of the ethnics of southern and eastern Europe in his book, *The Rise of the Unmeltable Ethnics*. He speaks of the 1970s as the "Decade of the Ethnics" and regards the rise in ethnic consciousness as part of a more general cultural revolution in America. His basic proposition is that ethnic identity has similar elements from one ethnic group to another and is a desirable antidote to the poisons of modern industrial society. He says,

> *The rise in ethnic consciousness is, then, part of a more general cultural revolution. As soon as one realizes that man is not mind alone, and that his most intelligent theories, political decisions, and works of genius flow from "intelligent subjectivity," attention to the roots of imagination, value, and instinct is inevitable. When a person thinks, more than one generation's passions and images think in him.*

The ethnic group, for Novak, lives in the individual in a mystical, nonrational way. He defines an ethnic group as

> *a group with historical memory, real or imaginary ... Ethnic memory is not a set of events remembered, but rather a set of instincts, feelings, intimacies, expectations, patterns of emotion and behavior; a sense of reality; a set of stories for individuals— and for the people as a whole—to live out.*

The racial and ethnic minorities who make up about one-third of the population of the United States have become actors on the stage of "cultural pluralism." The action has become so vigorous since 1960 that it is a major concern in domestic politics, in social ethics, and in education.

Robert J. Havighurst

Forms of Local Community Participation in Local School Affairs

The stage was set for a major trial of local community participation in local school affairs when, in 1967, the New York City Board of Education agreed to the formation of three "demonstration districts" in lower-income areas of the city. Each district was to consist of one or two junior high schools and several elementary schools whose students went on to these junior high schools. The Ford Foundation made grants to local groups of parents and citizens in the three "demonstration districts" to pay the costs of the experiment. The Ocean Hill-Brownsville area of Brooklyn had a population 75 percent black and 20 percent Puerto Rican. The northeast section of Harlem was 80 percent black and 20 percent Puerto Rican. The Two Bridges area in the lower East Side of Manhattan was 40 percent Puerto Rican, 36 percent Chinese, 12 percent black and 12 percent Anglo.

The Ocean Hill-Brownsville experiment attracted wide attention. In 1966, the United Federation of Teachers started a teacher-parent joint action program in the district that used picketing and other demonstrations to secure the removal of an unpopular school principal and the provision of some special services from the Board of Education. Meanwhile, a group of social workers and parents affiliated with Brooklyn CORE (Congress of Racial Equality), aided by a white priest, Father John Powis of the Church of Our Lady of the Presentation, formed an unofficial "people's board of education" for the Ocean Hill area. These two groups came together and secured a grant of $44,000 from the Ford Foundation in the summer of 1967 to pay the costs of a "demonstration district" to include two junior high schools and six elementary schools in the Ocean Hill-Brownsville area.

The Ocean Hill group formed a "planning council" consisting of several teachers in the local schools and parents active in the "people's board of education." Their first action was to employ a unit administrator, who would be paid by the Board of Education to administer the demonstration unit of eight schools. They worked hard at this during the summer of 1967, with the aid of Father Powis and a black activist teacher, Herman Ferguson. Since it was summer vacation, the teacher delegates were seldom present at meetings, and the planning group employed Rhody McCoy, a black schoolman who was acting principal of a school for disturbed boys in Manhattan, as administrator. A plan was drawn up to elect a governing board of twenty-four members, one parent and one teacher from each of the eight schools, five community representatives to be chosen by the parent members of the board, two representatives chosen by school supervisors in the district, and one delegate from a university to be chosen by the board as a whole. The council advertised an election for August 3 and set up ballot boxes in the schools. The voting was light, and for two more days members of the council collected votes by calling on parents. Eventually, about a quarter of the parents voted. The elected parent representatives were all mothers, and several were on welfare. They named five community leaders to the board, including Father Powis, Assemblyman Samuel D. Wright, who was a lawyer and representative of the district in the State Legislature, and Rev. C. Herbert Oliver, a black pastor of the Westminster Bethany Presbyterian Church, recently arrived from Alabama.

Four of the school principals asked to be transferred out of the district, and a fifth vacancy was created by the opening of a new intermediate school. McCoy proposed and the new board approved the appointment of five men to fill vacancies. Only one of the five was on the city school system's list of persons who had passed examinations for the principalship. This list contained several hundred names, with only four blacks. Two of the five new principals were black, one was Puerto Rican, and one was Chinese. Those whose names were not on the civil service list were given the title of "Demonstration Elementary School Principal" which could be assigned to anyone without a licensing examination, temporarily.

This was the first of many actions of Rhody McCoy and his governing board that had doubtful legality. The New York City Board of Education did not state just what the powers of the governing board or the unit administrator were, but simply accepted their recommendations, at first. Later the city Board refused to approve some of the actions of the district governing board. All but one of the new principals won approval from the teachers, parents, and other administrators with whom they worked. Nevertheless, the Council of Supervisory Associations (a kind of union consisting of principals, assistant principals, bureau chiefs, and other supervisors) instigated a lawsuit to oust the new

Ocean Hill principals as illegally appointed. The Council was joined in this lawsuit by the teachers' union, even though it had generally opposed the Supervisory Associations.

The teachers' union, which had originally favored the Ocean Hill experiment and helped to set it up, had changed its position by the fall of 1967, and forbade union teachers to become members of the governing board. The reason for this action was that the parent and community members of the board tended to be critical of at least some of the teachers and made them feel uncomfortable in board meetings. It was becoming clear that the governing board would soon move to replace those teachers against whom there was hostility from parents or pupils.

Also, in November, all eighteen of the district's assistant principals applied for transfers, claiming that some of them had been harassed (by anti-Semitic insults, among other things) and that McCoy was not supporting them. This meant that all the schools had to be staffed with new assistant principals, some of them inexperienced. The result of these changes, along with the uncertainties about the power and responsibilities of the various persons and groups involved in the experiment, was internal chaos in most of the schools.

The first few months under the governing board were taken up with efforts to get the schools to operate smoothly with new principals and acting principals. Progress was being made, and a number of new programs of compensatory education were started. Then, in April of 1968, there were setbacks. The assassination of Martin Luther King increased hostility toward white teachers. A fire in the new intermediate school one afternoon forced the children out of the building for two hours, after which they swarmed back without adequate supervision by teachers, and produced a minor riot. Some teachers who had gone home instead of staying to maintain order were criticized. About this time, the governing board became more aggressive, though a minority led by Assemblyman Wright urged patience and conciliation. The majority of the governing board recommended "the removal from our district" of 13 teachers, five assistant principals, and the one surviving preproject principal. This recommendation started a confusing chain of events, in which the governing board insisted on its right to discharge personnel without formally bringing charges against them. Eventually, the teachers' union called out all teachers in the demonstration district, and some 350 of the 500 teachers were out on strike for the last month of the school year.

During the summer of 1968, efforts were made by Mayor Lindsay, by State Commissioner of Education James Allen, by the city Board of Education, by the Ford Foundation, and by the Ocean Hill-Brownsville Governing Board to settle the dispute over the removal of the ten teachers. (Of the original thirteen, one was reinstated by the governing board, and two accepted transfers out of the district.) The Board of Education appointed a retired black judge, Francis Rivers, to examine charges that McCoy had agreed to bring against the teachers. On August 26, Judge Rivers found the charges inadequate and denied McCoy the right to transfer any of the ten teachers. The Ocean Hill Governing Board voted not to accept Judge Rivers's findings, and also not to reinstate about one hundred teachers who had struck against the district during the preceding May and June.

Accordingly, the United Federation of Teachers responded with a city-wide strike, and nearly 54,000 of the city's 57,000 teachers stayed out on the opening day of school in September. After two days of negotiation, the Board of Education signed an agreement with the union that sent the teachers back to the schools. But the union teachers in Ocean Hill were systematically threatened at a teachers' meeting by community residents of Ocean Hill, including about 50 men, some wearing helmets and carrying sticks. In some schools teachers were given police protection, but were not allowed to teach. A second and a third strike were called, altogether keeping the city schools effectively closed for two months.

Finally, the State Department of Education, the State Board of Regents and Mayor Lindsay settled the strike and started the school again in mid-November by placing the Ocean Hill-Brownsville district under the direct supervision of the State Department of Education, while a state supervisory commission would maintain the rights of the teachers in the local schools. The Ocean Hill schools gradually settled down, with the governing board headed by Rev. Oliver continuing to function, with some turnover of principals and teachers, until 1970.

The growing hostility between the advocates of local community control and the United Teachers Federation resulted in a deep division within the group that had originally been united in favor of racial integration and liberal socio-political policies. This hostility was illustrated by the action of the New York Civil Liberties Union in publishing a report on October 9, 1968, in the midst of the teachers' strike, attacking the teachers' union and arguing that the teachers' union and other groups had brought on the chaos of Ocean Hill by efforts to undermine local community control of the schools. The New York Civil Liberties Union is a strong local branch of the American Civil Liberties Union, but does not speak for the national organization on the issue of local community control. The New York branch report was entitled *The Burden of Blame: A Report on the Ocean Hill-Brownsville Controversy.* This report was foreshadowed by an article by the journalist Nat Hentoff in *The Village Voice* on September 26, entitled *Ad hoc Committee on Confusion* which attacked a group of socialist leaders for their advertisement in *The New York Times* in support of the teachers' strike. Hentoff was one of the leaders of the New York Civil Liberties Union who favored local community control. Answering Hentoff, in *The Village Voice* for October 3, 1968, Michael Harrington, National Chairman of the Socialist Party, USA, said,

> *I am for opening up new channels of innovation and popular participation. But there can be no decentralization in New York City based on breaking the union; there can be no decentralization based on vigilante control of the schools; there can be no effective decentralization apart from a long-range program to end the slums.*

These events illustrated the kinds of problems that were likely to occur when local communities of disadvantaged minorities suddenly assumed control of local schools. But these events also may have helped other communities to avoid some of these problems, or at least to reduce them.

The community participation movement took the form, generally, of "school advisory councils" created by boards of education with definitive functions and powers. These councils were formed, after 1968, in Chicago, Seattle, Los Angeles, and a number of other large cities. Council members were elected from parents, teachers, and local community leaders. In some high schools, students were also elected to the local council.

The functions of the advisory councils were exercised mainly in their influence over the curriculum and over the appointment or discharge of teachers and principals. In some cases, they were given some small influence over expenditures. It. was made clear when councils were created that they were *advisory* to the board of education, which retained full authority over the schools. For instance, if a vacancy in the principalship arose in Chicago, the local council might *nominate,* but the superintendent must recommend and the Board of Education must give final approval to the appointment of a new principal. Furthermore, the council must make nominations from a list of eligible candidates certified by the Board of Education.

Functions of Local Community Control

The effectiveness of local councils is being studied on the basis of as much as five years' experience in some communities, but no general judgment can yet be recorded. Allan Ornstein, writing in 1973 said:

> *As of now we have no research evidence that decentralization and community control improve education; this is especially true with community control. . . . Until the evidence is clear, we should proceed with caution. The point is, the so-called "solutions"— decentralization, community control, even community participation—are mainly slogans rather than closely worked out concepts with consequences understood and accounted for.*

In 1973 Don Davies, formerly Deputy Commissioner of Education for Development in the U.S. Office of Education, became Director of the Institute for Responsive Education at Yale University, and in 1974 moved to Boston University. He has been surveying advisory councils. He proposes the following areas of involvement for such councils:

· *School Objectives:* Identifying educational needs; determining goals, objectives, priorities; monitoring and assessing progress toward achievement of goals.

- *Personnel* (Principal, teachers, other staff): Defining qualifications (within state law); reviewing candidates; selecting candidates; evaluating performance; deciding about tenure, reassignment, removal; determining personnel policies; planning and conducting staff orientation and training; negotiating with employee organizations.
- *Budget:* Identifying resource needs of school; setting budget priorities; reviewing and adopting budget; monitoring use of funds.
- *School Program* (curriculum, extra-curriculum, student services): Planning and developing new or revised programs; preparing and approving proposals for special projects; monitoring and evaluating programs; determining program priorities; approving participation in research projects.
- *Facilities:* Establishing priorities for rehabilitation, equipment; selecting building sites; planning for new or remodeled buildings.
- *School-Community Relations:* Identifying community needs, explaining school policy programs; securing support and services from parents, students, teachers, community residents; serving as ombudsman for individual students or parents; planning and conducting orientation and training activities for parents and community; sponsoring social activities; raising money for the school.

A more convinced protagonist for local community control is Kenneth W. Haskins, in 1973 Vice Superintendent of Schools in Washington, D.C., who is a leader in the black movement for self-determination. Presenting "A Black Perspective on Community Control," he is not content for blacks to accept the concept of a school advisory council as satisfactory. He wants full control of black schools by a black community. He quotes with approval a document from AFRAM Associates (Harlem, New York City, 1970) entitled *Action Stimulator #32: A Twenty Point Program for Real School Community Control.* Some of these twenty points are:

1. District boundaries defined by the communities themselves—organized on the basis of one district for each intermediate or junior high school complex.
2. School board election procedures developed by the school

communities and held by the communities. This includes determining number of members, qualifications, and voter eligibility.

3. Full employment of community residents. All available positions to be filled by residents *first*.

4. Accountability of all administrative and teaching staff. Teachers must believe in our children's ability to learn; teachers must respect the children and the community.

. . .

7. Abolition of all testing until tests can be developed which are relevant and geared to the requirements of individual communities.

. . .

9. Free breakfast and lunch programs for all children. No more soup and bread and butter sandwiches. Nutritious and appealing meals, including soul food, rice and beans, and Chinese food, will be served.

10. Establishment of educational programs which teach modern awareness of the real world. This includes Puerto Rican, Black, and Chinese culture and history, problems of unemployment, poor housing, malnutrition, police brutality, racism, and other forms of oppression.

11. An end to all suspensions, dismissals and other abuses against children until fair procedures can be devised to deal with each individual case.

. . .

13. Establishment of student participation in the decision-making process, both at junior high and high school levels.

. . .

15. Immediate changes in the teacher and supervisory licensing and certification procedures so as to eliminate practices which have been used to exclude minority group persons from teaching and supervisory positions. Abolition of the Board of Education, which exists only in New York City.

16. Development of bilingual classes and programs at all levels.

. . .

19. Free access to their children's records for all parents, as is their legal right. Nothing to be put in children's records unless approved by parents.

20. Abolishment of the tracking system which was declared unconstitutional and discriminates against Black, Puerto Rican, and poor.

How Does Local Community Participation Actually Function?

Three areas of school administration which are of special concern to the local community are budget, personnel, and curriculum. Some experience in these areas is available to be used as a basis for tentative conclusions concerning the effectiveness of local community participation.

Budget

The budget of a local school is generally determined almost entirely by the central administration, which allocates funds for salaries on a standard basis of a certain number of pupils to a teacher, and a certain number of administrators, counsellors, librarians, office personnel, and maintenance personnel, depending on the enrollment of the school. Not much can be done by a local community group to change this, since every school must have the same claim on the total school budget, based on its enrollment, unless it has special needs that are recognized by other schools; or unless it receives special grants outside of the regular budget from the federal government or other sources. Such special grants are likely to flow toward schools in low-income and ethnic areas, since they are most likely to qualify for extra funds under Title I of the Elementary and Secondary Education Act, the Bilingual Education Act, or the American Indian Education Act.

Decisions must be made about the use of these special funds, and the school principal and his staff have some influence on these decisions. The advisory council may have a part in making these decisions, which depend mainly on the curriculum and program of the local school.

The Board of Education may give each school a small fund for use at its own discretion, and the advisory council may have some influence on the use of such a discretionary fund. It may also organize local fund-raising events to secure money for its discretionary fund.

Curriculum and School Program

It is here that the representatives of the local community can work most constructively with the school teachers. Schools in low-income areas have special access to federal government and other funds outside of the regular school budget. These funds may be used for a variety of purposes: for remedial teaching; for enrichment in home economics and industrial arts; for teacher-aides; for bilingual teaching; for helping parents or preschool children to relate their children more effectively to the school. The local community representatives can help the teachers to diagnose community needs, and to choose effective procedures to meet these needs.

But those who have studied the actual attempts to bring teachers and parents into fruitful cooperation are more realistic than optimistic. For instance, the University of Wisconsin at Milwaukee cooperated with the Racine, Wisconsin, public schools in a "Parent School Study-Action Project." Warner Bloomberg, Jr., and John Kincaid worked on this project. They reported a good deal of mutual suspicion and misunderstanding between parents and school staff. Their report, "Parent Participation: Practical Policy or Another Panacea?" concludes that,

> *The success or failure of efforts to improve education in ghetto schools through parent participation projects seems to depend largely upon four main factors: (1) The kind of understanding and skill that can be developed among organized residents; (2) The resources and capacity for persistence that they can develop and maintain; (3) The receptiveness or refractoriness of teachers and administrators to efforts by parents to engage in what amounts to systematic evaluation of the staff's effectiveness as educators and to enter into what has normally been the staff's sole domain; and (4) the extent to which the decision making that can be affected is most relevant to underlying causes of educational problems in the ghetto.*

They note a tendency for administrators and teachers to be skeptical about any good coming from the involvement of slum parents in the making of educational decisions.

> *Teachers and administrators tend to view angry parents as ignorant, and dissident groups as automatically hostile. They also believe that parental agitation makes their already difficult student control problems even worse by appearing to legitimate the various forms of guerrilla warfare conducted by the large number of pupils who are "behavior problems." Already feeling*

like losers, most of them see nothing to be gained and even more
to be lost should "parent power" be intruded into the daily life
of the school.

Personnel

The most controversial aspect of local community participation
has to do with selection and evaluation of principals and teachers.
This is especially difficult when the parent group is mainly of
black or Spanish descent, and the teachers and pupils are mainly
Anglos. It is a natural thing for a council consisting of parents
and other local community members to want the principal and a
number of teachers to be of their own ethnic group. There are
sound reasons to support this, and also sound objections to it. Not
only are the seniority rights of the present school staff involved,
but also an experienced teacher who has really worked hard to
understand the local community and its culture may be very useful to help some students succeed in the larger community to
which they must go for economic improvement. Probably a teaching staff with a variety of ethnic and social class backgrounds is
desirable in practically all schools, if the goal is democratic social
integration, but the movement for cultural pluralism tends to
emphasize the desirability of having school personnel of the same
culture as the local community.

It is a common experience that one of the first acts of a
local community council is to bring in teachers and a principal
of their own ethnic group, with resultant conflict and tension, as
was seen in the Ocean Hill-Brownsville controversy.

This conflict was noted in Chicago by a seasoned observer
of the Chicago schools, Professor Mark Krug of the University of
Chicago. In an article in the September, 1974 *Phi Delta Kappan*
entitled "Chicago: The Principals' Predicament," he reported
that the school principals are bitter and angry over what they see
as abuses in the process of removal or "transfer" of principals.

Legally, the school councils only nominate the new princi-
pals but, in practice, they choose the principals because the general
superintendent has approved virtually all the "nominations."
The difficulty began when the Board of Education gave
the school councils the power to select the principal when, as the
guidelines put it, "a vacancy exists." Some school councils or

community groups sometimes decide to create a vacancy by forcing the ouster or the transfer of a principal so that they can choose one more to their liking.

In Area A alone, in the last five years, about 20 principals have been removed by some form of community pressure. Since these principals have tenure and an earned status classification, they are transferred to other administrative jobs at the same pay.

It is the process followed in the removal of principals that has created a great deal of resentment and which has adversely affected the morale of their colleagues.

While most of the principals that we talked to work with obvious zeal and enthusiasm, often in spite of difficult conditions, they are angry and distressed by the well-publicized cases of unfair treatment of school administrators accused of a variety of charges. Some principals say they intend to retire before the mandatory age of 65 or as soon as their pension rights would not be seriously affected.

For those principals who have been forced out of their jobs by what is usually referred to as "community pressure," this has been a cruel and trying experience. They assert that they have been denied due process of law.

The injustice is compounded because "transferred" principals, especially those charged with "racial prejudice" or "insensitivity to the needs of the community," have few prospects to be selected by other local school councils. Their professional career is either ruined or tainted because of charges brought against them.

Krug goes on to say:

It must be emphasized, however, that evidence indicates that on the whole local school councils have selected well-qualified principals for their schools. This is especially the case when vacancies have occurred and when the selection of the principal was done without undue pressures and when the interest of the children was the paramount criterion in the final choice.

The Importance of Balance between Local Community and Other Factors

This consideration of local community participation in the conduct of the schools emphasizes balance among a number of factors that have importance for an effective school system. The contemporary trend toward cultural pluralism gives the local community greater importance, at the risk of giving the local community too much importance.

There is a continuing need for a balance among several interest groups: the local community, the students, the teachers, and the administrators. Most of the controversies over local community control since 1965 have resulted from conflicts and rivalries among these interest groups.

Most likely to be neglected is the major socio-political unit of an urbanized society—the city as a whole, or perhaps the metropolitan planning agencies which are concerned with the economic, commercial, and cultural development of the area; such goals as racial integration, and economic opportunity for low-income groups; and wise use of rivers, lakes, and forest preserves. Facilities for higher education, adult education, vocational education, education of the handicapped and the gifted need to be organized and administered on an area-wide basis. Therefore, the central educational authority must be able to coordinate the work of elementary and secondary schools in local communities, and must relate the programs of these schools to the educational opportunities and the social needs of the larger area.

A weak board of education at times may seem to facilitate local community participation in local schools, but very few local schools can prosper under a weak central authority. A strong board of education and a strong central administration can cultivate and enhance the area-wide educational program, and also cultivate local community participation in local school affairs.

Also, there are non-school solutions to social problems which will facilitate the work of the schools. In general, raising the income of poor families is likely to do more for the school achievement of their children than spending to reduce class size or provide remedial instruction. Measures to reduce the number of one-parent families may be the most effective ways of improving the school performance of children.

The chart that concludes this paper attempts to orient the reader to the bibliography which follows. Most of the authors cited in the list of references are placed on this chart in relation to the positions they advocate with respect to local participation in educational affairs.

Positions with Respect to Local Community Participation
in School Affairs

Favor Local Control

Academicians	*Ethnic Separatism*	*Maximize Individual Freedom and Small Group Control*
Marilyn Gittell	Kenneth Haskins	Paul Goodman
Mario Fantini		(mini-schools)
Don Davies		Nat Hentoff
		(New York Civil
		Liberties Union)

Balance of Local Community and Central Office Authority

Kenneth B. Clark—Teach the Basic Mental Skills
Fred Hechinger—De-bureaucratizing without De-schooling
Luvern Cunningham—Responsible Autonomy
Carl Marburger—National Committee for Citizens
    in Education
Allan Ornstein—Research on Decentralization
Bernard Bard—Between the professionals and the parents—
    there is no match.

For Teacher and Professional Leadership

Albert Shanker—New York Teachers Union
Irving A. Yevish—New York City Teacher

For Non-School Solutions
(End Poverty, Eugenics, etc.)

Michael Harrington
Maurice J. Goldbloom

REFERENCES

Allen, James E. *The Special Educational Needs of Urban Puerto Rican Youth.* Introductory Comments. New York City: ASPIRA, 1968.

Bloomberg, Warner, Jr., and John Kincaid. "Parent Participation: Practical Policy or Another Panacea?" *Urban Review* (June, 1968), pp. 5–11.

Brooks, Thomas R. "Can Parents Run New York's Schools?" *Reporter* (January 11, 1968), pp. 20–22.

Clark, Terry N. "On Decentralization." *Politics* 2 (1970), pp. 508–514.

Davies, Don. "The Emerging Third Force in Education." *Inequality* 15 (November, 1973), pp. 5–12.

Fantini, Mario. *The Reform of Urban Schools.* Washington, D.C.: National Education Assoc., 1970, pp. 51–61.

Fantini, Mario, Marilyn Gittell, and Richard Magat. *Community Control and the Urban School.* New York: Praeger, 1968.

Goldbloom, Maurice J. "The New York School Crisis." *Commentary* (January, 1969), pp. 43–58.

Gurule, Kay, and Ortega, Joe. "Los Angeles Decentralization with Problems." *Inequality* 15 (November, 1973), pp. 43–44.

Halverson, Jerry F. "Los Angeles Decentralization with Promise." *Inequality* 15 (November, 1973), pp. 39–42.

Harrington, Michael. "The Freedom to Teach: Beyond the Panaceas." *The Village Voice,* October 3, 1968.

Haskins, Kenneth W. "A Black Perspective on Community Control." *Inequality* 15 (November, 1973), pp. 23–34.

Hentoff, Nat. "Ocean Hill-Brownsville and the Future of Community Control." *Civil Liberties* 260 (February, 1969), pp. 1–8.

Krug, Mark M. "Chicago: The Principals' Predicament." *Phi Delta Kappan* 56 (September, 1974), pp. 43–45.

Los Angeles Unified School District. *Summary of Major Suggestions for Further Decentralization of the Los Angeles City Schools.* Los Angeles: Decentralization Office, Los Angeles City Schools, January, 1971.

New York Civil Liberties Union. *The Burden of Blame: A Report on the Ocean Hill-Brownsville School Controversy.* New York: Civil Liberties Union, 1969.

Novak, Michael. *The Rise of the Unmeltable Ethnics.* New York: Macmillan Co., 1971.

Ornstein, Allan. "Research on Decentralization." *Phi Delta Kappan* (May, 1973), pp. 610–614.

Scribner, Jay D., and David O'Shea. "Decentralization of Administrative and Policy-Making Structures of Large City School Districts: A Theoretical Analysis," in *The Uses of Sociology in Education,* 73rd Yearbook of the National Society for the Study of Education. Chicago: University of Chicago Press, 1974.

Seattle Public Schools. *Guidelines for Citizens' School Advisory Councils.* Administration Regulation R–4500–3. December 17, 1970.

Strickman, Leonard P. "Community Control: Some Constitutional and Political Reservations." *Inequality* 15 (November, 1973), pp. 35–38.

"The Failure of 'Community Control'," *Council for Basic Education Bulletin* 13 (December, 1968), pp. 1–5.

Yevish, Irving A. "Decentralization, Discipline, and the Disadvantaged Teacher." *Phi Delta Kappan* 50 (November, 1968), pp. 137–138, 179–181.

Institutionalizing Community Participation in Education

Marilyn Gittell
Brooklyn College,
City University of New York

The 1960s contributed a new emphasis to the concept of citizen participation in public education. Office of Economic Opportunity programs had originally conceived the process of participation as advisory and peripheral to decision making. Experience in these programs, however, convinced the participants that without power in policy making they were performing a meaningless ritual. Many of the social engineers who conceived these programs to serve the cause of social and institutional change also recognized the need to specify a more direct role for those who were formerly powerless. Those who held power in existing institutions resisted any participatory role for citizens which would interfere with their power. They used the terminology of participation, but their definition excluded delegation of power. From the perspective of these various interests, the term "citizen or community participation" is subject to different interpretations. For the purposes of this chapter, community participation is defined as direct community involvement in decision making.

The extent and character of citizen participation must be addressed in all aspects of the educational policy-making process, at all levels and in all areas of decision making. No aspect of decision making should be totally isolated from consumer or citizen input and accountability. Any process that excludes participation of the people who are recipients of the service and who have a direct interest in policy decisions must end up lacking in responsiveness to needs.

Prevailing institutional arrangements emphasize the role of school professionals in policy making. Professionals control all levels and areas of decision making; they also have major roles in education interest groups. They advise state and local legislatures and administer educational policy on all levels down to the classroom. They are protective of their power, and defensive of the prerogatives they have established. Too often, this power is used defensively to protect the educational status quo with little regard for standards, outputs, goals, and procedures for accountability. In many ways, they have lost interest in the impact of their policies on the clients they serve and have substituted professional standards and goals. Added to this professional power structure is the growth of strong teacher organizations in recent years. They have become still another component in the professional ranks, with a vested interest which may be in conflict with consumer needs.

Effective community participation is a process which requires a clearly developed governance structure: some functions are allocated at the individual school level, some at the district level, and some at the state level. A balance of citizen and professional decision making can then be outlined in each circumstance. The structure must also insure that educational policy setting is an ongoing, dynamic process. It must allow for constantly evolving output from widespread discussion with a high degree of sensitivity to differences in needs.

Community participation, to be effective, must be institutionalized as a continuing process and must allow for constant feedback and ongoing revision of policy. Some of the specific experiences of the last several years outline the form community participation can take.

In New York City, there have been two major attempts to institutionalize community participation in school decision making. The first was the establishment of three demonstration school districts in 1968 (Ocean Hill-Brownsville, Two Bridges, and I.S. 201), which was planned to test the value of parent participation as a new factor in school decision making. This major experiment was the first along these lines, and was a product of grass roots demand and extended negotiations among parent organizations, the central board, the union, and the superintendent. No definitive delegation of powers was made to the district; some of those involved assumed no power would be delegated; others assumed a wide variety of powers would be forthcoming. The power the districts finally exercised was, in effect, taken by the locally elected community boards. Almost immediately, these newly elected citizen boards confronted the established system and its professional decision making, as well as its established standards. For the first time, a citizen board challenged the basis on which decisions had been made, and insisted that procedures be changed and participation in decision making be broadened. Parents in district schools were to be included in the selection of principals and review of teachers. The local school board members further asserted that they would take on new decision-making powers in areas of educational policy and budget.

In a three year evaluation of the impact of community participation in these experiments, I looked at the changes in personnel, budget, and curriculum policy to measure the effect. Were there changes in who participated, and did that produce changes in policy? With regard to budgeting, for instance, were new priorities developed? Were the same people making decisions about the allocation of resources? Who were the beneficiaries of such new policies or priorities? In the area of educational programs, I looked at the extent of change, particularly as reflected in the interest and flexibility in adopting new programs, and the sources of such innovation. The evaluation centered on client/consumer participation and attempted to determine whether power was redistributed, how broadly that changed policy, and who benefited from such changes. Clearly, it is difficult to totally isolate participation as an independent variable when so many other factors influence educational policy. The conclusions in *Local Control in Education*[1] suggested that there had been a fundamental broadening of participation in decision making in the demonstration districts, and that policy outputs in the areas of budget, curriculum, and personnel were changed. Innovation was markedly increased in education programs; selected personnel decisions were transferred to the community; principals selected by parents and the local board were more community oriented (although not necessarily any different in their educational approaches); allocation of resources was more emphatically directed toward increased employment of community people as paraprofessionals; and expenditures were increased for programs in basic skills development. These are only a few changes noted in the study. The most widely publicized change was the personnel decision to transfer thirteen teachers who the Ocean Hill-Brownsville board determined were not satisfactory. For some, that decision might be viewed as a militant act, a violation of due process; for purposes of my evaluation, I viewed it as a change in the policy output, which suggests the importance of methodology to the conclusion of any evaluation of community participation.

A comparison between the extent and kind of citizen participation in the demonstration districts with participation under the 1969 decentralization in New York City or decentralization in Detroit would show a difference similar to that between direct democracy and representative government. In the Detroit and New York City decentralization experiences, local board elections and a minimal delegation of powers from central to local boards were the major elements of those plans. Broadening of parent or community participation was virtually ignored, and no provision was made under either citywide plan to bring citizen participation to the individual school level.

In both cities, recommendations were made for more extensive citizen participation beyond board elections. The Bundy Plan in New York City emphasized the need to assure citizens roles in individual schools and on the district level. It called for parents to choose four of the nine local district board members. The report also stressed the need for technical assistance to be made available to local boards, and called for smaller districts (45 to 65 in number). The New York City plan retained its 30 (now 31) districts and Detroit established 7 districts. Neither city provided for technical assistance. The large districts and districtwide elections maintained under both plans, without provision for school governancy structures, did not allow fundamental change in parent roles. For example, the representation of minority groups on local boards in both cities was less than it had been on the citywide boards before decentralization. (See Tables 3–1, 3–2).

In contrast, in the demonstration districts, school structures were created to encourage broader parent participation. Only parents voted for a majority of board members in the demonstration districts, and the larger community voted for community representatives on the board. This system led to the election of board members more representative of the community as a whole. The demonstration district procedures also encouraged participa-

Table 3–1
Comparative Profile of Local School Board Members (Averages)

Area Represented	Occupation						Education			% Public School Parents
	% of Board Members in Professional, Technical, or Managerial Positions	% of Board Members Employed as Paraprofessionals or by Poverty Agencies	% of Members in the Clergy	% of Members Who Are Housewives	% of Members Who Are Laborers or Mechanics	Other	% H.S. or Grade School	% B.A. or M.A.	% Professional	
NYC Under Decentralization (1970)	63.8	10.3	5.3	16.6	4.0	10.0	33	56	23	46.8
Detroit Under Decentralization	61.3	—	3.2	12.9	22.6	—	50	44.1	5.9	67.6
Demonstration Districts NYC	16	44	9	22	3.3	6	78	6	15	85

Source: Marilyn Gittell, "Decentralization and Citizen Participation in Education." Reprinted from *Public Administration Review* © 1972 by The American Society for Public Administration, 1225 Connecticut Avenue, N.W., Washington, D.C. All rights reserved.

51

Table 3–2
Comparison of Ethnic Backgrounds of Local School Board Members (Averages)

Area Represented	% Pupil Population Non-White	% School Board Members Non-White
NYC Under Decentralization (1970)	34.4	17
Detroit Under Decentralization	63	30
Demonstration Districts NYC (Lay Members)	56	61

tion of parents and community members in *all* aspects of school policy. It was far from a perfect system, but it did achieve more community involvement. Realistically, one must recognize that the school crisis in 1968 in New York City encouraged participation and support in the demonstration districts, and the district leadership wanted to involve their constituents. One cannot avoid the conclusion, however, that a genuine commitment to community participation requires extensive attention to structures at the individual school and district level which encourage and support direct community roles in the selection and review of personnel, the determination of priorities in the allocation of resources, and the development of educational options.

Of primary importance in the development of a participatory system is the need to make information available and to provide technical assistance to new participants. Knowledge is a form of power, and citizens must be provided with full information on all issues if community participation is to be effective. The self-fulfilling failure model for community participation provides no technical resources, limits information flow, and keeps the governance structure simple to limit the avenues for participation. Public apathy and incompetence then can be blamed for failure.

No better argument can be made for this case than the recent events in New York City. Daily newspaper stories related the abuses and irregularities in local school board handling of funds and personnel decisions. Earlier concerns had centered around low voter turnouts and the lack of interest. The results are manifest in the statement of a former member of the city board, "Local autonomy in school as in governmental affairs, inevitably will lead to politics, to corruption and to inefficiency." [2]

Our two-year study of the New York City decentralization concluded that the status quo had been maintained in all but two districts. Those two districts had confronted the law and the system and had turned much of the decision making over to the parents in individual schools in their districts. These decisions were not part of the legislation, but were made by the local boards under pressure from well-organized parent and community groups. Neither of those districts has ever been cited in the various charges. In fact, charges are applicable to the districts that we concluded had made no effort to engage parents in decision making, and conducted business as usual. The District 23 board, interestingly enough, now controlled by a major opponent to the old Ocean Hill-Brownsville board, has been charged with major misuse of funds. Community groups in that area have claimed since 1969 that such practices were going on and that they have been excluded from the operation of the district. Information is not available, and the local board makes decisions in closed meetings.

The New York City Plan ignored all of the admonitions for guaranteeing parent and community participation; it made no effort to provide technical assistance; and to all intents and purposes, it made no effort to redistribute power to a broader cross-section of its consumers. The citywide plan merely created local elected boards and assigned them the single power of appointing a community superintendent. The Chance-Mercado court decision[3] was a far more important factor in expanding the power of local boards than the law itself because it invalidated the city examination procedure for selection of principals. As a result, local boards could choose principals under the more flexible state requirements. Only the two districts noted above took advantage of the decision to involve parents from individual schools in that process. Four or five other districts established parent advisory councils; the rest continued to operate as closed bodies in appointing principals.

None of the districts have really changed the budgeting process. Again, the two districts noted made adjustments in some priorities in a limited way. Under the present structure, however, at least 80 percent of the New York City school budget is earmarked, leaving little or no discretion for local districts. Without local control of funds, except for relatively minor expenditures by the district office, citizen roles in budgeting cannot be developed in any meaningful way.

Community School Boards (CSB) were to be involved in decisions with respect to both the expense budget and the capital budget. In the expense budget, teachers' salaries and established ratios for specialized personnel are beyond control of the CSBs; both items are determined by the union contract.

Unless citizen participation is an input to contract negotiations, a vital area of policy making with regard to budget and personnel matters is denied. Great effort was expended in New York City during negotiation of the last contract to include several local school board members, but even this minor adjustment was resisted by the union. Another central constraint on the budgetary discretion of CSBs is the requirement that excess personnel assigned from the district to the central board still must be paid from district funds. This obviously limits the local board in determining priorities in the allocation of resources, and also limits its personnel powers.

The central Board has also retained discretion in the distribution of Title I funds. Our report noted that, "For example, CSB 24 was promised last year [1972] that all disadvantaged children coming [based] into the district would be accompanied by title and state urban money. The city Board did send $100 of the $269 Title I funds per child, but the other $169 from Federal monies was never received." [4]

The CSBs have even less power over the capital budget. The decentralization law charges the city Board through the chancellor with the responsibility to develop the capital budget. The power delegated to the CSBs includes only the ability to submit proposals for projects within their jurisdictions. Final power to decide rests with the central Board and other city agencies.

The right to hire and fire teachers, principals, and other school workers is probably the most explosive of all the issues in which the CSBs have become involved. The question of teacher accountability to the community assumes that the community should have some power over teacher recruitment and selection. The original decentralization legislation in 1969 actually granted the CSBs almost no power over staffing. Central control of teacher hiring was retained, except in districts in which the students scored in the lowest 45 percent in reading achievement. In those districts, teachers could be recruited if they had passed the National Teachers Examination. Otherwise, the citywide teacher examination system was retained. In fact, districts found that union seniority rules and central procedures greatly limited their ability to screen and hire teachers.

This citywide examination system also minimized the recruitment of black and Puerto Rican administrators who were, after all, selected from the pool of teachers in another recruitment process. This became the subject of a suit by the NAACP in 1970,[5] which invalidated the examination procedure and opened the selection of principals to wider groups of applicants. (See Table 3-3).

In the demonstration districts citizen challenges to the selection of principals contributed to the court action and the change in policy. In Ocean Hill, the community was granted special permission to create a personnel category called "Demonstration School Principal." This category was subsequently declared invalid by the courts, precisely because it was a procedure which did not use the traditional examination-based selection procedure. The important point, however, is not that the procedure was declared invalid, but that an alternative approach was tried. In those districts where the challenge to established procedure was first made, a new way of selecting principals was instituted. The change was important not only in terms of not using the traditional, professional screening devices, but also in terms of who had the power to choose the principals. For the first time in New York City, community boards and parent committees were involved in the selection of principals.[6]

Any discussion of school personnel policy must deal with the role of professional associations and unions. These associations serve as the major checks on the limited power of the CSBs in the area of personnel policy. Restrictive provisions of union contracts,

Table 3–3

Comparison of Percentage of Black and Puerto Rican Principals to White Principals in Five Largest U.S. School Systems, 1970

City	*Total Number of Principals*	*Percent Black*	*Percent Puerto Rican*	*Percent Black and Puerto Rican*[a]
Detroit	281	16.7	—	16.7
Philadelphia	267	16.7	—	16.7
Los Angeles	1,012	8.0	1.7	9.7
Chicago	479	6.9	—	6.9
New York	862	1.3	0.1	1.4
City	*Total Number of Assistant Principals*	*Percent Black*	*Percent Puerto Rican*	*Percent Black and Puerto Rican*
Detroit	360	24.7	0.2	24.9
Philadelphia	225	37.0	—	37.0
Los Angeles	—	—	—	—
Chicago	714	32.5	—	32.5
New York	1,610	7.0	0.2	7.2

a Thus New York City has by far the lowest percentage of minority representation. The next lowest city, Chicago, has almost five times the percentage of minority principals in New York City. As is shown also in the table above, there is a similar imbalance of minority assistant principals.

Source: *Chance and Mercado* v. *Board of Education, 330 F. Supp.* (S.D. N.Y. 1971).

including seniority and historical practices of evaluation, have deterred any citizen role in the area of teacher recruitment or review under the decentralization plan. The Council of Supervisory Associations has critically reported on the hiring practices and limited capability of administrators chosen outside the traditional system.

Over the last few years under the New York City decentralization, efforts by local district boards to adjust the selection of staff and special personnel have been met by either union or bureaucratic stonewalling. One district refused to accept twenty-three curriculum specialists assigned to the district by central headquarters because none were black or Puerto Rican, and the district board judged those assigned to be inappropriate to district needs. That district was without curriculum specialists, the board unable to choose their own people. Districts that recruited bilingual staff were accused of bypassing regularly licensed teachers, and hiring unqualified personnel. Parent or citizen participation in personnel selection seemed to be particularly abhorrent to the school professionals. Concessions to local school boards were not readily made, and any effort to move even further toward more direct citizen participation was openly opposed.

The decentralization law granted the CSBs a greater degree of control over curriculum than over budget and personnel decisions. The law stipulates only that the chancellor will set minimum standards and will periodically review such standards. The determination of instructional materials lies essentially in the hands of the CSB. According to our study, local board members, in fact, perceive of their power as being greater in this area than in budget or personnel. When asked whether they had experienced any conflicts with the city Board in the area of curriculum, about 90 percent of the CSB members responded in the negative, or indicated that these conflicts were much less pronounced than those in the area of personnel and budget. Nor did parents perceive that CSBs were unduly limited in curriculum matters.[7]

Basic education programs and ancillary programs are two curriculum areas in which we reviewed community participation. The CSBs have attempted innovation in basic education with individual CSBs and schools involved in a number of innovative programs, including open classrooms, schools without walls, and mini-schools. In addition, a number of CSBs have prepared proposals for federal grants. If funding for a specific proposal is approved, the funds are completely under the control of the local board and are not subject to review by the central office.

Attempts at innovation, such as the open classroom, have been impressive, and seem to be the result of active community participation in the educational process. In the two districts which engaged parents directly, innovation was more prevalent. However, these efforts were the exception rather than the rule; most CSBs have not been active in the basic education area.

The CSBs have been more active in the area of ancillary programs. In this area more funds are available to the CSBs. Most local boards have continued experimental and innovative programs, such as special reading and math programs, assistance to underachievers, and after-school study centers. However, restrictions on the use of personnel are defined by contract provisions.

Despite the power that the CSBs have over curriculum, they have not exercised that power in the area of basic education programs. Citizen participation in educational program development has been minimal, although when it has been encouraged and technical assistance provided, the results have been positive. When parents who start out with traditional views on basic skills development are exposed to other educational options, they support innovation.

The experience of the three demonstration districts supported this conclusion. Ocean Hill-Brownsville was the first district in New York City to adopt bilingual schools and open classrooms, with parent encouragement and support. The I.S. 201 district was the first to adopt the Gaeteno method. Although the lack of a clear educational philosophy was a problem in the demonstration districts, just as is true in the CSBs, the demonstration districts implemented a greater variety of innovative programs.

The impact of community participation on the students at I.S. 201 produced a high level of student feelings of ability to succeed. An attitudinal study of these students conducted by Marcia Guttentag indicated that "there is strong evidence that the special climate which has been created by the decentralized community-controlled school has sharply changed the attitudes of children toward the school experience. This attitude shift is important, not only in itself, but also because these positive attitudes apparently precede higher academic achievement and non-traditional job choices." [8]

Our actual experience in the area of community participation in education has been limited. One would naturally assume that the rhetoric of the last decade must have been matched with a variety of programs which offer a laboratory of experience. However, on the contrary, our experience has been limited in scope and practice. As I have indicated, the citywide decentralization plans did not call for community participation beyond the elected local board level. The demonstration districts, which offered a real opportunity for evaluation, were short-lived and plagued by political controversy. Individual school experiments which did involve community participation, like Rough Rock in Arizona and Adams-Morgan in Washington, D.C., showed insignificant educational gains, but never went beyond their limited single school experience. The Boston and Milwaukee alternative school federations struggled with constant financial problems, although showing some of the same increasing participation as the demonstration districts. Recent results in East Palo Alto's Ravenswood district and the Crystal City, Texas, district indicate clearly that concentrated thoughtful pursuit of broadbased parent participation can turn the educational process around and bend it in new directions.[9] In both those districts, parents and community groups were part of the original struggle to gain control of their schools. These groups have used that power to engage parents on the school and district level in every aspect of school decision making, including teacher training, program evaluation, development of budget priorities, curriculum development, etc. Both districts embody a concept of community services that is the major thrust of educational philosophy. They have used political and educational power as a means to develop a participatory system. Their achievements and difficulties should be watched carefully to evaluate community control, because they are among the very few real experiences we have on which to base our conclusions. In large urban centers, individual school or district experiments are sparse, but significant. In San Francisco, recent reports showed the community school made the greatest advances in improving students' reading scores. Alternate schools in Rochester, New York, also demonstrated progress under parent direction. Unfortunately, the existence of these schools is now being challenged by the teachers' union.

From 1967 to date, the urban school reform movement has concentrated on increasing community control of the schools through expanded citizen participation in the decision process combined with a breakdown of large-city school systems to the local neighborhood level. The extent of power sought for neighborhood school boards varies according to particular plans.[10] The rhetoric, however, far exceeds action, and we have few models of effective decentralization and community control. It is easy to espouse support for the concept of decentralization, as many do, while at the same time denying the concept of local control. In fact, at least six large cities adopted what they describe as school decentralization plans; they are arrangements for administrative decentralization, but make no provision for increased local community roles. They do not seek to include any new public voice in the policy process to balance professional control of the system. The plans call for dividing the cities into districts and assigning district superintendents to field positions. In some cities even these field superintendents are maintained at headquarters and have little contact with the local community.

Administrative decentralization must be distinguished from political decentralization, particularly because compromise arrangements often call for administrative decentralization as if it could answer the demands of those seeking an increased community role in school decision making. Administrative decentralization means a shuffling of the bureaucratic and professional staff to provide for more direct field contact, which may involve the creation of field offices or merely the creation of field titles. Political decentralization, on the other hand, requires a shift in power from professionals to the community.

Often administrative decentralization attempts to forestall real local control or compromises between community pressure for policy control and professional defense of the status quo. In Los Angeles, the school board and the professionals twice defeated state legislation for a study of effective decentralization of the Watts district and instead encouraged administrative decentralization of the school system. Other cities responded to mounting community interest and pressure for local control with plans that called for dividing the city school system into districts or regions and assigning district superintendents to these field positions. None of these plans included a new role for the community or a balance of professional power with citizen participation.

In Philadelphia, Boston, and Los Angeles the professional school associations and the unions were instrumental in defeating efforts to move toward delegation of policy-making powers to the local communities. In several cities like Houston and Milwaukee, administrative decentralization was a reaction to pressure from local community groups. Neither plan provided for increased community participation. State studies of political decentralization have been conducted in California, Massachusetts, Illinois, and Wisconsin, but there appears to be little evidence that professional pressures opposing political decentralization can be avoided even at the state level. The results in California and Massachusetts suggest that the outcome in most states is more likely to be a plan for administrative decentralization of the city school system.

In any plan for decentralization which is committed to go beyond administrative restructuring, community participation in policy development can be accomplished in several stages. The first consideration is the preparation of the plan; this is probably the most crucial and the most difficult stage at which to involve the public. The planning phase is generally viewed by professionals as solely theirs, and dependent upon professional expertise. There may also be professional concern that early public participation can endanger or cause undue delay. There is increasing awareness, however, that the early involvement of community representatives is likely to result in the development of more realistic plans, supported by the community at critical stages. Early public participation can also be an effective means of broadening the base of participation in subsequent implementation. Engagement in the planning process assures fuller appreciation of the intricacies involved. In the Fort Lincoln project and the Anacostia district in Washington, D.C., community groups were involved in the planning period.[11]

The content of plans for decentralization provides another basis for evaluation of community roles and potentially provides the measure for its effectiveness. The extent of balancing of community and professional roles and of central and local power is the key issue. The major policy questions in any plan will be the setting of local boundaries, the system of representation and governance for the local agency, and the division of personnel and budget control between the central and local agency. Clearly, the size of districts and their constituency can influence the extent and character of community participation, as evidenced in the New York City and Detroit plans.

How the central and local boards divide responsibility for policy relating to personnel and budget will directly affect the extent to which new local units with increased community participation can achieve institutional change. If civil service, contract and budget constraints so completely delimit local policy roles as to make them nonfunctional, there is little reason to anticipate meaningful local participation. Much of the evidence suggests that if a central authority is retained close to its previous roles and new local decentralized units have little or no power, there will be no inducement to participation. The citizenry will quickly measure the investment of time in terms of ability to effect policy.

If the purpose of decentralization is to effect institutional change, shared responsibility between professionals and clients requires a redistribution of power. The division of responsibility between central and local agencies and the extent of control by local representative bodies, as well as the mechanism for broad participation as reflected in the plan, will determine the potential for these results. When central agencies are abolished, or diminished in size, these can be indications of significant potential shifts in roles beyond the specific delegations of power to local agencies. Provision for individual school governance is another indication of commitment. Such provision can be included in legislation or formal plans.

The final stage for evaluation of decentralization would be in the implementation of a plan. Even a limited delegation of power can be broadened in practice as indicated by the experience in Ocean Hill-Brownsville. Conversely, broad grants of power may not be fully utilized for various reasons. In the case of the three demonstration school districts in New York City, no specific power was delegated, but local strategists used harassment, pressure, and open confrontation to broaden their roles. The greater the direct involvement of community in the two earlier stages, the more likely it will be that local units will take on policy roles in the implementation. The broader the base of participation and the more highly organized the community is, the more probable that concern will be with local control over policy. Policy is also more likely to be changed under the above circumstances. On the other hand, those programs centrally established, with very limited or no local community participation, will generally produce little community interest or involvement at any stage. The chances for institutional or policy changes are also nil.

Restructuring the governance of American education offers the possibility of creating an environment in which priorities can be reordered and responsiveness to the various communities of interest assured. The dynamic of a viable social system, if it is to be functional, requires a constant reappraisal and adjustment of its institutions.

Those who control the schools have been unable to produce acceptable results; they have excluded the public and the students from a meaningful role in the policy process. The structure of schools must be adjusted to encourage the involvement of all interested parties, and to give the community greater control over educational institutions.[12] Participation in itself provides an involvement with the system which can diminish alienation and also can serve to stimulate educational change; it is itself an educational experience. Community participation implies a redistribution of power within the educational subsystem. The definition of "community" includes not only parents of school children, but also other segments of the public. It is directed toward achieving a mechanism for a participatory system which can deal with the political failure of educational systems. Community participation is intended to create an environment for development of meaningful educational policies and experimentation with a wide variety of alternate solutions and techniques. It also seeks to achieve a more equitable allocation of resources as a result of the redistribution of power. It seems plausible to assume that a school system that is devoted to community needs and serves as an agent of community interests will provide a more encouraging environment in which children can learn. This conclusion is based on the finding of educational research that child and teacher attitudes are the major influence in educational performance. In the community school environment, there is far better opportunity to achieve the more positive and sympathetic attitudes which will lead to a better performance and educational achievement.[13]

Properly instituted, community control is an instrument of social change. The redistribution of power is in itself an aspect of that change. If adequate provision is made for the technical resources to carry out this new role, community participation has the potential for providing new insights into our concept of professionalism as well as our general theories of educational expertise. If community boards have the resources to engage a variety of professionals in the policy process, institutional changes of all kinds can be anticipated.

NOTES

1. Marilyn Gittell, Maurice R. Berube, Frances Gottfried, Marcia Guttentag, Adele Spier, *Local Control in Education* (New York: Praeger Publishers, 1972).

2. *The New York Times,* October 29, 1974, p. 1.

3. Chance and Mercado v. Board of Examiners 330 F. Supp. (S.D.N.Y. 1971).

4. Marilyn Gittell et al., *School Boards and School Policy* (New York: Praeger Publishers, 1973), p. 56.

5. Chance and Mercado v. Board of Education.

6. Gittell et al., *Local Control in Education,* p. 9.

7. Gittell et al., *School Boards and School Policy,* p. 80.

8. Gittell et al., *Local Control in Education,* pp. 116–127.

9. See Tim Parsons, "The Community School Movement," *Community Issues* 2 (Flushing, New York: Institute for Community Studies, Queens College, City University of New York, December 1970), pp. 69–71; and Herbert Hirsch, Armando Gutierrez, and Santiago Hinomosa, "The Lion and the Cricket: The Making of Militants in Crystal City, Texas," in Don Davies, ed., *Schools Where Parents Make a Difference* (Boston: Institute for Responsive Education, 1976), pp. 77–89.

10. Marilyn Gittell, "School Decentralization Today," *Community Issues* 3 (Flushing, N.Y.: Institute for Community Studies, Queens College, City University of New York, November 1971); Parsons, "The Community School Movement."

11. Mario D. Fantini, Milton A. Young, and Frieda Douglas, *A Design for a New and Relevant System of Education for Fort Lincoln New Towns* (Washington, D.C.: School District, 1968).

12. Rod Lewis, "Indian Education Legislation," *Inequality in Education* 10 (December 1971): 19–21; Dan Rosenfelt, "New Regulations for Federal Indian Funds," *Inequality in Education* 10 (December 1971): 21–25.

13. The work of Eugene Litwak and Henry Meyer has suggested that the joint functioning between bureaucratic and community primary groups is generally neglected in sociological theory. They hypothesize that social control and goal achievement in modern society are accomplished through the joint contributions of both types of social forms and that optimal control and achievement will be obtained when these forms are in balance. Eugene Litwak and Henry J. Meyer, "A Balance Theory of Coordination Between Bureaucratic Organizations and Community Primary Groups," *Administrative Science Quarterly,* 11 (June 1966): 58. See also Eugene Litwak and Henry J. Meyer, *School, Family and Neighborhood: The Theory and Practice of School-Community Relations* (New York: Columbia University Press, 1974).

The Future of
Community Participation
in Educational
Policy Making

David Selden

Former President, American Federation of Teachers

Local Control: Middle-Class Involvement

From its earliest beginnings in the small towns of New England to the present, public education has been governed by local school boards. Local control of education is based on the fact that in the past, money for schools came almost entirely from local property taxes. Local control continues, even though monies for schools now come mostly from state sources, and education is legally considered a state responsibility.

Because local school boards meet publicly, with their actions becoming public record, it is often assumed that there has been a high level of public participation in school affairs. In fact, however, public participation in school decision making, whether as school board members, voters, or otherwise, has been mainly concerned with fiscal and budgetary matters. Except for public outbursts every now and then against "progressive education" or some other program thought to be too extreme, what actually happens inside schools and what educators are trying to do have largely been accepted without protest.

Another restriction on public participation in school policy making, official or informal, has been the fact that what participation there has been has come traditionally from the middle class. School board members tend to be lawyers, real estate operators, college-graduated housewives, or owners of small businesses. It is not surprising, therefore, that public schools have been middle-class in their purposes, values, and modes of functioning.

Educators vs. Taxpayers: The Rise of Bureaucracy

The history of American education might be thought of as a long contest between the school establishment and the public: educators versus taxpayers. Educators, fulfilling their mission as the standard-bearers of civilization, have constantly sought to expand the educational enterprise to meet the increasing needs of American society, while school board members, legislators, and other representatives of taxpayers have just as constantly sought to limit the costs of schooling.

As our educational structure expanded and added more teachers, administrators, specialists, and clerical and maintenance personnel, our school systems became more bureaucratic. Lines of responsibility, rules, hierarchical arrangements, and standard procedures evolved, and role functions of staff members became more specialized. The process became more standardized and impersonal: the larger the system, the more bureaucratic it became.

"Bureaucratic" has become a pejorative term, but bureaucratic structures are not without merit. They serve to establish order, responsibility, and equity in management structures which otherwise might be capricious, inefficient, and riddled with political influence and favoritism. The school systems of New York, Chicago, Boston, and literally hundreds of smaller school districts often seemed corrupt and ineffective until bureaucratic order was established.

Nevertheless, bureaucracies do tend to develop internal lives of their own which have little or nothing to do with the purposes for which they were created. When this happens only some outside force—the state legislature, the state department of education, or a local citizens' movement, for instance—can correct the situation.

The Education Establishment: Power to the Powerful

The basic structure of school systems became fixed sometime around World War I. Schematically, school systems closely resemble the structure of typical medium-sized corporations in private enterprise. Boards of education correspond to boards of directors; presidents or executive vice-presidents of typical corporations correspond to school superintendents. Each structure has central staff departments and localized branches with school principals performing many of the functions of branch managers. In school systems, teachers are production workers, pupils are products and the general public is the consumer.

As the structure of the educational enterprise became more stable and the hierarchical role-functions more standardized, a parallel structure of voluntary associations developed which connected persons in similar status roles horizontally throughout the nation. Most of these associations were clustered within the National Education Association (NEA). Until recently their chief officials, along with administrators and school board members in the enterprise itself, constituted the educational establishment. However, two groups were excluded from the establishment: teachers and the public.

Most teachers belong to the state associations affiliated with the NEA. Until recently, these associations were dominated by principals, superintendents, and other management personnel. A more or less benign relationship between teachers and their supervisors was maintained by various devices of compulsion "for the good of the system." This arrangement was highly satisfactory for the members of the establishment, but was completely inadequate for teachers.

Within the establishment, the only national organizations representing the public were the state and local board associations, whose interests were almost entirely fiscal and managerial, and the National Congress of Parents and Teachers. The latter organization was more often a servant to the rules of the establishment than a real force for improvement of educational quality, or an advocate of educational reform. Although there have been a number of reform-minded organizations of citizens in big cities which have refused to be tools of the local establishment or of its critics, efforts to link these local groups into a nationwide force have never been successful.

After World War II: The Old Establishment Under Siege

Regardless of their other effects, wars are powerful change agents of society. They also serve as historical watersheds. Time, in terms of social history, tends to be counted as "before the war," or "after the war." World War II certainly had this impact on American education.

Before the war the authority of the educational establishment was virtually unchallenged. The war brought the baby boom and the demand for vastly increased school facilities. It accelerated migration, particularly of blacks and members of Hispanic groups, from the rural South, Puerto Rico, and Mexico to the big cities of the North, California, and the Southwest. It brought the cold war between the United States and the Soviet Union.

After the war, as schools became more crowded, turbulent, and less able to meet the new needs of American society, the old establishment was increasingly under siege from military leaders, teachers, and civil rights organizations in the new urban communities. The main stress of the new pressure on education was felt in the big cities where new militant black organizations sprang up in the postwar period and where the new militant teacher movement had its base.

Initially, the civil rights movement was primarily concerned with fighting racial discrimination in transportation and public accommodations, and the problem of school integration was left to the more established organizations, such as the National Association for the Advancement of Colored People and the Urban League. But as social equality, distinguished from desegregation, became the overriding goal of black organizations, the crucial importance of public education became more apparent. The inferior education available to blacks in the segregated schools of the South and in the schools of the black slums of the North would have to be greatly improved, if blacks were to achieve social, economic, and political equality with whites.

The educational establishment was slow to adjust to the demands of the new militant civil rights movement. The establishment, while strongly favoring better schools, did not associate educational quality with integration, in spite of many Supreme Court decisions affirming the interdependence of the two goals. In fact, many components of the establishment were themselves segregated, and the establishment as a whole had accommodated itself to discrimination in education. While many were talking earnestly about the "teaching profession," increased professionalism was not associated with raising the economic status of teachers or with giving them a share in educational decision making.

The struggles of black organizations and other ethnic group organizations outside the establishment and of teacher organizations to gain power within the educational establishment dominate the history of education during the 1960s. Under the impact of those struggles, profound changes have taken place in the establishment itself, and more changes will certainly occur in the future.

Community Control: Beginnings in New York

Both the militant teacher movement and the militant black movement for school reform emerged in New York City in the early 1960s. The chief goal of the militant teacher movement was collective bargaining; the chief goal of militant black organizations was community control of education.

Soon after the United States Supreme Court outlawed racially segregated schools in 1954, the New York City Board of Education declared its intention to eliminate de facto segregation from the school system. To most school reformers this meant that not only would all-black schools be eliminated, but also that the admittedly substandard schools in the slum areas, where most blacks lived, would be upgraded. Black children, regardless of the school they attended, would thus receive the same quality of education as white middle-class children, it was widely assumed.

Integration and quality education quickly became intertwined as goals. The right of all children to equality of educational opportunity, regardless of race or ethnic background, was the basis for the Supreme Court's ruling. According to the ruling, racially separate schools are illegal because they cannot be equal, and furthermore, integration would make it difficult to discriminate in the distribution of educational services. If equality of educational opportunity did not mean that black children would learn and achieve as much as their white counterparts, what *did* it mean?

The years following the New York City School Board's integration declaration saw a growing skepticism that equality of educational opportunity would be achieved without a drastic over-hauling of the entire school system. One proposal after another to integrate the schools was rejected or proven to be ineffective, and resistance to integration, even as a goal, increased in white middle-class areas. On the other hand, demands for improving the quality of education in the slum schools by adding services invariably floundered for budgetary reasons.

To blacks and many non-black social reformers, the failure of the city to integrate or to improve instruction in slum schools was a manifestation of white racism. Educational writers not only blamed "the white power structure" for failing to live up to its high-sounding objectives, but they also blamed racism in the school system itself for the low academic achievement of black children. The kids were not learning, they said, because the teachers, overwhelmingly white, either did not think black kids were capable of learning, or worse, because white teachers just did not care about black kids.

In other words, the school system, from top to bottom, had rejected blacks; blacks should, therefore, reject the system. They should take over the schools in the ghettos and run them to suit themselves. The teachers then would be forced to teach black and Puerto Rican children. Integration could wait. "They" were not going to do anything about it anyway. Enter community control.

A Theory Is Born: *Reconnection for Learning*

The theoretical basis for the community control movement was set forth in *Reconnection for Learning* (Ford Foundation, 1967), known familiarly as "The Bundy Report." McGeorge Bundy, President of the Ford Foundation, was named by Mayor John Lindsay in 1967 to be chairman of a panel to study possible de-centralization of the New York City school system. The panel's report was *Reconnection,* and its principal author was Marilyn Gittell.

Reconnection stated that the New York City school system had become too large, too insensitive, and too remote for its clien-tele, and that this alienation was mainly responsible for student academic retardation. At least three previous major reports had complained about the isolation of the school bureaucracy, but *Reconnection* differed from these previous analyses in its proposed remedy.

For years it had been taken for granted in educational circles that one way to improve the quality of education was to reduce the number of school districts by consolidating small districts to form larger districts. Many believed that large districts could achieve economies of scale which were beyond the reach of small districts. Large districts could also give improved service through greater professionalism of staff, and they could provide a more varied curriculum for students.

But following World War II it became obvious that there was such a thing as being *too* big. The economies of large scale operation were offset by bureaucratic delays and snafus, and that ever-present hazard of big bureaucracies, graft. Staff professionalization in New York especially had brought increased rigidity, inbreeding, and resistance to any kind of structural change. Previous studies had pointed out these factors, but remedial proposals had been limited to suggested changes in administrative structure and procedure. In general they advocated that final decision-making authority, tightly held at central headquarters at 110 Livingston Street, Brooklyn, should be parcelled out to the thirty field superintendents and to school principals where feasible.

Reconnection, while generally agreeing with these previous diagnoses of the system's ills, proposed that decentralization be accomplished by giving decision-making power to "communities." Adding the element of community control to the already widely accepted concept of decentralization did not seem like a radical new step. The community control spokespersons claimed that they only wanted for New York City communities what suburban and rural communities had always enjoyed.

Mass movements usually depend upon intellectuals to articulate basic concepts, to rationalize internal conflicts, and to convince skeptics. In this case the embryo of the community control movement was aided by planning grants and seed money from the Ford Foundation, headquartered in Manhattan, under whose guidance the movement soon took on a form and substance it otherwise might not have attained. Since reason had been tried and found wanting in the struggle for equality of educational opportunity, militancy and direct action became the mode.

Teacher-Community Conflict: War and an Uneasy Truce

While civil rights and community leaders carried on their war against the board of education, teachers continued their struggle against the same adversary. Even though they had won collective bargaining rights late in 1961, teachers continued to move from one crisis to another as they sought to negotiate higher salaries and improved conditions in the schools.

Throughout the early stages of the community control struggle, the teachers and their union, the United Federation of Teachers (UFT), were supportive of the movement's aims, which seemed only an extension of their own objectives. Teachers wanted schools in which they could teach successfully, and community leaders wanted schools where children could learn. Teachers, therefore, initially viewed the community control advocates as possible allies.

But in the eyes of the leaders of the community control movement, the UFT was part of the New York City school establishment. As the community control movement became more militant and strident, its cutting edge was directed more and more against the teachers and their union. After several early clashes over proposed changes in teacher and pupil assignment policies and demands for reform in the examination system for selecting teacher and supervisory personnel, the showdown came in the bitter Ocean Hill-Brownsville strikes in the spring and fall of 1968.

The battle of Ocean Hill-Brownsville resulted in concessions and losses on each side. The United Federation of Teachers successfully protected its collective bargaining rights and the right of individual teachers to "due process" when charges are brought against them; in the aftermath of the strikes the community control forces persuaded the legislature to institute a modified form of community control on a city-wide basis.

Much of the bitterness of the struggle in Ocean Hill-Brownsville remains on both sides, however. An uneasy truce rocks along from year to year, with neither side accepting the other's basic premise. Community control advocates still maintain that low student achievement is primarily due to isolation of the schools from the communities they serve, and that community control is necessary to force teachers to "shape up or ship out." The teachers, for their part, just as stoutly maintain that degrading social and economic conditions, lack of proper compensatory education programs, and unwarranted community hostility toward teachers are the main sources of underachievement. In the meantime, blacks and Puerto Ricans continue to achieve less than their white middle-class counterparts.

A Tenuous Theory—and a Troublesome Reality

One of the reasons that community control, or any form of community participation, for that matter, has not made greater headway is that the theory underlying the movement is tenuous at best. There seems to be no hard evidence that community control, or even community involvement, has ever been responsible for increased academic achievement by students. It is true that self-confidence is highly correlated with achievement, but it has yet to be demonstrated that self-confidence can be transmitted from a community to an individual child.

Furthermore, it seems logical that to have community control there must be a community. Slum communities are notoriously unstable. Many slum schools have 50 percent or more turnover in pupil enrollment during the school year. Under such conditions it is impossible to establish a sense of community comparable to that which exists in small towns and suburbs.

Again contrary to the assertions of its advocates, community control of education in its present context is not the same thing as the local control we have known. Historically local control is rooted in taxing authority. If the community boards had to raise their own funds through taxes on property within their boundaries the effect would be devastating. Most slum districts would be even worse off than they are now.

It must be recognized, too, that our time-honored system of local control has not been an unmixed blessing. Local school boards have been responsible for much that is mean, petty, and repressive in American education. It has been local boards of education, for the most part, that have banned and burned books, fired non-conforming teachers, and restricted educational opportunity for reasons of race or social class. Quite contrary to our democratic principles, small school districts have often served as havens for hoarded wealth and privilege.

Breaking up large school districts to form smaller ones would also seriously interfere with efforts to integrate students. There may be cities where integration is a practical impossibility, but there are many others, some of them under federal court order to desegregate, where integration is still a real possibility.

Yet there remains the troublesome fundamental truth of the indictment leveled by *Reconnection:* big city schools, with rare exceptions, *are* isolated from the communities they serve. This cannot be good for the schools, the students, or the communities.

Toward Coalition: Compensatory Education and Parent Participation

Experience with community control of education over the past ten years has failed to reveal any instance where community control has raised pupil achievement levels or has even been able to function from year to year without a great amount of assistance from outside the community.

On the other hand, there are many examples of continuing community involvement in school-level decision making short of actual control. The difference between control and participation or involvement is that instead of tearing the system apart and installing a new set of bosses under the rubric of community control, the community is allowed into the existing decision-making structure.

Although a community control experiment in Chicago did not succeed, the city does have a form of community participation. School councils elected by parents have functioned successfully for several years. The councils meet monthly and the school principals report to them. The meetings provide forums where parents' complaints can be heard. At least 60 percent of the membership of each council must be composed of parents with children in the school. The councils have the right to hire principals from the official list when vacancies occur. Teacher collective bargaining is undisturbed.

The experience with community control and participation has shown that neither alone can improve the achievement of children. Community and parent participation cannot substitute for adequate school staffing, good instructional facilities, and relevant curriculum. Parents and teachers should and can agree that children outside the majority middle class for which our schools were designed must have a much more intensive educational experience to compensate for the social handicaps associated with economic deprivation.

Any successful scheme of parent or community participation in school decision making must take into account the changes which have occurred within the educational establishment and in American society since World War II. The most notable change has been in the racial and ethnic composition of the populations of American cities. Most American cities are slowly—in some cases swiftly—becoming mainly black, Hispanic, and Oriental, and this shift will have lasting effects on the American political structure. In some cities—Gary, Detroit, Newark, Washington, Baltimore, and Atlanta, for instance—the change in the political power base has already occurred. In many more it is about to happen.

The most notable change within the educational establishment is the rise of teacher power. The old relationships based on status and authority have been swept away and teachers, through collective bargaining and political action, have achieved a large measure of autonomy and a greater share in decision making. That new-found power is not likely to go away; more likely it will continue to increase.

Taking into account the changes in the educational establishment and the changes in American urban society, it seems obvious that the future of both society and education can best be served by forming a new coalition, based on mutual respect, between teachers and leaders of the new urban power structures. In New York City and perhaps some other cities, the hostility between teachers and the new urban majority may appear too wide to be bridged, but this is not so in Chicago, Gary, Newark, Atlanta, and many other places. However, those who should be fighting for better education often are too busy fighting each other. In the meantime, millions of American children fail to get an adequate education.

The Role of Professional Teacher Organizations in Encouraging Community Participation in Education

James A. Harris
Former President, National Education Association

Community participation in education is as desirable as it is necessary. Education belongs to the people, and their participation in it is part of our tradition as a free society. Education is essentially a state function, with administration being delegated to the state education agency and in turn to the school districts created by the state. The organized teaching profession recognizes the control of education—determination of the broad goals of the schools, establishment of financial support, administration through local school boards—as being a public function and so states throughout its resolutions. The National Education Association (NEA), which counts most of the nation's teachers among its members, believes that the professional teacher associations "must promote public understanding of education and encourage wide public and parental participation in solving education's problems" and that "a representative, nonpartisan board of education in each school district also has a responsibility to promote public understanding of the schools." (Resolution A–7)

I will discuss here three primary areas of community participation: school budget development; personnel selection, deployment, and evaluation; and determination of curriculum.

School Budget Development*

Traditional school budgeting has been described as "a process that culminates in the adoption of a fiscal document that reports a plan for expenditure of funds equivalent to anticipated revenue, has a

---

* This section is based on "School Budgeting: Best Practice," by Sol Levin, a paper prepared for the NEA's 14th National Conference on School Finance.

specified time frame, and requires . . . legislative or public approval." In this age of accountability, many school boards now endorse the concept of program budgeting, which "can be defined very narrowly as costing-out programs, or very broadly as planning a systems approach to planning" a school district's future.

Some people consider program budgeting to be a temporary nuisance that will disappear when the accountability movement has run its course. Others are convinced it is here to stay. What follows is a sketch of the budget development process in a fast-growing suburban school district in the northeastern part of the country. The community is generally middle and upper class but has a small black ghetto from which comes about 10 percent of the student population. The budget process is in transition to Program Planning Budgeting System (PPBS). Budget development for the subsequent fiscal year begins in October and ends in May, it is hoped, with a public vote of approval.

In planning the overall strategy, the first product is a calendar of what to do and when. It includes descriptions of the roles of the board, the superintendent and his or her cabinet, the major administrative divisions (construction, personnel, community relations), and most importantly, the board's negotiating team. Next comes preparation of statistical backup data for use by the superintendent, the board, and the negotiating team, and for use subsequently at public hearings. The data include enrollment projections, a ten-year chart of expenditure and revenue categories on a per-pupil and percent-of-budget basis, expenditure data of selected comparable school districts, personnel inventory, and staff ratios.

Projecting fiscal limits in a world of political realism is an essential part of the budget development process. A way to do this is to construct a simple budget model against which to test the developing budget. The first part consists of the built-ins onto which more will be built later, including the legally mandated expenses and what was agreed on at last year's negotiations. Basically, it is last year's budget with certain required items automatically included. In the revenue part, there are certain assumptions —continuation of state aid, continuation of the previous tax rate, sure revenues, and some surplus. Next come projected negotiation results at the strike-limit level, and then adjustments for inflation. And, of course, if enrollment is up, at least the same staff and service levels must be provided for the additional children as for the continuing student body. Other possible revenues are state aid increases, the elastic limit of the local tax generator, and federal grants, which provide the fiscal perimeters of the probable real-world budget.

Involving staff in budget development used to be an act of *noblesse oblige* by the superintendent because he was taught to do that in his professional training. Now, every employee has the right to be involved. However, the privilege channel—which goes through the chain of command—continues, as does the right channel, which is through negotiations with the various employee groups. For example, the administrators talk with principals about new programs and get their ideas, and later they sit across the table negotiating on the same issues. In the near future, students and parents will be similarly involved.

In the privilege approach to involvement, forum and individualized channels are used. For example, principals and other administrators discuss priorities and terms of change; then the special-interest groups (elementary principals, secondary principals, supervisors, district-wide personnel) meet with their division people to discuss general priorities, and their recommendations are recorded for the superintendent's information. Through the individualized channel, the staff makes individual requests for their school departments. Because the district is going PPBS, the budget request forms are designed to solicit requests for existing as well as proposed programs. This encourages involvement of people in the lower operating levels in the school structure, by school and by area of instruction. Other support program requests are submitted by the respective departments, such as transportation. For new programs that are proposed or for significant changes, a program analysis is required.

Some allocation guides on a per-pupil or per-staff basis are used for certain continuing programs. However, these guidelines are subject to change on documentation of special needs. Per-pupil guidelines are used also for certain allocations to encourage schools to budget up to these levels. How the supervisors involve their staff is up to them and, of course, this varies from school to school and department to department. And while this privilege channel is going on, discussions are also taking place across the negotiating table.

How does the superintendent involve the Board of Education? He has about five meetings with the board as a whole and with his top administrative staff, at which times he presents the prepared statistical data. At this point the board is not involved with the minutiae of budget requests. During these meetings the superintendent reports to the board on the status of negotiations on items with major budgetary implications, and elicits fiscal and program priorities from the board. At intervals, summations of budget requests based on the negotiation input are prepared. Finally the superintendent tries to reconcile his position with the board's position in the package he submits as his recommended budget.

Planning is very important in PPBS. Proposals for new programs or major changes in existing programs are funneled through a planning board representing teachers, principals, and the superintendent. Any building principal or department supervisor may submit a request through his/her organization channels or to the program planning board directly. For example, if someone suggests that third-grade reading be changed and everyone agrees that this change is essential, the planning board appoints a subcommittee with the responsibility of investigating and producing the necessary curriculum change. Action of the planning board is strictly advisory.

The next procedure is to take all the requests from the individual schools, departments, and negotiating teams and put them together to test them against the "maybe" budget. The directors review this budget with the principals and supervisors to get it down to district priorities. Here there is consideration of trade-offs and cutbacks. Negotiators are then given the board's final negotiating position. At this stage the employees' union and the board's negotiators may engage in mediation and fact-finding. There may be very little, if any, new money available after negotiating salaries, benefits, and working conditions, meeting legal mandates, making adjustments for inflation, and providing for additional pupils. There are alternative considerations, trade-off considerations, and these may be good; and then talk starts on trade-offs and cutbacks and it is back to negotiating.

The community as a whole comes in for the concluding process. The assistant superintendents submit to the superinten-

dent their division and departmental final budgets, and the negotiating team submits contract settlements. There is a final exchange
of points of view between the superintendent and his staff, and the
superintendent then makes his final decision on the budget he will
submit to the board. The board may also make some changes
at this point, and then the budget is submitted to the voters.
About a month before the elections, the school administration
mails brochures to every taxpayer in the community, and regular,
legally-required public hearings are held. The administrative
staff and board members meet with civic groups in all school
buildings. If the public votes down the budget, the board may implement what is called an austerity budget—95 percent of last
year's budget.

How to reconcile two opposing forces—the output priority
of PPBS and the input priority of negotiations—will continue to
be the key in implementing program budgeting. There are other
problems not so basic, such as the legal structure of the budget
and the "common law" attached to it. The fiscal year is a constraint because PPBS is a continuing process with a long-range
perspective. Another problem is the traditional accounting mentality—the self-contained business office. And a final problem is
the illusion that PPBS can take place in every school system. If
there is no provision for time, qualified personnel, and money
assigned for the task of planning, you can have no planning.

The NEA "believes that planned program budgeting systems . . . are often used in a deleterious manner as vehicles for the
introduction of de facto performance contracting or for the implementation of plans for holding teachers accountable without
permitting them to share in the process of educational decision-
making." It urges that no such system be undertaken or continued
unless (a) the local teachers' association is a full partner in planning and implementation; (b) performance objectives, if utilized,
are defined by certified staff directly affected; (c) the community is
kept fully informed and its cooperation actively sought; (d) the
level of funding ensures maintenance of constructive teaching
loads and adherence to professional salaries; and (e) the plan does
not involve performance contracting.

"The Association is aware of the misuse of PPBS plans and
will assist its affiliates in correcting such abuse."

Personnel Selection, Deployment, and Evaluation

Kenneth B. Clark, in his introduction to *Community Control and the Urban School,* says that "community control of schools is a given in many of the towns, smaller cities, and suburbs of the nation. If an epidemic of low academic achievement swept over these schools, drastic measures would be imposed. Administrators and school boards would topple, and teachers would be trained or dismissed. If students were regularly demeaned and dehumanized in these schools, cries of outrage in the PTAs would be heard—and listened to—and action to remove the offending personnel would be taken immediately." We have never used terms of "community participation" or "community control" when talking about the suburban situation. It has been an understood and accepted fact.

In the nation's suburbs and small cities, the basic overall personnel policies essentially are decisions made by the board of education and the central office administration. These bodies are responsible for the selection, deployment, and evaluation of school personnel. Residents are assured that the best available staff are recruited to carry out the goals, objectives, and curriculum set by the institution, that the staff who are hired for managerial or teaching positions are in agreement with the values of the community and will work to foster and promote an accepted and entrenched way of life.

If and when the community feels there has been a change in board or administrative policy, or that an action is planned which is unacceptable and threatens to damage existing values or academic standards, a swift and an organized reaction occurs to challenge and counter such changes and decisions. The community becomes an active participant in the democratic process—contacts are made with the board, the administrators, and others who make the final decisions. A responsive and organized community exists, not only concerning single issues, but on a continuing basis. It seeks to oppose undesirable changes and is the agent that prods for additional resources and needed personnel. The maintenance of high scholastic achievement is demanded by the educated and informed parent group and by the community at large for their own purposes, and also to attract new residents who are like-minded and will help to maintain quality standards in the schools.

This watchful eye of the suburban community, which can influence school policy, presupposes that all citizens are aware of how the democratic process works and can organize for action to influence existing practices, or to pressure for additional needed services. Until recently such organized efforts were not present in large urban centers. Historically, the low-income, poorly educated community of the inner city (or other poor area) was keenly aware of being an uninformed audience that listened to the decisions made but did not contribute to the scene. They mistrusted the authority of institutionalized governance but felt defenseless to influence decisions.

When the Coleman report was published in 1966, detailing the differences in student achievement and inequality of social forces, one of the grounds for attack was that it considered only the "existing differences." The report did not project the effects of new and experimental remedial programs. Conclusions were then drawn which placed the fault for poor student achievement with the institution rather than with the learner. During the late 1960s, in an effort to remedy existing ills that were made public by Coleman and others, federally funded projects were established under both the Elementary and Secondary Education Act and the Office of Economic Opportunity—projects which offered organizational patterns new to urban communities for the purpose of giving people a voice in the decision-making process. In addition to new curricular projects, there were guidelines and budgets for community involvement and for the establishment of home-school-community liaison groups. The guidelines encouraged participation by local citizens. Liaison groups were created not only to better inform parents, but to help them succeed in making decisions which affected their children's education. The community's role had had no official sanction before these anti-poverty programs.

In federally funded projects, adult involvement was emphasized partly as an educative process, so that advisory groups could propose action from an information base rather than from emotional reactions to unsatisfactory situations. Also, informed parents could become something more than interpreters of school district policies. In Florida, in each of approximately twenty Follow-Through projects, a Parent Advisory Committee participated in the selection of teachers. This particular action became a joint one between the school administration and "parent educators." Administrators and the Parent Advisory Committees formulated selection criteria and then interviewed candidates together.

In this period of urban militancy and federal and foundation funding, groups of parents became involved, informed, and active. In a newly found and organized voice they expressed dissatisfaction with existing professional staff. Early on, complaints were leveled mainly at school principals rather than at other administrative staff or specific teachers. Several urban principals were dismissed, forced from schools, or were made powerless in their positions by parent groups. The immediate community had no authority to make such sweeping changes, but insisted these school personnel had been found sorely lacking in responding to the needs of the student population. From such situations emerged the issue of central administration decision-making power versus control by community school boards. Solutions were sought through the establishment of district-wide committees, policy advisory committees, and various school councils, but whatever the group's composition or name and whatever their mode of operation, final decisions about professional staff lay with the central administration and central board of education. No legal power for enforcement of personnel policies was given to community groups until these groups insisted on such decision-making power.

The situation described above held true in many cities. In Washington, D.C., the Board of Education, through an agreement with Antioch College, established an experiment in community action at the Adams-Morgan School in an attempt to give authority to a decentralized operation. When the community school board became dissatisfied with the services of the project director, they voted to dismiss him. Their authority for such action had not been previously established or granted, but Antioch College did not assign a new director. The community school board, in a bid for broad and strong decision-making powers, selected a new school principal and sought to control all staffing policies. It believed that it must determine the number and the type of personnel needed, and also their qualifications for specific positions. They believed that the school must reflect and serve the community in which it existed.

Evaluation of the staff after one year of service was based on their willingness to experiment with new approaches to classroom practices, on extra efforts to improve the school, and on the long hours needed to fulfill the assignment. In addition, it was often felt that teachers needed to put the needs of children above their own and feel a responsibility to the school and to the community.

Local school boards have run a collision course with central administrations in the selection, deployment, and evaluation of school staff. In large urban areas there are political realities of continuing control over personnel policies by the central administration. Where minority parents feel that teachers or supervisors do not have to meet district certification to be qualified for school openings and have appointed their own selections, the district has not considered such appointments valid and has withheld payment for services. Community criteria for selection are mainly that personnel be from the same minority group as the school population—black teachers with black children, Puerto Rican teachers with Puerto Rican children, Chinese teachers with Chinese children. Where school populations are mixed, it has not been possible to carry out this policy. In these cases, community boards have made allowances for personnel who have a commitment to the education of minority children and have an understanding of minority children's abilities and aspirations. They have been insistent that applicants believe in the principle of community involvement in the educational process. These attributes appear to be more important to selection committees than does an overall educational philosophy. In the main, selected personnel believed strongly that proper schooling for poor children can make a difference educationally.

In New York City many ghetto parents and members of decentralized governing boards have felt that teachers are the key personnel in schooling. Where there has been a problem of middle-class teachers expecting and therefore getting minimum achievement from poor black children, the decentralized boards have wanted the right to dismiss such teachers. Chinese groups, on the other hand, are satisfied with the status quo and align themselves with middle-class school personnel who work through the policies and practices of the "establishment."

Mario Fantini has stated that acceptance of school personnel should be moved away from traditional credentialing and systematized advancement through the system. Instead, emphasis should be placed particularly on performance with students and with parent-community groups.

A director of the Madison Area Project in Syracuse, New York, Fantini states his belief in the rights of community representatives and parents: "If we do not provide superior education for your children, you have a right and responsibility to replace us with others who can. We are accountable to you." In the same context, there is a need to retrain teachers and other school personnel already in the system to work with minority children and in poverty area schools.

The NEA "believes that the educational decision-making process must be as close as possible to the citizens and professional staff directly served by, or involved in, local communities within the cities," and has recommended decentralization of the process within large cities.

We endorse the concept of "appropriate delineation of authority and power between a central city board of education and . . . smaller and more viable units of school governance and administration which will make large city schools more responsive and accountable to the various groups they must serve."

The NEA "also believes that elected community boards of education possess clearly defined authority in the areas of curriculum, educational materials, school program, and personnel, with negotiation rights and procedural due process guarantees for the educators of the city." (Resolution A-6)

The NEA insists, of course, that personnel policies be developed in cooperation with the local education associations, with "cooperative annual review" and "improvements . . . made through the negotiation process" where it exists. (Resolution E-7)

Although the selection, deployment, and evaluation of school personnel are activities in which the public must share, these matters also fall within the realm of what is known as "professional governance" and are (or ought to be) much more in the domain of the profession. The public, through its duly elected boards of education, plays significant roles in the selection of key administrative staff—the superintendent of schools, for example. But in the selection of most other staff, the professional secretariat to the board (the school administration) is expected to have the expertise and professional judgment requisite to the task that laypeople (board members are laypeople vis-a-vis the teaching profession) might not be expected to possess. This is even more important in the complex areas of staff deployment and evaluation where the highest levels of professional expertise ought to be brought to bear on the decision making.

Determination of School Curriculum

Community participation in curriculum development is by no means a new concept. Since the 1930s, many widely differing kinds of school-community relationships have developed over the country. While some of these have decreased the distance between school and community, genuine lay involvement in curriculum is still in the beginning stages.

Traditionally, the curriculum was designed to transmit "the American culture" and to prepare students for college, because a college degree was a passport to a good job in an affluent society. Although the typical parents placed high value on schooling, they were content to be represented in decision-making councils by boards of education. The extent of their own responsibility was to send the kids to school, provide a place for them to study at home, check their report cards, and support education through taxes and the PTA. Curriculum was the domain of professionals and boards of education, and the American system of "universal public education" was widely acclaimed as the best in the world.

Then came Sputnik and an ensuing sense of national urgency concerning education. Rapidly changing social forces made very different demands on the schools. New types of children with myriad kinds of needs came into the classroom. Black parents in the ghetto and white students on campuses began to revolt. They questioned the purpose of school, the quality—and the *equality*—of American education, and above all, the relevance of the school curriculum. The traditional curriculum was no longer viable for self-propelling personalities with different values and belief systems. The role of the teacher had to change. No longer a mere dispenser of facts and of a single culture for all students, the teacher is now becoming a diagnostician, guide, and resource person. His or her task is to assist students in planning what William Alexander, professor of education at the University of Florida, calls a "personal curriculum continuum" of their own.

In this new role the teacher needs information and active participation from parents, and as a consequence, the parent's role has also changed. It is no longer a parent's responsibility just to know how the child is doing in school but also to share with the teacher how the child is doing at home with the family, on a trip, or in the street and how the child reacts in the public library and museum or before the TV set. The parent must assist the student in selecting learning activities. This kind of sharing in education is said to help bridge the generation gap, providing children and parents with common purposes and understandings. Teachers increasingly recognize the educational possibilities of varied experiences in different places, utilizing many kinds of media, and working with community persons and agencies in cooperative sharing of resources.

In models such as "schools without walls" (in Philadelphia, Berkeley, Chicago, and elsewhere) curriculum events take place wherever most desirable and useful to the student. Thus a hospital, a shop, or an insurance firm may serve as a classroom. A recent issue of *Learning* magazine calls the modern museum a "new partner in curriculum," and cites examples of ways in which teachers and museum personnel coordinate visits and loans of materials. Thus, museum exhibits and school programs come alive for the students. In Sturbridge Village, Massachusetts, for example, students can cook, weave, and work with farm tools of colonial times—or can spend the night in the village to round out a 24-hour day in the eighteenth century. In the Boston Children's Museum, students explore the underground network of city cables, sewers, and subways beneath modern Boston. In the Fort Worth Museum of Science and History, workshops range from weather to animal care. The walls of the school are being expanded both to bring the community in and to move school activities out into the community. Alvin Toffler, author of *Future Shock*, even predicts that advanced technology will make it possible for most of a person's education to take place away from the school building.

A good deal of education will take place in the student's own room at home or in a dorm, at hours of his own choosing. With vast libraries of data available to him via computerized information retrieval systems, his own language laboratory, and his own electronically equipped study carrel, he will be . . . freed of the lockstep of the classroom.

All of this is part of a concept, which again has been appropriately named by Dr. Alexander, "the school as a learning management center." With growing recognition of the need for lifelong training in this changing society, continuing education for adults is becoming an integral part of public education. The school must become a dynamic resource center staffed by teachers who are social engineers. Teachers as specialists in various areas surrounded by many different kinds of resources would assist learners of all ages in planning and implementing a "personal curriculum continuum." Their goal would be to facilitate learning—from womb to tomb.

Such a future-oriented idea will undoubtedly seem too far out to some people. Certainly, it would require extensive reform of teacher education curricula and massive programs of on-the-job training for educators. On the other hand, such a model obviously has potential for genuine lay involvement in curriculum planning, and it could prove a viable response to the increased furor and demands of educational consumers today.

Increased consumer awareness in education, vigorously stimulated by Sputnik, was encouraged by the federal legislation which followed, and is an impressive part of the current scene as evidenced by both individual and group criticism of the school. Some of the discontent is real and is caused largely by the inability of schools to respond to the changing needs of society. Much of it, however, emanates from a loss of faith, a feeling of helplessness on the part of segments of the community who have not been full participants in the society. They often view community participation in curriculum as synonymous with control of the curriculum. However, improvement in the level of trust comes from shared responses to recognized needs. In the curriculum process, it begins with shared determination of goals and requires involvement and coordination of all resources in a community.

Without describing in detail any particular approach for

community participation, a brief look at some of the varied and many-faceted efforts since 1930 may be useful. These efforts might be viewed as signposts to models of community involvement.

The cooperative problem-solving approach of the TWA in the 1930s was one of the earliest examples of school and community efforts to help people solve real problems in all areas— economic, social, and educational. It embodied two important concepts: realistic problem solving and continuing adult education.

Another early model, the community school developed in Flint, Michigan, brings the community into the school for education, recreation, and cultural enrichment. Parents also use the school to discuss and plan activities and as a forum to solve a variety of community problems.

The use of paraprofessionals and volunteers in the school has lent impetus to the movement and has helped to ready the community for meaningful involvement in curriculum. Decentralizing the schools, as discussed earlier, has brought decision making closer to the local community with increased involvement. Guidelines for federal legislation, such as the poverty program with "maximum feasible participation" mentioned earlier, and the burgeoning number of alternative schools, are indicators of accelerating community involvement in what schools are all about —the curriculum.

Probably the most widespread of all vehicles for participation of community representatives in decisions about curriculum is the Curriculum Advisory Council. It is sometimes a citywide council with lay and professional representation from varying cultural and ethnic backgrounds. Many people believe that there should always be area and local school building councils serving as the base of the central council, because experience has shown that *involvement is most genuine and meaningful when it is related directly to the child, to his or her parents, or to the special-interest group concerned.* For this reason the local school committees sometimes have subcommittees in each area of specialized interest—the arts, service areas, occupations, and other categories. Thus, lay and professional persons serve as resources in the areas of their competence and have representatives at the building, area, and school district levels.

Finally, PACTS, a school reform plan proposed by Superintendent Barbara Sizemore for the District of Columbia schools, is called "a process of consensus." It involves *P*arents, *A*dministrators, *C*ommunity, *T*eachers, and *S*tudents in the decision-making processes of the schools. One important goal is to reorganize the curriculum by grouping similar subjects together and placing "emphasis on concepts instead of facts." While only in the beginning stages, PACTS already demonstrates potential for change because it "has people working together rather than apart." According to the personnel involved, it is significant because it represents the sharing of power by the administration rather than community demand for power.

Society increasingly demands that schools accept the mission of developing lifelong learners. We have seen that this concept requires a broader grouping of curricular opportunities than in the traditional system and infinitely more alternatives from which to choose. It necessitates, in addition, community planning groups facilitated by competent professionals to provide feedback and evaluation. It can succeed only if students are motivated and possess the basic skills to continue learning.

Preparing Teachers
for Parent Involvement

Daniel Safran

*Center for the Study of Parent Involvement
Oakland, California*

This paper asks and attempts to answer five questions:

   I. Why should parents be involved in the formal education of their children?
  II. Why should teachers be trained to involve parents?
 III. What competencies do teachers need for working with parents?
 IV. How can teachers be helped to achieve these competencies?
  V. What can be done to enable schools of education to meet the challenge of preparing teachers for parent involvement?

Why Involve Parents?

The involvement of parents in the formal education of their children is good for the children, good for the parents, good for the teachers, good for the schools, and good for the community. This generalization is elaborated below.

Good for the Children

Children profit from almost every opportunity parents may have to demonstrate an interest in them. Parents' increased understanding of school programs and their participation as school resources and change agents contribute to better preparation of preschoolers and make schools more responsive to children's needs.

Miriam Stearns has published an excellent framework for examining the potential impact of parent involvement on the achievement of children in compensatory education programs.[1] She analyzes three roles commonly played by involved parents: tutors to their own children; paraprofessional employees; decision-makers. Dr. Stearns outlines the hypothetical links in the chain leading from each role to increased child achievement. The framework is based upon the assumptions of parent involvement advocates and the rhetoric of project proposals and various agency guidelines. In some cases it is hypothesized that children do better because of improved self-image; in other cases it is because of improved parent self-image; in still other cases it is due to program adaptations brought about because parent perspectives influence decisions.

Dr. Stearns summarizes the research in these areas and indicates where research has been conclusive or insufficient. A high degree of the research cited uses test scores as the measure of how "good" parent involvement may be. Unrecorded but pervasive empirical evidence suggests that parent involvement is good for the children irrespective of test score criteria.

Good for the Parents

The benefits accruing to parents from their involvement in their children's educational programs range from individual self-satisfaction to the ability to prevail over oppressive circumstances. In addition, there are vast learning opportunities, whether in formal parent education programs or through informal interaction with staff and their materials.

Good for the Teachers

How parent involvement is good for teachers can be summed up as follows: it enables teachers to draw upon supplemental and often unique adult resources; it provides teachers with additional information on the children they teach; it permits teachers to understand more about the community served by the school; it opens up opportunities for dialogue between the providers and consumers of educational services, encouraging teachers to recognize other perceptions of what they do; it makes possible political alliances between teachers-as-workers and parents-as-consumers in contending with school bureaucracies.

Good for the Schools

Though negative, an appropriate question may be: "Is uninvolvement and apathy good for the schools?" Public and private schools require effective community support for maintaining and expanding educational services. Few groups comprising the general public have the potential that parents have for mobilizing support for (or, at times, opposition to) school activities and affairs. Parents have the power to shut schools down (as attested to by the tragic battles over integration in Boston and textbooks in Charleston) or to keep an entire educational program in operation without financial assistance (as the Mississippi Head Start parents demonstrated in 1966 and 1967).

Parents are capable of devoting considerable energies to schools in the non-political arena as well. Tutoring programs, playground construction, and fund raising are but a few of the contributions parents make to the improvement of schools—to say nothing of the role which parents play in demystifying the schools by the questions they ask.

Good for the Community

Since many of the social benefits of parent involvement are implied in the above paragraphs, only a few additional examples will be cited here. What parents learn about schools and teachers is rarely kept a secret. Whether it is called "gossip" or the "diffusion of ideas," parents spread the word about what schools are doing. Involved parents will spread that word accurately, reducing the possibility of disruptive and demoralizing rumors. On the positive side, few people can sell the community's educational resources to prospective residents as persuasively as parents of school children. Involved parents tend to have a stake in the schools and, when the schools are good, parents are eager to proselytize.

For many parents, involvement in school affairs leads to

participation in other areas of civic responsibility. The experiences of interacting with school personnel and with other parents during meetings offer parents a form of "reality training" in citizenship. Bad or good, these experiences are learning opportunities for parents to test out and strengthen their leadership capabilities.

Schools can become development institutions. A significant portion of the community's human and financial resources is already used to provide educational services. With effective and creative parent involvement, any school can be the catalyst for a community's improvement—or survival.

There are those who may look at these paragraphs and decry the implications of additional work for the "overburdened" teacher or the "undertrained" administrator. Others may moan that to pay all of this attention to parent involvement negates the mission of the schools: to educate the child. The assumptions on which this paper is based are that the child is brought up by the family, lives in the community, and attends school—in that order. No slap at the school is intended. Educators simply need to be reminded that their perspective is institutionally centered. A *child-centered* perspective necessitates parent involvement and community development.

There is another reason for parent involvement which, because of the highly publicized confrontations between parents and schools, should be obvious. Edgar and Jean Cahn, writing in the late 1960s, pointed out that "Citizen participation is a nuisance. It is costly, it is time consuming, it is frustrating." [2]

> [Yet] *citizen participation—real, genuine, meaningful, total—is probably the only guarantee, frail though it may be, that people will be willing to abide by the terms of today's social contract and have sufficient faith in the system to feel that it is in their best interest to wait for the next round of negotiations to press for still better terms within the framework of orderly dialogue and negotiation. Otherwise, the dialectic, the bargaining process shifts to the streets—and the barricades. And citizen participation takes on another and more sinister meaning: civil disorder. The participants term it* rebellion.[3]

Notwithstanding the fact that "rebellion" is a scare-word even to citizens of a nation born of rebellion, there is a more immediate historical context within which to advocate parent involvement. The 1960s provided us with a legacy: the rebirth of national experimentation in social programming; the civil rights movement; new forms of minority group consciousness; and the growing awareness by consumers of the need for collective action. These "social actions" provided a basis for revitalizing citizen participation in the design, implementation, and evaluation of human services. In education parents, particularly members of ethnic minorities, began to challenge large public school systems to make local schools responsive to local traditions and values.[4]

In the mid 1960s the federal government legitimized parent involvement through its policies and guidelines for the Head Start and Elementary and Secondary Education Act (ESEA) Title I programs. Public and professional interest in parent involvement was further aroused by the controversies over decentralization and community control, controversies which clearly are still with us.

As the 1970s began, state education agencies developed their own policies on parent involvement. In a survey conducted in 1973 by the Center for the Study of Parent Involvement, fourteen states indicated the existence of legislation demanding or recommending some form of parent involvement. The same survey asked each State Education Agency for information on

any policies or regulations specifically regarding parent involvement in the classroom, in the local school, on school advisory committees, on district advisory committees, in curriculum development, in principal selection, in budget determinations, in school design, and in teacher contract negotiations.[5]

Eighteen states reported some kind of policy in at least one of these nine areas. Significant in its own way was the fact that 48 State Education Agencies responded to a four-page, mailed questionnaire entirely devoted to parent involvement.[6]

Thus, in recent years, state and federal education agencies, researchers as well as ethnic constituencies, the organized teaching profession, and the general public have been paying considerable attention to parent involvement. During 1973, three organizations with a national perspective on the subject were created or revitalized: the Institute for Responsive Education (Yale University);

the National Committee for Citizens in Education (Columbia, Maryland); the Center for the Study of Parent Involvement (Oakland, California).

While certainly not of "movement" proportions, a momentum has been building to encourage, mandate, and study parent involvement. Yet, somehow, incredibly, this tide of activity and concern seems to have been rising around teacher education virtually unnoticed. Despite the growing interest in and demand for parent and community participation in schools, and despite the continuing controversy over school governance issues and the extent to which parents should or should not be involved, teachers are no more being prepared to work with parents and facilitate community participation now than they were ten years ago.

Teachers, particularly elementary school teachers, must be trained to understand and work in the "community domain" if parents are to be involved and if the anticipated benefits of this involvement are to be realized.

Why Train Teachers to Involve Parents?

Why not forget the teachers and train the administrators, parents, community liaison workers, or other paraprofessional personnel? A decade of work with parents (in many parts of the United States, of diverse ethnic and socioeconomic backgrounds, and with a great variety of school experiences when they were children), convinces me that teachers can play the most significant role in educating, activating, and involving parents.

Parents tend to have a "wishful respect" for their children's teachers. That is, parents want to believe that their children's teacher is skillful as an educator, sensitive to the needs of individual children, successful in moving their child at a pace equal to or better than other children, and competent to supplement parental guidance and authority. For most parents the teacher is the significant link between them and the education of their children. While many parents are sophisticated enough to see the influence of systemic, institutional, and cultural forces on their children's formal education, the vast majority of parents want to see the teacher as the key component.

But perhaps there is something akin to a love-hate relationship between parents and teachers. Waller's observations in his classic *Sociology of Teaching*, written over forty years ago, may sound quaint but they have a familiar ring:

From the ideal point of view, parents and teachers have much in common, in that both, supposedly, wish things to occur for the best interests of the child; but, in fact, parents and teachers usually live in a condition of mutual distrust and enmity. Both wish the child well, but it is such a different kind of well that conflict must inevitably arise over it. The fact seems to be that parents and teachers are natural enemies, predestined each for the discomfiture of the other. The chasm is frequently covered over, for neither parents nor teachers wish to admit to themselves the uncomfortable implications of their animosity, but on occasion it can make itself clear enough.[7]

Elements of this conflict are still with us. Waller points to the reinforcement parents and teachers receive from their respective social groups. As a result, he sees futility in parent-teacher work since it is so often directed "at securing for the school the support of parents, that is, at getting parents to see the children more or less as teachers see them." [8]

In his 1932 work, Waller proposed a solution which, though simple, could to this day contribute much to improved relations.

If parents and teachers could meet often enough and intimately enough to develop primary group attitudes toward each other, and if both parents and teachers might have their say unreservedly, such modifications of school practice and parental upbringing might take place as would revolutionize the life of children everywhere.[9]

In 1969, Humanics Associates of Atlanta, Georgia, received a grant from the Office of Child Development to provide training and technical assistance on parent involvement to parents and teachers in Head Start programs in several southeastern states. The proposal for which the grant was awarded suggested that training be applied differentially in each setting to see whether different impacts might be perceived. Thus, in one community assistance was provided in each Head Start center only to parents, in another community only to teachers, and in a third community to both parents and teachers. In a fourth community, assistance was provided differently on a center by center basis.

The emphasis in this project was training, not research. But the project staff (who were early childhood and adult educators) wanted to assess the impact of their efforts. What they discovered was that any training for teachers in working with parents produced new awareness on the part of the teachers, an increase in parent-teacher dialogue, and more parent involvement. When parents alone were trained, teachers were ill-equipped to engage in dialogue and the parents, with their newly developed competence and self-confidence, perceived the teachers' behavior as arrogant and reacted with hostility. Training for both parents and teachers produced the best results: there were major changes in the behavior and attitudes of both parents and teachers, and the changes seemed more enduring than when training was directed toward one group or the other.

Perhaps, to overcome the "enmity" cited by Waller or the apathy and anxiety observed by so many, parents and teachers must receive special assistance. Inservice training, I have found, is not only too little, it is too late. Teachers must be prepared for work with parents *before* they start teaching. By the time most teachers are on the job, they have been prepared *not* to work with parents. Teacher educators must begin to specify competencies for teachers which will enable them to reach out to the community and involve parents.

There is a model which may be useful for the task of developing the competencies advocated here. The following list was designed by the author to "train the trainers" of community development workers:

Community workers must be . . .

1. Conscious of their own values, how they perceive others and how they, in turn, are perceived by others;
2. Skillful in making meaningful individual contacts with people of diverse backgrounds and personal capabilities;
3. Capable of bringing people together around common interests and common problems;
4. Perceptive in understanding group behavior and skillful in assisting and strengthening a wide variety of groups;

5. Knowledgeable about existing community resources, confident in the always vast potential of human resources, and creative in facilitating the development of new resources;
6. Capable of enabling individuals and groups to understand and prevail over dehumanizing institutional behavior and oppressive social conditions.

With the help of this framework, it may be possible to specify a useful sequence of competencies expected of teachers working with parents.

What Are the Parent Involvement Competencies?

Seven competencies are listed below. These are proposed as "working statements," and are neither polished nor completed.
Teachers must demonstrate the ability:

A. To understand and overcome the barriers to open communications between teachers and parents;
B. To engage in one-to-one communication with parents in a variety of settings, so that the judgmental nature of the experience is minimized and the parent's sense of competence is maximized;
C. To interpret various educational and institutional practices to parents of diverse socioeconomic backgrounds;
D. To define and explain specific meaningful tasks for parents in their roles as educators of their own children, as school resources and as decision makers;
E. To bring individual parents together and facilitate their addressing and resolving common problems;
F. To work with parent groups and develop the leadership skills of their members; and
G. To understand the nature of educational systems and assist parents in comprehending and modifying the schools so that they can better serve the needs of the children and the community.

The professional socialization of most teachers is a process which confirms the prevailing role model of "school teacher"—a role which emphasizes the mystique of classroom programming and all but ignores the community context of education. The teacher possessing the competencies listed above will understand the importance of family and community variables to the development of the whole child. This understanding must be profound enough to compete with—and overcome—the constraining parochialism common among the subculture of many elementary school teachers.

Future teachers must recognize that they are but *one* factor affecting the life of a child. This recognition is not advocated as a means of humbling teachers (too much of that goes on already) but rather to make more explicit the multiple factors affecting the child's development. As the most significant professional persons contributing to child development, teachers should be attempting to facilitate and integrate many variables which optimize a child's chances in life. The family and community are key variables which demand certain minimum skills and knowledge.

Teachers need to be aware that they "walk in a long shadow." That is, because they are perceived as "teachers," their interactions with parents are affected from the start. As much as they may wish to escape from the "shadow," it remains intact, since the role model and behavior of "teacher" are familiar, almost indelible, features in our social consciousness. Future teachers need to recognize the impact of this social perspective on their role and its possible effect on communications with parents.

Teachers will also need to understand what lies behind certain parental behaviors in their contacts with the schools. For example, when speaking with teachers for the first time, many parents tend to be deferential, even a bit passive. Teachers, on the other hand, are perceived by parents to be confident and, at times, arrogant. Yet, when a problem arises involving the safety of the child or an issue suggests culpability of the school, parents become aggressive while teachers assume a passive or defensive posture.

One of the prime occasions for parent-teacher communications is the conference. Rather than serving as an occasion to exchange information about the progress of the child (which many conferences are purported to do) and, as such, to be a source of mutual good will, conferences tend to be formal affairs and a time for mutual anxiety. Teachers often feel ill-prepared and parents feel judged. In fact, many parent-teacher transactions are formal and somewhat uncomfortable. Titles and last names are used, social amenities are sparse, and the parameters of conversation are very limited. Teachers must learn to elevate these communications to a more human and productive level.

Teachers have traditionally been "sole proprietors" of their respective classrooms. Future teachers need to learn how to educate and encourage parent aides and volunteers. An understanding of task analysis is essential so that assignments to parents serve to meet the educational goals for students, as well as to increase parental interest, skills, and confidence. An *adult* relationship must be established with parents. Too often, many teachers forget this and treat parents like kids.

Teachers need to learn group formation skills in order to help parents work on school and community issues. The value of using individual parents as resources can be multiplied by drawing upon their cumulative talents. Moreover, the job of organizing a parent education class or policy council is too important to be left to chance. These groups need help in getting organized, in maintaining themselves, in focusing on common needs and problems, in discovering and utilizing community resources, and in evolving responsible and effective leadership.

Teachers, functioning as they do in a social context, need to recognize the community development potential of the school. The children they teach ultimately will be far more affected by social, economic, and political forces in the community than by the latest changes in curriculum or teaching methodology. This is not intended to suggest that what teachers do is not essential and valid, but rather to suggest that societal pressures on the growth and development of a child require far more attention from teachers than hitherto has been the case. What this means is that teachers need to learn how to assist parents in improving the educational services provided to their community. Teachers need to know how to build upon the concerns parents have for their children's welfare, how to involve parents with one another to insure that welfare through educational and social action, and how to take the risks required by these tasks and implied by a professional calling.

How Can Teachers Achieve These Competencies?

The college or university which includes in its teacher preparation program a component on parent development will have to start by helping their students *unlearn* some major conceptions of what a teacher is and what a teacher does. Few other occupations are so clearly conceived in the minds of its novices as is the job of "teacher." From the moment that students identify with the image of teacher, the training they receive will be influenced by the experiences they have had throughout their own school years. A new role model must be established immediately and vividly. Students should be encouraged to scrutinize "classroom" and "community" models of "teacher" (as well as any other concepts of the role of educator) in order to discern how widely any concept can be interpreted. Students must be helped to refer to their feelings about becoming a teacher, drawing upon both the fears and the promises.

A more difficult unlearning which must take place is the alteration of existing conceptions of professional status. Students must learn that professionalism can be a liability, in that it sets the teacher apart from ordinary people, particularly the parents of the children they will teach. Teacher education has the task of assisting student teachers to realize the dangers of professionalization as well as its benefits. Teachers who work with parents must have a value orientation which is non-elitist and which accepts and respects the parents and community of the children they teach.

Three techniques familiar to teacher education could be extended to the new objective of preparing teachers to work with parents:

A. Role playing to simulate teacher-parent interactions and enable students to experience some of the emotional dynamics.
B. Supervised fieldwork with parent and community groups.
C. Working with "master teachers," not necessarily as role models to be emulated, but as representatives of existing professional values to be challenged.

Role playing is described by Matthew Miles as:

... essentially an action, doing *technique ... Role playing mem-*
bers react to each other spontaneously within the framework of
a defined situation which is provisional, or "not for keeps." In
this way, behaviors of people can be examined with a minimum
of threat, and their approach to the problem can be improved
after discussion and analysis.[10]

At a minimum, teacher preparation should include the
following role playing situations to prepare teachers for the competencies proposed above:

- A parent-teacher conference
- Encountering an angry parent
- Encountering a passive parent
- Encouraging parents to participate as classroom observers
- Encouraging parents to perform specific educational tasks with
  children at home and in school
- Encouraging parents to participate with other parents in exist-
  ing school or community organizations
- Assisting a parent chairperson in planning a meeting
- Maximizing the value of chance meetings with parents.

These experiences, while simulated, should enable students
to appreciate the multiple human relation factors in teacher-
parent transactions. Moreover, many subtle dynamics of these
interactions can be addressed during the analyses succeeding each
role-playing experience.

Supervised fieldwork with parent and community groups
should combine students' observations of and participation in
groups with increased sensitivity to their participation in their
own groups. Prospective teachers should be encouraged to re-
examine their own group experiences—in social clubs, professional associations, church groups, etc.—in any formal settings.
Student teachers should have the opportunity to work with parents on community issues. Moreover, students and parents should
be helped to meet together to share their perspectives of school
activities.

The technique of working with master teachers is a little
more complicated than obtaining guidance from an experienced
professional. In this case, the professional is less the guide than
the participant in a dialogue. Many of the suggestions made in

this chapter have been criticized for "leading the lamb to slaughter." Or, to quote a colleague, "Do you realize that the minute your parent involvement teachers get to their schools, the old 'warhorses' will cut them to ribbons?"

Student teachers need to be prepared for encounters with the old warhorses. They need to be strengthened for the culture of the school, particularly the debilitating and depressing aspects of institutional behavior which tend to dampen the ardor of new teachers, especially those with innovative approaches. One exercise, which has provided support to new teachers in inservice training, I call "The Teachers' Lunchroom Experience."

"The Teachers' Lunchroom Experience" places a new teacher in the midst of Anyschool's teachers' room during his or her first week. In the exercise, the student is encouraged to engage other teachers in conversation about a serious educational issue such as irrelevant textbooks, inadequate services, incessant demands for records, or insufficient parent involvement. The student is urged to make some recommendations rather than to simply gripe about the problems. The "other teachers" (usually fellow trainees or training staff) have been programed to respond in a number of "typical" (usually mildly exaggerated) ways. Most of these responses are thus "tedium," "impatience," "don't bother me," "silence." Finally, one of the "teachers" will come over to the "new teacher" and, placing a hand gently, but firmly, on one shoulder will say: "I used to be enthusiastic like you are honey, but you'll learn; just stay here a while and you'll learn!"

Can the student teacher be prepared for this kind of difficult encounter? Or should new teachers be permitted to face reality when they arrive at their first job?

The culture of the schools can be made an overt subject of teacher education. Master teachers can be engaged in discussions not as supervisors having evaluative control over student teachers' freedom of speech, but as professionals whose views are sought and whose perceptions are accepted as interpretations rather than truth. The simulation described above can be made a part of students' experiences *before* they leave teacher education. Value conflicts can be exposed rather than glossed over.

Perhaps the best preparation student teachers can have for contending with experienced teachers is to establish links with parents from the outset. Such links can demystify the gobbledygook which student teachers get as part of their indoctrination. A concept of accountability, based upon mutual trust between teachers and parents, can be created so that new teachers can turn to someone other than old teachers.

How Can Schools of Education Be Moved in This Direction?

In its study, *State Education Agencies and Parent Involvement*,[11] the Center for the Study of Parent Involvement found that only five states (California, Florida, Massachusetts, South Carolina and Pennsylvania) responded "yes" to the question: "In teacher preparation and certification activities are there any specific competencies identified which address themselves to work with parents?" (N = 48; Ohio and New York never responded.) Among the fourteen states reporting legislation on parent involvement, only two (California and Florida) said that they had such competencies; of the eighteen State Education Agencies with policies or regulations on parent involvement, there were three (California, Florida and Massachusetts) possessing parent involvement competencies. No states indicated any legislative or state education agency compulsion on schools of education to extend teacher training to the community domain.

An impressive record of institutional change has been brought about through legislative and administrative mandate. Local school districts and many individual schools have gone through some changes since the advent of Head Start, Follow Through, and Title I. Many other human services institutions—including colleges and universities—have changed their practices because of external directives. Schools of education could use such directives in order to extend their concept of what kind of teacher they are preparing.

My first proposal to move schools of education toward a greater parent and community awareness in teacher education is to mandate some form of consultation with parent and other lay groups in the design, implementation, and evaluation of teacher training activities. This is currently taking place, in a modified form, in California.

The Commission for Teacher Preparation and Licensing (Ryan Commission) requires the following prior to approving program plans for teacher education:

1.1.2 *Cooperating communities, school districts, teachers, and teacher candidates, carefully selected, involved in, and committed to program development.*

Between the institution, school system, and community: The involvement of school district personnel, teacher candidates, and community agencies in program development, implementation, and evaluation should be reflected in the program activities as stated. School districts should insure minority participation in proportion to minorities in the communities served. Communications from the school district should include responses from parents and groups in communities served. Evidence should be provided to show the contributions from all groups were included in developing the program.[12]

Though there is a burden on the teacher training institution to document the involvement demanded above, the effectiveness of the intended participation is in question. Schools of education have had so little experience in working with lay groups that, without either more directive guidance, technical help, or both, there is little likelihood that parents and other community representatives will play a meaningful role. The Commission has at least established the principle of inclusiveness. Time and experience may see parent and community involvement in teacher education become a fact.

My second proposal for reorienting schools of education toward parent involvement is to include parents as teacher educators. Parents are resources for student teachers; they can be paid consultants and can perform formal roles as lecturers or seminar leaders; they can participate in discussions of methodology, curriculum development, classroom management, and professional development. They can even supplement the work of field instructors by observing classroom performance and participating in supervisory conferences. Student teachers should be able to experience parents as people with diverse interests, values, perspectives, and talents; stereotyping would become more difficult and the process of professionalization could proceed on a less elitist basis.

My third proposal begins with the implementation of the ideas discussed above. Parents could be involved in re-training *teacher educators*. While institutional practices must change if schools of education are to prepare teachers to work with parents, so must the perspectives and practices of individual faculty members. I am not proposing that education faculty enroll in any classes or field work activities, because such a proposal would go unheeded save for the least status conscious professors. I am proposing that interaction be facilitated between parents and education professors so that these faculty members, who operate far from the community and its reality, have the chance to reorder their concepts of the teacher.

Some form of training would be valuable for teacher educators if they are to rethink and restructure the preparation they offer to others. Thus, a fourth proposal is to invite teacher educators to attend workshops designed to draw upon their experiences and knowledge so that we can prepare teachers to work with parents. Such workshops are already taking place to assist practitioners and staff development personnel on an inservice basis. (The Home and School Institute, Washington, D.C. and the Center for the Study of Parent Involvement offer educational opportunities of this kind.) Associations of teacher educators may need to be nudged a bit if teacher trainers are to take advantage of this form of training.

My final proposal is to place the burden, once again, on parents. Parents can ask some amazing questions of the right person in the right place. Perhaps they should begin to attend meetings of teacher educators, maybe even a faculty meeting. After all, the teachers being produced this year will be teaching their children in the years to come. The restructuring of teacher education so that teachers are prepared to work with parents might begin like this:

(Dean Strumpht) "But . . . . What . . . . ? Who . . . . ?"

(Spokesperson) "Yes, I realize that you are a busy person, but everyone thought that if anyone knew the answers to our questions it would be you. Some of us have been getting tired of the same old hassles at the school every year. In fact, several of our parents said that they have had the same kind of hassles at the other schools their children went to before moving here."

(Dean Strumpht) "What . . . . ? Where . . . . ?

(Spokesperson) "We don't want to bore you with the details, but we do want to know how teachers are being trained here

111

at Happy Valley. After all, some of your students may be teaching at Kinder Hollow Elementary School next year or the year after and we want to know whether you're preparing them for what they're going to face."

(Dean Strumpht) "Kinder Hollow . . . ? Is that far from here?

(Spokesperson) "Now, Dean Strumpht, let's not get off the subject. We want you to tell us what you do here. Isn't that right parents?"

(Thirty Parents) "Right." "Sure." "Right on." "Let's hear it, Deano!" "Tell us what you do here!"

(Dean Strumpht) "Well, you see, that's a very complicated question. First, there are philosophical, psychological, sociological, methodological, geographical . . . considerations to be considered."

(Spokesperson) "Dean Strumpht, we just came from the Dean's Office at the University; they ran the same stuff on us and even said 'phenomenological'; now are you going to talk with us or at us?"

(Dean Strumpht) "Uh . . . Umm . . . Nothing like this has ever happened here before. Would you like to visit some of our classrooms and talk to our students and faculty members?"

(Spokesperson and Thirty Parents) "Hey-hey, Deano, you're okay! The Dean is together; we're finally getting inside to see what they do. Far out!"

Such a scenario is unlikely because so few parents see the school of education as the most immediate cause of woe. Their problem is their children's teachers and the local school. However, I predict that parents will soon take on the places where teachers are trained—not because training results in bad teachers, but because parents need strong teachers with whom to ally in fighting the educational inadequacies and inequities in their communities.

The teacher—as a professional person and as a concerned human being—is in a unique position to improve the life opportunities for children. Schools of education need to broaden the concept of what teachers are and what teachers do so that dialogue is the mode through which teachers and parents interact. Professionalism based upon self-interest is a far cry from the ancient "calling" to which people have always responded in their desire to become teachers. Dialogue with parents draws teachers toward the community where all must strive together on behalf of all our children.

Founding itself upon love, humility, and faith, dialogue becomes a horizontal relationship of which mutual trust between the dialoguers is the logical consequence.

Pedagogy of the Oppressed
—Paulo Freire

NOTES

1. Miriam Stearns et al., *Parent Involvement in Compensatory Education Programs* (Menlo Park, California: Stanford Research Institute, 1973).

2. Edgar and Jean Cahn, "Citizen Participation," in *Citizen Participation in Urban Development,* ed. Hans B. C. Spiegel, I (Washington, D.C.: National Institute of Applied Behavioral Science, 1968), p. 218.

3. Ibid., p. 222.

4. "Began" is not to be taken literally. Recent efforts by minority parents are more like a renascence. See Nicolaus Mills, "Community Schools: Irish, Italians and Jews," in *Society* (March/April, 1974) for a brief study of New York City's "troubles" during the past 120 years.

5. Daniel Safran, *State Education Agencies and Parent Involvement* (Berkeley, California: Center for the Study of Parent Involvement, 1974).

6. Daniel Safran, *Evaluating Parent Involvement,* Issue Paper #1 (Berkeley, California: Center for the Study of Parent Involvement, 1974).

7. Willard Waller, *The Sociology of Teaching* (New York: John Wiley & Sons, n.d.), p. 68.

8. Ibid., p. 69.

9. Ibid.

10. Matthew B. Miles, *Learning to Work in Groups* (New York: Teachers College Press, 1959), pp. 191–192.

11. Daniel Safran, *State Education Agencies and Parent Involvement.*

12. State of California Commission for Teacher Preparation and Licensing, *Manual for Developing, Evaluating, and Approving Professional Preparation Program Plans for Multiple and Single Subject Credentials* (rev. 1973).

FOR FURTHER READING

Groteberg, E. H., ed. *Critical Issues in Research Related to Disadvantaged Children*. Princeton, N.J.: Educational Testing Service, 1969.

Groteberg, E. H., ed. *Day Care: Resources for Decision*. Washington, D.C.: Office of Economic Opportunity, 1971.

Hoffman, David B. *Parent Participation in Preschool Day Care*, Monograph #5. Atlanta: SE Educational Labs, 1971.

Michael, John. *Conceptions of Childhood and Parent Participation in Schools*. Paper presented to the American Sociological Association, Denver, August 1971.

Vollner, Howard M., and Donald L. Mills. *Professionalization*. Englewood Cliffs, N.J.: Prentice-Hall, 1966.

Wilson, Gary B. *Parents and Teachers*. Atlanta: Humanics Press, 1974.

Partnership

*A Proposal to Minimize
the Practical Constraints
on Community Participation
in Education*

Carl A. Grant

University of Wisconsin, Madison

Democracy is the form of government in which each individual, either directly or through an elected representative, is empowered to participate in those governmental decision-making processes which affect his or her life. Although we are wont to speak of American democracy, we sometimes fail to acknowledge that democracy, in most instances, is the goal rather than the reality: most systems purporting to be democratic have never really approached the theoretical limits of democracy. For instance, bureaucratic decision making is often beyond the purview of both citizens and their elected representatives. This is but one example of the kinds of restrictions on a person's right to participate in those decisions which affect his or her life—and as long as such restrictions exist, democratization is incomplete.

Citizen participation is, theoretically, fundamental to American democracy. However, the extent of community participation in governmental institutions and the form it should take have been and continue to be much disputed. Because there is a lack of consensus on this issue, many citizens, both today and in the past, have been prevented from participating in community affairs. For instance, constitutional amendments were necessary to ensure that non-white persons and women could avail themselves of the fundamental right of all citizens in a democracy to vote. In addition, disparity in the distribution of political resources has hindered (and continues to hinder) effective participation.

Today's citizens who wish to exercise their right to participate in community affairs are hampered or constrained by such forces as racism and bureaucratic politics and distrust. Twentieth-century Asian, black, native, and Spanish-speaking Americans and poor Americans of every color are particularly subject to discrimination when attempting to exercise their right and responsibility to participate. Nevertheless, they are today seeking a greater degree of participation in community affairs, especially in the schools. A technological and increasingly complex society makes education a necessity. People are interested in the schools both because they consider education to be an important factor in the achievement of success, and because at some time in their lives they are legally obligated to attend them.

The attempts of minorities and the poor to achieve more than a token voice in school systems are blocked, however, by three basic practical constraints: their lack of knowledge, their lack of representation, and their lack of financial resources. Only with the necessary knowledge, representation, and funds can minorities and the poor attain viable participation in school systems. For as political theorist Robert Dahl has noted, ". . . until and unless we reach much greater parity in the distribution of political resources, other steps toward democratization are like treating tuberculosis with aspirin, or airdropping marshmallows to famine victims." [1]

For the purposes of this paper, viable participation is that in which citizens and social agencies affected by schools are partners in making such important school policy decisions as budget and curriculum planning, selection of school personnel, and plans for racial integration. With the goal of discussing practical constraints to viable participation, the failure of past attempts to bring it about, and a possible means of achieving it, I have divided this chapter into three sections. The first section describes how insufficient knowledge, representation, and finance by minorities and the poor constrain their relationship with the school. The second section delineates the weaknesses of techniques that the schools have begun to adopt from other social agencies, and explains the failure of these techniques to bring about viable community participation. The third section discusses a practical school-community partnership that could successfully overcome the three previously discussed practical constraints.

Practical Constraints upon Citizen Participation in Schools

Lack of Knowledge

Knowledge about the policies and procedures of community programs is crucial to viable community participation, yet people from low income and minority backgrounds are often unaware of essential information about the programs. In discussing citizen participation, Martin Anderson emphasizes that it must include:

> *. . . assuring that the community as a whole, representative organizations, and neighborhood groups are informed and have full opportunity to take part in developing and carrying out the program.*[2]

Minorities and the poor are often excluded from receiving this knowledge by surreptitious methods and devices. An examination of the most recent explorations into community participation indicates that many community groups are not given the information they need for meaningful participation, nor are they told where they can find it. It has even been suggested that the guidelines of many federal programs have intentionally been withheld from minorities and the poor. In the early 1960s when the federal government began to require "maximum feasible participation," school officials began to make the guidelines themselves more available, but effectively blocked participation by not assisting citizens in understanding them. Consequently, citizens were allowed to attend meetings, but, as Arnstein notes, "It was the officials who educated, persuaded and advised the citizens, not the reverse."[3] Reed and Mitchell have also commented upon this phenomenon:

> *School administrators were slow to establish the required new advisory councils and even slower to grant them the considerable authority over Title I that the new guidelines allowed. Title I was a complicated program; the comparability regulation made it even more complicated. With some exceptions, the school officials did little to help citizens to understand the program. Many found it much easier and more convenient to comply with the letter of the law without complying with its spirit.*[4]

Lack of knowledge serves as an additional constraint when proposed programs are presented to community groups using technical language and professional jargon that is difficult to understand. While we have all been subjected to the speaker or writer who presents materials in a manner which is incomprehensible to the audience being addressed, there is no justification for such egocentricity in community affairs. Information that people need about factors influencing their lives should be presented to them in a clear, direct manner if they are to be expected to understand it.

Misleading or outdated knowledge also constrains community participation. Concerned citizens who attend meetings to resolve issues that disturb them are often stymied by false or misleading statements. For example, officials mislead them into thinking that no persons or procedures are available to help them, when, in fact, personnel have been employed and procedures have been instituted to resolve the problems.

The incomplete knowledge that parents receive from their children about school systems brings about misunderstandings that hamper community participation in the schools. In fact, parents receive twice as much information from their children than from any other source, even when school personnel attempt to contact parents directly.[5] Consequently, a large part of their knowledge about the school is both unofficial and incomplete. This indirect and partial knowledge about school policies and procedures further inhibits the development of a viable relationship between community members and the schools.

As further proof that lack of knowledge constrains community participation, I would like to examine traditional types of communication between the school and community in terms of (1) school services to the community and (2) community services to the school.

The most obvious school services to the community, beyond the educational and custodial, are social, such as graduation ceremonies, open houses, and sporting events. These activities do bring some community members into the school, but they usually involve only the parents of children attending them. These parents are there, however, merely as spectators, because these events are neither designed nor planned to provide an opportunity for community input. Unfortunately, school officials parade this type of superficial involvement in school affairs as genuine citizen participation.

Schools also serve the community by distributing report cards and organizing conferences between parents and teachers or principals. In both of these services minority and poor people, in particular, are on the receiving, not the participating, end. The parent-teacher meetings generally have two common features: ". . . the teachers do most of the talking, and the parents are vaguely anxious and a little fearful about their child's performance, but often do not have a clear idea about what might be done to change or improve it." [6] Consequently, little useful communication occurs at these meetings, which if appropriately organized, could serve as a direct line of communication between school officials and parents. For example, in addition to each child's progress, the goals of both the school and parent and plans to effect them could be discussed.

The third type of school service to the community involves knowledge that is released by the administrative head of the school district—the superintendent. The superintendent serves as spokesperson of the school board and as the official link between it and the community. Often being the architect, implementor, and chief interpreter of school policy and procedure, the superintendent is in a powerful position to control, censor, and interpret the information about school programs given to community participants. Because of this control, the superintendent often singlehandedly shapes and focuses school programs. The superintendent's use of the knowledge he or she controls can be a major constraint to community participation.

There are, at present, few community services to the school. Those that do exist—the PTA and fund raising groups, for example—are school-directed and rarely representative of the community as a whole. According to Reed and Mitchell, this token community participation is recognized and accepted by all parties involved:

> . . . they are led by a fairly small group of leaders who do virtually all of the planning for the group; they see themselves, and are seen by school personnel, largely as "communication links" through which information about the school program is disseminated to the community.[7]

As long as the public accepts these situations, viable community participation in the schools will be blocked because administrators will quash complaints of nonparticipation by publicly praising the activities of these groups and the citizens involved.

In sum, people from low income and minority backgrounds are blocked from viable community participation because they are often unaware of or prevented from acquiring the knowledge needed to participate in community affairs. The two basic modes of communication between the school and the community currently in use are ineffective in bringing about the knowledge needed to participate effectively in community affairs. The first, school services to the community, is superficial, school-directed, and closed to citizen input. The second, the so-called community services to the school, are as shallow and school-directed as the first, but, even worse, parade as viable community participation. Perhaps this token participation unwittingly diverts community members from genuine involvement in community affairs.

Representation

To deny citizens a voice in school affairs, whether by subterfuge or diversion, is to deny them a voice in a major tax expenditure. Historically, for various reasons, minorities and the poor have been denied their fundamental right to viable participation in community affairs and have only recently been encouraged to participate, as a result of the federal guidelines established in the Economic Opportunity Act of 1964, Title III of the Elementary and Secondary Education Act of 1965, the Demonstration Cities and Metropolitan Development Act of 1966, and the Office of Economic Opportunity education amendments of 1974.

Title III, for example, specifies that grants may be made to local agencies "... only if there is satisfactory assurance that, in the planning of that program or project there has been, and in the establishment and carrying out thereof there will be, participation of persons broadly representative of the cultural and educational resources of the area to be served." [8] Unfortunately, the practice of having selected community members "sign off" on grant proposals —thus effectively thwarting viable community participation—has become so widespread as to render this proviso meaningless.

The communication gap between citizens and their representatives is one of the major constraints to viable community participation. Community representatives must make certain that they are truly representing the views of the community. Too often the views of such important groups as the elderly, youth, and the unemployed are not openly sought. Consequently, their needs are not reflected in community programs that affect their daily lives.

The communication gap between community members and their representatives is caused in part by the methods and procedures frequently used for collecting information. Survey questionnaires and interviews, for example, are very popular, but close attention must be given to their inherent disadvantages. The mailed questionnaire assumes that the respondents are not only literate, but literate in the language in which the questionnaire is written. Another of its disadvantages is the low rate of return.[9] Sax explains additional weaknesses of the mailed questionnaire and brings out the importance of people's attitudes toward the usefulness of replying:

> *The usual expectation for mailed questionnaires is that fewer than half of the respondents may reply the first time they receive a questionnaire, the percentage of returns depending upon such factors as the length of the questionnaire, the reputation of the sponsoring agency, the complexity of the questions asked, the relative importance of the study as judged by the potential respondent, the extent to which the respondent believes that his responses are important and the quality and design of the questionnaire itself.[10]*

In addition, the impersonal methods of surveys and interviews often exacerbate misunderstandings between community members and their representatives because they do not create the sense of trust needed to win the interest and support of low income and minority community members. Also, as Sax notes, the personal characteristics of an interviewer may bias the responses:

> *The personal characteristics of the interviewer can (and often do) determine the validity of the responses. It is important, then, to select and train interviewers who can obtain valid responses.[11]*

Of the eight variables Sax presents that influence the responses, racial background and socioeconomic status are the most important to this discussion. He states, for example, "Responses of Negroes differ depending upon whether they are interviewed by Caucasians or other Negroes." [12]

Another constraint to representation is the inhibiting attitude of those in power. For example, racist, sexist, or paternalistic attitudes may be manifested by school officials either openly or through their apparent unwillingness to relinquish any of their power in order to foster viable community participation. School officials are most often seeking rubber stamp participation; their paternalistic attitudes cause them to encourage participants to choose among alternatives developed for them rather than to co-operatively develop ideas. Reed and Mitchell have noted:

> *In traditional participation, communication is* from *the school principal and the other school officials* to *the parents and citizens, and it is either a matter of informing them about school plans and programs or sounding them out on contemplated policy and programs. Communication from parents to the school officials is largely personal and represents complaints or compliments that are evaluative of school programs only in a very narrow sense. In this way citizens rarely, if ever, initiate policy or prevent its implementation.*[13]

A third constraint to viable participation in community affairs is the scheduling and operation of meetings. They are frequently held when many community members, especially minorities and the poor, cannot attend, without enough advance notice so that they can arrange to participate. In addition, many citizens do not know how to place items on the agenda, nor are they told how to do so. To increase community participation in school affairs, officials must not use parliamentary procedure to thwart citizen participation; rather, they should familiarize citizens with it, in order to facilitate their participation. Also, school officials must provide ample time for a dialogue on important issues and hold meetings at times and places convenient for citizen participation.

In addition, when citizens organize themselves to respond to issues that they feel school officials are mishandling, their efforts toward debate in the presence of the officials are often diverted into petty disputes over the proper form their opposition should take. The officials insist that a referendum or advisory committee should be established to deal with the problem so that they can gain control of the opposition and keep the disagreement low-keyed. The problem is shunted into the oblivion of committee-hood, and thus the basis for the existence of the citizen group is undermined. Sooner or later a report is filed, watered down resolutions are passed, a new committee is formed, and the citizens, faced with the uselessness of their efforts, retreat into frustrated disinterest and apathy.

In sum, methods of collecting information, school officials' inhibiting attitudes, the scheduling and operation of meetings, and the undermining of community groups often prevent the type of community representation needed for viable community participation.

Finance

Once minority groups and the poor have the knowledge and representation needed to participate in community affairs, they are faced with the third major constraint: lack of finance. Community members are in a paradoxical situation: their tax dollars provide revenue for school programs, but as an organized group they are usually without funds. Money is vital to the implementation and maintenance of a viable program of participation. Often lack of petty cash prevents viable participation from taking place. For example, many minorities and poor people are unable to assume the cost of transportation to a meeting, pay for child care, or take time off from work to attend community meetings because they would not be financially compensated for it. Thus, out-of-pocket expenses discourage their participation in community affairs. School officials, on the other hand, may actually receive payment for attending meetings. This practice further alienates parents from the school system because they consider it unfair. In addition, school officials have access to effective means of communication which are usually unavailable to community groups. Information is power, and without at least a room with a bulletin board and a telephone, community groups may find that sources of information are too diffused to be useful to their members. Community groups must have money in order to see that their tax dollars are well spent.

Techniques Employed to Encourage Citizen Participation

Acknowledging their need for the taxpayer's support, schools in the past did not remain completely blind to the citizen's demands for viable participation in them. The post–World War II population explosion, for example, increased demands for schooling so much that schools, unable to meet these needs, initiated community relations programs to raise funds. The Parent-Teacher Association (PTA), in particular, and other committees and associations whose members are appointed by school officials, arose as part of this movement to provide a communication link between parents and the school. School officials reasoned that if citizens had even a minor decision-making role in forming school policy, they would be more willing to support such things as the bond referenda necessary for the continued growth of the schools.

These groups, however, for the most part involved only middle-class citizens. Because they had the time, political influence, knowledge, and money to intervene in school affairs, their demands were heeded by school officials. On the other hand, the great numbers of minorities and the poor who had migrated from rural areas to large, industrial cities after the war had no voice in either the schools or any other area of community affairs.

Both the poor and the middle class—black and white alike —have viewed the schools as bridges to social equality and rungs on the ladder of upward mobility. Although many initial efforts to create social equality focused on social, economic, and political changes, education soon became an important factor in bringing about such changes. However, as the minorities and the poor attempted to improve their schools and the quality of education they provided, they were halted by discriminatory school policies such as district gerrymandering. Despite their widespread, justifiable opposition to these policies, little change would likely have occurred in the schools without the passage of federal legislation requiring community participation as a condition for federal funding. These federal mandates, referred to earlier, gave minority and low-income groups the legal right to demand viable participation in both the schools and community affairs in general. Spurred both by the fear of losing federal funds and the conflict and turmoil of the 1960s, some schools have begun experimenting with several techniques reportedly used by other social agencies to encourage citizen participation.

These techniques—nominal group methods, marathon sessions, surveys, interviews, and advisory councils[14]—increased, at least superficially, citizen participation in the social agencies. The effectiveness of this participation is, however, questionable. With all five techniques the final outcome was determined by the social agencies themselves, reducing the citizen's participation to mere tokenism. Since the use of these techniques presents no substantive threat to the existing decision-making process, while offering enough opportunity for citizen involvement to satisfy public demand, schools have begun to try them.

The first of the five techniques, the nominal group method, breaks a large meeting into smaller discussion groups to stimulate creative thought. Each member of a small group prepares a list of needs for a particular program or project. These needs are then discussed in the small groups, and needs expressed by only a few are eliminated from each group's composite list. Next, the large group is reconvened and someone from each small group presents its list. The process of eliminating items held by the fewest number of people is repeated, creating a master list for the large assembly. Each item on the list is then included on the agenda for the large assembly meetings. There are two major drawbacks to the nominal group method. First, many important, though less widespread, needs are filtered out in this repeated elimination. Second, those needs that are included on the agenda are, in the end, subject to final approval by the school.

The second of the five techniques, the one or two day marathon session, is an intensive discussion held under the guidance of a group facilitator. Representatives of both the school and the community are present at the sessions and cooperatively draw up recommendations for future school policy. In the final analysis, however, the marathon sessions remain mere talk because the participants have no means to implement their recommendations. All the ideas that stem from the sessions are subject to final approval by the school board itself which can compromise or veto them.

Two additional means of including citizens in the decision-making process are the survey and the interview. The schools can ascertain overall public opinion by mail or through field interviews.

The survey might also be designed to interview only representatives of established community groups. Both these techniques, however, present the inherent drawbacks discussed earlier. They may seem unimportant and impersonal, and they are subject to bias and misrepresentation.

The fifth means of involving citizens in school affairs is the creation of advisory groups for each school. However, school officials have tended to use advisory councils to project the appearance of community involvement, while in actuality the advisory councils are often very restricted in both their membership and the range of topics on which they may advise. Guidelines for Local School Councils in Chicago[15] state that, "Membership in the Local School Council should be broadly representative of the community within the school district." Elsewhere, however, they state that, "The participating voters in the organizational meeting must be parents of students in the school," thus denying many community members the right to vote on the expenditure of their tax dollars. In addition, while assenting to community participation in decisions about such topics as local school curricula, these same guidelines note that "fiscal policies" are beyond the purview of the Local School Councils.

In summary, while the techniques cited above do offer a means for increased citizen participation in school affairs, each technique is, at best, only a token effort. These token efforts are of great concern because they short-circuit real participation, while at the same time allowing school officials to claim that participation exists.

Partnership as an Effective Means of Overcoming Practical Constraints

I have defined viable participation as that in which citizens and social agencies affected by schools are partners in making school policy decisions in such important areas as budget and curriculum planning, selection of school personnel, and plans for racial integration. In order to achieve viable community participation, I am suggesting the implementation of a three stage model. The stages include (1) identifying the problem, (2) organizing for action, and (3) gaining independence.

Stage One: Identifying the Problem

Community participation that will lead to partnership with school officials will not occur until community members recognize and understand that the injustices they are encountering will not be eliminated unless they themselves make the alterations. Frustration at continued high pushout rates and low achievement scores may cause parents and community members to focus their attention on the schools. Outside organizers with a genuine concern about the injustices a community is facing may help to make community members increasingly aware of how important the schools are in remedying injustice. No matter who identifies the problem, however, it is vital that everyone in the community understands the nature of the problem, because such a unity of understanding is a necessary base for a strong organization.

Stage Two: Organizing for Action

Organization is one of the more formidable obstacles to meaningful community participation. Organizing is not, however, always as simple as declaring that it shall be done. First, a group must organize around substantive issues—rather than vested personal interests such as common skin color or economic status—if it is to be politically effective. If leaders cannot be identified, leadership must be given time to evolve. Structure is also necessary, for, as has been noted, so-called structureless organizations usually develop an internal tyranny detrimental to effective action. An equitable procedure for decision making by the group's members is necessary. This mechanism could include anything from Robert's *Rules of Order* to "rapping" an issue until a consensus is reached. Mechanisms should also exist to assure the continued existence of the organization; these might include a written constitution and bylaws, and an ongoing commitment to recruiting new members. Continual communication between leadership and rank and file members of the organization is also vital, so that every member continues to feel that this is his or her organization, not "theirs."

Finally, the process of developing a cohesive organization should not be patronizingly viewed as beyond the capabilities of any particular community or group of people. A new organization may encounter difficulty in achieving all its goals, but we can learn from our mistakes, and if we do so, we become stronger.

Stage Three: Gaining Independence

Once a community has identified the problem and organized, it must establish its independence. The community needs to be independent with regard to both representation and finances. In addition, it must maintain its own identity by refusing to be absorbed or co-opted by any other group.

Representatives and other resource people need to be accountable to the community. In order for this to happen, the community must be able to reimburse its leaders for expenses such as supplies and child care. The community also needs to be able to pay resource people, for example, lawyers, for the time they spend working on community business.

Where will the community obtain the money necessary for the above? While outside grants and donations may be helpful, no community can truly be independent until it raises some of its own money. Collecting and redeeming empty pop bottles, holding car washes and selling candy bars may not generate huge sums of money, but they do provide an organization with funds to operate. For instance, independence will be further achieved and demonstrated when the community has an office with a telephone and other supplies. This will enable community members to have a place of their own to gather, and to call to receive information.

Independence also needs to be exercised by community organizations when they are invited to join with other groups. Forming coalitions with other groups may appear very tempting and worthwhile. Nevertheless, caution must be exercised because community members may become involved in time-consuming political maneuvering and lose sight of their own goals.

Community groups must also avoid being duped into making unnecessary political trade-offs. Many politicians, for example, are happy to speak to an organized audience. They will frequently promise anything within reason for prospective votes, and then conveniently forget their promises after the election. Additionally, community members should only accept "no strings attached" money or gifts. It might be very important to have a new copy machine, or to have the phone bill paid. It is more important, however, to realize that "there is no such thing as a free lunch."

Conclusion

In order to eliminate the practical constraints on community participation in education, the model proposed in the preceding pages should be given serious consideration for several reasons.

First of all, it gives low-income and minority community members a strategy for overcoming the three practical constraints —insufficient knowledge, representation, and finance—to viable participation in schooling. Second, it encourages community members to develop the independence and confidence to seek bargaining power necessary to deal effectively with school officials. Third, it advocates that citizens work within the existing system so that their tax dollars are put to use where they deem most appropriate.

Once organized, a community is assured a greater opportunity for representation in official school policy making. For example, it can nominate candidates for the school board or attend meetings en masse to bring pressure to bear on school officials. By organizing communal baby-sitting groups, the community can greatly increase its attendance at meetings. With their concern and interest clearly evidenced by the large numbers of residents present, school officials would not, at least as easily as in the past, be able to ignore items that the minority and low-income groups want discussed, and would be less able to surprise them with unexpected, unwanted, and unsought changes for their community.

The traditional communication gap between the community and the school administration would be lessened because citizens could personally outline their complaints and desires to school officials, thus preventing any misunderstandings resulting from unrepresentative surveys or biased interviews. In addition, racism, paternalism, and sexism—all extremely effective against individuals—become more difficult to employ against an organized, vocal group.

With funds available to pay a few community members or to hire experts, community members could acquire the knowledge they need about school policies and procedures to promote the interests of their children. Lawyers hired by the community could amass information about the legal means of bringing about citizen participation and explain to the community how to use them. They could help slice through technical jargon and circumvent diversionary tactics by school officials. These experts would have the legal recourse to sue school officials for needed information and the professional expertise to recognize and demand more than token participation when proffered by school officials. They could act as professional organizers by teaching community leaders where to find meetings; how to handle themselves in them; how to introduce items on the agenda; and how to cope with diversionary tactics by school officials, question their statements, and follow through with their requests. Once they have provided this instruction, the lawyers might be consulted only when necessary, in order to reduce community expenditures.

The self-reliance these measures would give communities could overcome past ineffectiveness in dealing with school systems. Armed with the knowledge needed to influence schools to follow federal mandates requiring viable citizen participation, and the organization and interest to provide that participation, community members would be in a position to bargain intelligently and effectively with the schools. They could become equal partners with school officials in determining policy in areas such as budget and curriculum planning, selection of school personnel, and plans for racial integration. For the first time since it was coined, the phrase "maximum feasible participation" could become a reality.

NOTES

1. Robert A. Dahl, *After the Revolution?* (New Haven: Yale University Press, 1970), pp. 162–163.

2. Martin Anderson, *The Federal Bulldozer* (New York: McGraw-Hill, 1967), p. 18.

3. Sherry R. Arnstein, "Eight Rungs On the Ladder of Citizen Participation," *Citizen Participation: Effecting Community Change*, ed. Edgar S. Cahn and Barry A. Passett (New York: Praeger, 1971), p. 75.

4. Douglas B. Reed and Douglas E. Mitchell, "The Structure

of Citizen Participation: Public Decisions For Public Schools," in *Public Testimony on Public Schools* (Berkeley, California: McCutchan, 1975), p. 190.

5. Paul F. Kleine et al., "Citizen Views of Big City Schools," *Theory Into Practice* 8 (October 1969): 225, cited by Reed and Mitchell, p. 206.

6. Reed and Mitchell, "The Structure of Citizen Participation," p. 207.

7. Ibid.

8. *Elementary and Secondary Education Act, U.S. Code,* Vol. 20, Sec. 844(a) (1970).

9. Gilbert Sax, *Empirical Foundations of Educational Research* (Englewood Cliffs, N.J.: Prentice-Hall, 1968), p. 215.

10. Ibid., pp. 215–216.

11. Ibid., p. 213.

12. Ibid.

13. Reed and Mitchell, "The Structure of Citizen Participation," p. 208.

14. These five techniques were suggested by John Urich, Director of the City of Madison, Wisconsin, Planning Department.

15. "Revised Guidelines for Local School Councils," Chicago Public Schools, December 1972.

Education as War

American Indian Participation in Tribal Education

Patricia Locke

Director of Education Policy Planning and Programs
National Tribal Chairmen's Association

Definitions and Background of the Issues

The essence of community participation in the education process for American Indians means that the mature members of a tribe, through concentrated involvement and consensus decision making in every aspect of education, will determine the direction and process of schooling in their tribal governments in order to reaffirm the social and cultural integrity of that tribal-specific group and to ensure its continuity.

American Indians have been historically and systematically denied community participation in education as it is described in the foregoing definition. Many Indians have perceived this denial as yet another battlefield strewn with dead languages, extinguished cultures and nearly assimilated sons of warriors. But as the Lakhota holy man Black Elk predicted, some living roots persist in the earth below the tree that seems to have been withered. After the long nights of defoliation, green shoots of life appear above ground in the shielding tree.

This chapter will discuss the historical and current policies behind the continuing denial of Indian tribal control over Indian education, contemporary efforts by various tribes and organizations to achieve control, and finally, alternatives that Indians must consider in order to achieve a quality education on Indian terms.

American Indian education is a misnomer since such tribes as the Cree, the Arapaho, the Miccosukee, and the Navajo may all have differing perceptions of education that arise from their diverse languages, life ways, and value systems. To impose uniform educational programs for all tribes is ethnocentric in the extreme, yet until as recently as nine years ago, education for American Indian tribes followed a monotonous and nearly deadly northern European curricular model that was totally outside the control of Indian parents and tribal members.

American Indians today consist of 481 federally recognized tribal entities; 51 officially approved organizations outside of specific federal statutory authority and 255 traditional organizations having recognition without federal approval of their organizational structure.

Of an estimated populace of one million American Indians, approximately 5 percent of the tribal members are living off-reservation some part of the time. A few tribes have thousands of members while many have less than 200. One-half the population is under sixteen years of age. In 1971, approximately 250,000 identified Indian, Eskimo, and Aleut children attended this nation's public, federal, and private schools.[1] Nearly 70 percent of the children attend public schools, 25 percent attend federal schools operated by the Bureau of Indian Affairs and 5 percent attend religious and other schools.[2] It is estimated that 10,000 Indian youngsters from the ages of six to eighteen do not attend school at all.[3]

Beginning in 1966, American Indians began to work systematically to achieve participation in and control over their educational systems. As of March 1978, there were approximately sixty-three Indian-controlled schools that were members of the Denver, Colorado–based Coalition of Indian Controlled School Boards (CICSB). In addition, there were some 160 members of the CICSB that were in various stages of assuming control and management of their educational systems.[4] These member schools are controlled by parents and concerned tribal members who are living on reservations and in off-reservation communities.

The concern of Indian participation and control of the educational process also extends into the arena of postsecondary education. In the academic year 1974–75, there were an estimated 25,000 American Indians in college.[5] In 1973, approximately 170 Indian studies programs in the nation's colleges and universities responded to a survey conducted by the Western Interstate Commission for Higher Education (WICHE). These programs varied widely in program complexity, numbers of students, and curricular offerings. A very small number of these programs had significant tribal community involvement or American Indian advisory boards.[6] An updated survey conducted by the Planning Resources in Minority Education program at WICHE in August 1974 revealed that numbers of Indian faculty had increased substantially and that community participation had increased only slightly.[7]

Indian controlled community colleges on the reservations are beginning to emerge. As of March 1978, twenty-one tribes had resolved to charter community colleges located on the reservations. Tribes initiating these postsecondary institutions are the Standing Rock Sioux, the Turtle Mountain Chippewa, the Sisseton-Wahpeton Sioux, the Fort Berthold Mandan-Hidatsa, the Cheyenne River Sioux, the Pine Ridge Sioux, the Rosebud Sioux, the Winnebago, the Omaha, the Santee Sioux, and the Navajo, the Keweenaw Bay Chippewa, the Devil's Lake Sioux, the Mississippi Band of Choctaw, the six tribes of the Minnesota Chippewa, the Lummi, the Inupiat Eskimo, the Tanana Chiefs, the Hualapai, the Havasupai, the Salish-Kootenai, the White Mountain Apache, the Blackfeet, the Fort Peck Assiniboine and Sioux, the Fort Belknap Tribes, the Northern Cheyenne, and the Colorado River Tribes. These tribes have elected to provide postsecondary programs on their reservations in order to locally serve their tribal members. Boards of Regents of these colleges are composed of elected and appointed tribal members. In 1970, Dr. James Wilson, a Pine Ridge Lakhota, who then headed the Office of Economic Opportunity's Indian Desk, convened a dozen Indian educators from throughout the United States to project future postsecondary initiatives that would encompass the concepts of Indian control and community involvement. It was projected that at least four Indian controlled regional universities and research institutes would be needed in the near future. In a project backed by the Fund for the Improvement of Postsecondary Education, Dr. Arthur McDonald, a Lakhota, researched tribal needs for a University of the Northern Plains. Such an upper division and graduate institution would serve culturally similar tribes of the northern plains and Rocky Mountain states. At present, Indian educators are projecting six to eight regional or upper division and graduate institutions that would be responsive to various cultural and linguistic tribal entities.

The few Indian communities and tribes that have so recently managed to assume participation in and control over their educational systems have been forced to view education as war. Scores of other tribes are currently engaged in battles to achieve even a minimal involvement in their elementary and secondary educational systems. Protagonists appear from the local school district level as well as from the state and federal levels. That American Indian children have been the losers and the victims of this war is well documented in the 220-page report, *Indian Education: A National Tragedy—A National Challenge.*[8]

Federal Policies and Legislation

Since the first days of European immigration, non-Indians have viewed the aboriginal inhabitants of this country as impediments to their concepts of "manifest destiny." Education has been utilized as a tool to "civilize" the American Indian so that resistance to land and resource exploitation would be diminished. Overall, federal policies toward American Indians have vacillated between extermination and assimilation since the American Revolution.

In 1819, Congress passed a law which provided for the administration of an educational fund for the "civilization" of Indians. The $10,000 annual appropriation was channeled through Christian religious and mission groups that proceeded to divide Indian country among themselves for proselytizing purposes.

The authority for the regulation of American Indians by Congress was delineated by Chief Justice Marshall who declared: "That instrument [the Constitution of the United States] confers on Congress the powers of war and peace; of making treaties, and of regulating commerce with foreign nations and among the several states and with the Indian tribes. These powers comprehend all that is required for the regulation of our intercourse with the Indians. They are not limited by any restrictions on their free actions; the shackles imposed on this power in the Confederation are discarded."[9]

Beginning with an Indian treaty submitted to the Senate by President Washington on May 25, 1789, the President and the Senate entered into some treaty relations with nearly every tribe and band within the territorial limits of the United States.[10] Part of the consideration for the treaties' promises of education was the cession by various Indian tribes of almost one billion acres of land to the United States. Technical education in agriculture and the mechanical arts were emphasized in treaties such as the Treaty with Sacs and Foxes, March 6, 1861 (school and teacher); Treaty with Crows, May 7, 1868 (teachers); Treaty with Northern Cheyenne and Arapahos, May 10, 1868 (teachers); Treaties with Sioux, April 29, 1868 and March 2, 1889 (teachers); Treaty with Chippewas, March 19, 1867 (school or schools); and Treaty with Navajos, June 1, 1868 (teachers).[11]

In 1879, the House Committee recommended the establishment of industrial training schools for Indian youth so that "by a removal of the children from all tribal influence during the progress of education, . . . educators can command all the time and attention of their pupils." The committee would utilize abandoned army barracks, stating,

> *Is it not wise economy to occupy these government buildings for the objects contemplated, and employ army officers who are fitted as teachers and otherwise, in connection with such schools, and to vigorously and adequately provide for and enforce the treaty stipulations recited; thereby not only discharging a solemn government obligation and duty, but speedily accomplishing the education, elevation, and civilization of all the savages in our land?* [12]

In 1893, Congress authorized the Secretary of the Interior to "withhold rations, clothing, and other annuities from Indian parents or guardians who refuse or neglect to send and keep their children to proper school age in some school a reasonable portion of the year." [13]

Until the Citizenship Act of 1924,[14] all Indians did not have the right to attend state-supported schools, even though citizenship had been conferred on some tribes by treaty. The limitation of state power over Indians is described in United States v. Kagama:[15]

> *It seems to us that this is within the competency of the Congress. These Indian tribes are the wards of the nation. They are communities dependent on the United States; dependent largely for their daily food; dependent for their political rights. They owe no allegiance to the States, and receive from them no protection. Because of the local ill feeling, the people of the states where they*

*are found are often their deadliest enemies . . . The power of the
General Government over these remnants of a race once powerful,
now weak and diminished in numbers is necessary to their protection, as well as to the safety of those among whom they dwell. It
must exist in that government, because it never has existed
anywhere else, because the theatre of its exercise is within the
geographical limits of the United States, because it has never been
denied, and because it alone can enforce its laws on all the tribes.*

Four federal programs that support the public school education of Indian children are the Johnson-O'Malley Act of 1934,
the Impact Aid laws, the Elementary and Secondary Education
Act (ESEA), Title I and the Indian Education Act, PL 92-318.

The Johnson-O'Malley Act of 1934

The Johnson-O'Malley Act (JOM) authorizes the Secretary of the
Interior, through the Bureau of Indian Affairs, to make contracts
with states "for the education, medical attention, agricultural assistance, and social welfare of Indians."

For years, Indian people had felt that the millions of JOM
dollars were not reaching their children. These suspicions were
confirmed in a study, *An Even Chance,* sponsored by the NAACP
Legal Defense and Educational Fund and the Center for Law and
Education at Harvard University. Mr. Leonard Bear King, field
director, and twenty-nine Indian community interviewers gathered documents and interviewed state and local officials in sixty
districts in eight states, as well as 445 Indian parents. The study
found no accountability for JOM funds by state or local school
districts, nor accountability by the Federal government. Neither
the Bureau of Indian Affairs (BIA) nor the Department of the
Interior had ever conducted audits of JOM expenditures at the
state or local level. Flagrant misuse of funds by local officials,
sanctioned by the states, was found consistently.

Indian parents were found to be largely unaware of the
possibilities for using JOM to meet the special needs of their
children.[16] Interviews revealed that although parents were keenly
interested in education, they were alienated from the public
schools, and were systematically excluded from decision making
in education. Parents were found to be afraid to talk with inter-

viewers for fear of harassment of their children and loss of jobs. Parents were not involved in Title I or JOM programs despite federal regulations calling for their participation.[17] Further, though Indians comprised a substantial part of the school enrollment, they were typically unrepresented on school governing boards and excluded from administrative and teaching positions and from the PTA. They were not represented on JOM or Title I–required advisory committees. Local school boards in districts with heavy concentrations of Indian people usually had little or no Indian representation on the school board. Many Indians and non-Indians alike erroneously believed that Indians are not eligible to vote or run for office because Indian-owned property is exempt from local property tax.[18]

Following several lawsuits involving violations of the JOM regulations in 1973, the BIA was instructed to reform JOM regulations. The BIA delayed so long that numerous Indian organizations concerned with education approached the Native American Rights Fund (NARF) in Boulder, Colorado to request legal action against the BIA. On January 11, 1974, BIA Commissioner, Morris Thompson, published revised JOM regulations and invited comments on them. Concerned Indian people met in Albuquerque on February 7 and 8, 1974, to develop an Indian version of the proposed regulations. Thirty-eight Indian organizations that became known as the "Red Regs" group submitted their consensus version to Commissioner Thompson on February 28, 1974.[19] The Red Regs group did not use the "BIA's Proposed Rules" as a departure point because they were felt to be totally inadequate. Section 33.3, "Community Participation" as recommended by the Red Regs group stated that maximum self-determination was a primary goal. By requiring contracting directly with Indian groups, parents would have substantial input and control over JOM programs. All community education committees and parent contracting institutions would be nominated and selected by procedures determined by the Indian community affected. These procedures would be sanctioned by the tribal governor where necessary.

Each community education committee would be authorized to make an initial assessment of the needs of Indian children in the community affected; participate in negotiations concerning contracts; participate in the planning, development, evaluation, and monitoring of programs; hear complaints by Indian students and their parents; meet regularly with the professional staff serving Indian children and with the local educational agency; establish rules for conducting its offices; and have such additional powers as are consistent with these regulations.

As a backup, Mr. Charles Wilkenson, a NARF attorney representing the Indian Red Regs group, sent a letter to Commissioner Thompson outlining basic inequities.[20] Documenting the arbitrary and random distribution scheme, he stated that in the fiscal year 1971, Alaska and Iowa received $932 and $616 per pupil respectively, while Nevada and Oklahoma received only $70 and $58 per pupil respectively.

There were other issues as well. The BIA had failed to promulgate legally acceptable standards for monitoring and review. It was illegally limiting JOM assistance to those areas near "large blocks of non-taxable Indian-owned property," which negatively affected California Indian children. Finally, provisions concerning parent participation must be set forth in the regulations and not just in the BIA manual.

The BIA accepted the Indian citizens' version of the revised regulations almost in toto, becoming effective on September 20, 1974. After a four year war, a major battle had been won.

Impact Aid

An Even Chance also documented glaring misuse of Impact Aid monies as they affect Indian children. Two Impact Aid Laws affect children whose parents live and work on federal property. PL 874 provides funds to local school districts for general operating expenses paid in lieu of local taxes, and PL 815 provides for school construction in districts where there are "federally connected" children. In the fiscal year 1969, the federal government provided $27.9 million for school districts on the basis of eligible Indian students.[21] In 1953, PL 815 was amended to include districts where Indian children were not in public schools because there were no facilities for them. Between 1953 and 1966, the federal government spent $55,223,523 for schools for 48,497 pupils.[22] Although Indian children in the Gallup-McKinley County School District in New Mexico brought in $306.70 per child in

Impact Aid Funds in 1970 as compared to $127.00 per non-Indian child, Indian children were in overcrowded and substandard facilities with inadequate supplies and materials, inadequate and insensitive teachers, and a lack of special programs and classes. Meanwhile, a school attended predominantly by non-Indians only five miles away could boast a carpeted music room, a carpeted library, uncrowded and well-equipped classrooms, a gymnasium, and a separate cafeteria.[23] No accountability was required by the Office of Education.

Elementary and Secondary Education Act—Title I

Educationally deprived Indian children are also entitled to aid from Title I of the Elementary and Secondary Education Act. Both BIA and public schools receive funds from this program based on their Indian enrollments. More than two-thirds of all public school districts participate in Title I programs; nine million students in both public and private schools were receiving $1.5 billion in Title I services in the 1970–1971 school year. A study of school districts in eight states found widespread violations of the law as it affects Indian children. This law forbids use for general aid and specifies that projects must be designed to meet the special educational needs of educationally deprived children. [24] *An Even Chance* exhaustively documents widespread misuse of funds.

Title I regulations as of 1970 required the creation of parent advisory councils.[25] As of 1974, American Indian parents were found on numerous JOM advisory boards throughout Indian country. Parent participation is more prevalent in schools on or near reservations where family income is below $2,000 per year. Often the same persons sit on JOM and Title I advisory boards as well as on Title IV committees. Transfer of the decision-making abilities that positively affect the quality of educational programs is evident at many Indian schools.

Title IV—The Indian Education Act

The Indian Education Act of 1972 (P.L. 92–318) establishes a National Advisory Council for Indian Education and an Office

143

of Indian Education within the Office of Education. Part A provides formula grants based on the number of Indian pupils enrolled. These grants are allocated to local school districts to meet the particular needs of these children, with a special provision allotting up to 5 percent of the funds to Indian controlled schools located on or near Indian reservations.

Part B authorizes grants made on a competitive basis directly to Indian tribes and organizations, and to state and local educational agencies. The purpose of these grants is to support special programs and projects aimed at improving educational opportunities for Indian children. Part C authorizes funds for special programs relating to adult education for Indians.

Indian people within the Office of Education cooperated with Indians from throughout the country in developing the concepts embodied in the Act and in fighting for the release of appropriated funds impounded by then President Nixon. Indian people representing various tribes and organizations traveled to Washington, D.C., to learn the lobbying process. Herschel Sahmaunt, who was then president of the National Indian Education Association, coordinated lobbying efforts. There had not been such a coordinated and widespread attack by Indian people since the antitermination battles of the Eisenhower administration. Two major legal suits were brought against President Nixon that combined efforts of several tribes and Indian organizations. These legal actions resulted finally in the release of appropriated funds.

There was broad, nationwide participation by tribes and Indian organizations in the nomination of respected Indian people to sit on the fifteen-member National Advisory Board on Indian Education mandated by P.L. 92–318. Indians had long planned for such a board which would influence and represent their concerns for all federal education programs affecting Indian children. The final appointments to the National Advisory Board made by the White House did not reflect the wishes and recommendations of the tribes. In the fall of 1972, several hundred tribes and Indian organizations submitted nominations to the Office of Education. From this list, thirty-nine names were culled that had been most frequently nominated. Twenty-five of the thirty nominees that were submitted by the Secretary of Health, Education and Welfare were rejected. New names were picked by the White House, and telegrams of support were solicited as late as May 4, 1973, one day before the appointments.[26] There was widespread disillusionment and disappointment with non-Indian and even some Indian politicians who had not shown understanding of the concept of fair Indian representation and participation. But there was such relief that the legislation was going to be finally implemented that Indian educators moved forward to program planning and implementation.

The Indian Education Act is now judged by most Indians to be successful. The Office of Indian Education of the Department of Health, Education, and Welfare employs Indian consultants as readers. In the field, Indian people plan the projects and, for the most part, hire Indian program administrators and staff, except where there is a scarcity of Indian linguistic specialists, teachers, and administrators. Indian tribal members living in off-reservation communities and in the cities are being reached as never before. The Indian Community School in Milwaukee, funded by Part B, in 1974 had seventy-six students in grades 1–12, with a waiting list of over 100. Every subject taught has an Indian base. The school's board of directors is composed of members of the Oneida and Chippewa tribes. Its advisory council is composed of both Indian and non-Indian people.[27]

Title IV—The Indian Education Act is the first federal legislation *requiring* active participation by Indians and Alaskan natives in projects to advance their children's education supported under the act. But there are still a few shadows. Some school administrators have avoided applying for Part A entitlement funds, just as JOM monies are avoided. Many Indians feel that the main reason behind this refusal to accept available funds is rooted in racism. Some school administrators would rather do without school funding than accept Indian participation. In 1977, the National Indian Education Association and the National Congress of American Indians proposed some twenty amendments to the Indian Education Act to improve its scope and function.

Programs That Work

The Indian-controlled elementary and secondary schools and the twenty-one tribally chartered community colleges are proving that the best way to improve the quality of Indian children's education is to place the control and the decision-making power in the hands of the tribes and the Indian people. The Indian programs funded by The Indian Education Act are also proving that strong tribal and Indian participation in planning, implementation, and evaluation of their programs is the only answer to quality education.

There are several outstanding examples that prove this point. These include the Rocky Boy School District near Box Elder, Montana; the Rough Rock Demonstration School near Chinle, Arizona; the Busby School in Montana; the Miccosukee School in Florida; and several of the Indian community colleges including Navajo Community College at Tsaile Lake, Arizona; the Lummi School of Aquaculture in Washington; Sinte Gleska College at Rosebud, South Dakota; and the Lakhota Higher Education Center at Pine Ridge, South Dakota. Since these programs have been established longer, it is easier to point to their successes. The other tribally-controlled schools that have been more recently initiated already show the same success patterns.

All the schools can point to sharply increased retention rates. While the attrition rate for Indian students between the first and second years of college is an alarming 78 percent, the attrition rate at Sinte Gleska College is 5 percent! The College Board of Regents, which is composed of elected tribal members, feels that to give their children an opportunity to continue their education in a supportive environment is important. Curriculum is devised to meet individual student needs. More importantly, it is designed to meet the short and long range cultural and economic goals of the tribe.

The Rocky Boy School in Montana was formally approved as a reservation school district in 1970. The principal benefits have been emphasis on individual instruction, heavy reliance on Cree-speaking teacher aides, and attention to the Cree language and culture as an integral part of the curriculum.[28] Rocky Boy is considered to be a national model for the development of Indian curriculum.

The Rough Rock Demonstration School is a bilingual school. Dillon Platero, the first director of the school, stated that, "Rough Rock is an extension of the child's normal world, in which he is competent to communicate and react in fashions sanctioned by his community and culture."[29] Fluency in both

Navajo and English is stressed. As soon as the parents at Rough Rock had control of the school, the Navajo language ceased to be considered as a patois to be eliminated.

Conclusions

The major problem confronted by the Indian community controlled schools is the precariousness of funding. The schools are primarily dependent on unstable federal and state financial assistance. The BIA has only recently begun to plan or modernize its school system, and most Indians fear that there is a covert plan to phase out the BIA education function. This fear was fanned when the National Council on Indian Opportunity recommended that "All programs involving the education of native people through public school organizations be administered or coordinated by the Bureau of Indian Education in the United States Office of Education under the direction of a new Deputy Commissioner, and that responsibility and authority vested in the new Bureau specifically include the management and distribution of Johnson-O'Malley funds." [30]

The Minnesota Chippewa Tribes and the Lac Courte Oreilles Tribe of Wisconsin sent strong letters and resolutions of total opposition to this recommendation. Their prime concern was that such a change would abrogate the unique federal responsibility to the education of Indian children.

It seems likely that the trend toward Indian tribally controlled schools will continue. If so, within the next five to ten years, there could conceivably be at least two hundred tribal elementary and secondary schools, as many as thirty Indian community colleges, and from six to eight regional upper division and graduate Indian universities. Funding must be equitable and adequate.

On September 29, 1976, Senator James Abourezk of South Dakota introduced a Senate bill to provide for grants for certain Indian controlled post-secondary educational institutions, which would appropriate $21 million in each of the first two full fiscal years following enactment of the bill, and $22 million in the third fiscal year. Indians hope that special monies will be appropriated for Indian colleges, since their programs tend to fall between the cracks when they compete with other colleges. The Indian College Bill has been revised and is still before Congress as of the spring of 1978. Indian tribes are beginning to consolidate their education programs under divisions or departments of tribal education. The Navajo, Blackfeet, Standing Rock Sioux and approximately a dozen other tribes have developed working models.

Indian controlled schools must solve the problems of teacher competencies, and tribes in concert must quickly develop comprehensive accreditation systems. Non-Indian accreditation associations are reluctant to accept the diverse Indian languages as valid means of communication. They are reluctant to accept American Indian belief systems and philosophies as valid spheres of study. They are also reluctant to recognize eminent Indian persons without "credentials" as faculty members. Two interesting and recent exceptions are the medical schools at the University of Oregon and the University of Utah. These institutions allowed that faculty status would be granted to widely respected Indian "medicine men."

Finally, Indians must help the BIA to correct its impression that Indian educational services are a privilege. Education is a right and an entitlement that was agreed to by the United States government in legally binding treaties with the tribes in exchange for the real estate on which it stands.

NOTES

1. Report from the Committees on Labor and Public Welfare and the Committee on Interior and Insular Affairs, on S. 248s, S. Doc. 384, 92nd Congress, 1st Session, October 1, 1971, pp. 13–15.

2. U.S. Department of the Interior, *Fiscal Year 1971 Statistics Concerning Indian Education*, p. 1.

3. Interview with George Scott, Assistant Director, Education Programs, Bureau of Indian Affairs, October 10, 1974.

4. Interview with Betty Gress, Director, Coalition of Indian Controlled School Boards, October 8, 1974.

5. *United Scholarship Service News* 2 (April 1974).

6. Planning Resources in Minority Education at Western Interstate Commission of Higher Education, *A Survey of College and University Programs for American Indians*, June 1973.

7. Planning Resources in Minority Education at Western Interstate Commission of Higher Education, *A Survey of College and University Programs for American Indians,* August 1974.

8. *Indian Education: A National Tragedy—A National Challenge,* S. Rep. No. 91–501, 91st Cong., 1st Sess.

9. Worcester v. Georgia, 6 Pet 515 (1832).

10. Felix S. Cohen, *Handbook of Federal Indian Law* (Albuquerque, N.M.: University of New Mexico Press, 1942), p. 91.

11. Daniel·Rosenfelt, *Indian Schools and Community Control,* 25 Stanford Law Review 489, April 1973.

12. *Industrial Training Schools for Indian Youth,* H. Report No. 29, 46th Congress, 1st Session, June 14, 1879.

13. 27 Stat. 628, 635. 25 USC. 283.

14. 43 Stat. 253. Nationality Act of October 14, 1940, reenacted in the Act of June 27, 1952, 6 USC. 1401(a)(2).

15. Cohen, *Federal Indian Law,* p. 116.

16. NAACP Legal Defense Fund, *An Even Chance,* 1971, p. 26.

17. Ibid., p. 42.

18. Ibid., p. 48.

19. Proposed Johnson-O'Malley Regulations. Available from the Native American Rights Fund, Boulder, Colorado.

20. Letter from Charles F. Wilkenson to BIA Commissioner Morris Thompson, April 17, 1974.

21. NAACP Legal Defense Fund, *An Even Chance,* p. 6.

22 USOE, Administration of Public Laws 81–874 and 81–815, 196 (Table 15), 1969.

23. NAACP Legal Defense Fund, *An Even Chance,* pp. 8–9.

24. Ibid., pp. 27–40.

25. Elementary and Secondary Education Act Advisory Statement of Policy of Parental Involvement in Title I, October 30, 1970.

26. Coalition of Indian Controlled School Boards, from a congratulatory letter to the advisory members from Gerald Clifford. *Newsletter* II (June 16, 1973).

27. American Education, Department of Health, Education and Welfare. *Indians In Charge Here* 10 (October 1974), p. 8.

28. "We'll Do It Our Own Way Awhile," *Race Relations Reporter* 3 (January 3, 1972).

29. *Indian Voices* (San Francisco: The Indian Historian Press, Inc., 1970), p. 133.

30. *Between Two Milestones: The First Report to the President of the United States.* November 29, 1972 (recommendation #4). Congressional Record, 119 (Thursday, March 29, 1973).

School and Community

Boss-Worker or Partners?

Manuel Montano

University of the Pacific
Stockton, California

Since the advent of federal funding of school programs for the poor, questions regarding the relationship between the school and the community have become increasingly louder. Previously, any questions related to the community's role in the educational process remained in abeyance for a number of reasons. The poor were politically quiet, inept, or both. For example, even if they rejected the practice of imposing middle-class values and skills on their children, they did not fight to prevent this practice. Silence remained their dominant response. Regardless of whether their silence constituted consent, or apathy, or merely reflected the acceptance of a subordinate position in society, schools tended to treat this silence of the poor as indicative of their consent. The middle class took a more active interest in the school. The value reciprocity, political activism, and skill to battle bureaucracy provided the middle class with control of schools and the educational process, while the poor remained quiet.

Recently, the issue of the poor community's role in education has been debated widely across the United States. New demands from a number of cultural and racial groups with special needs have emerged as a result of this debate. Prominent among these groups has been the Chicano. In addition to the domination of middle-class values, which has been endured by the poor in general, Chicano children also have been deprived of their language. Although federally-supported schools in the possessions and territories of the United States have been bilingual, Spanish-speaking populations within the United States generally have been forced to speak only English in schools. Samoan children could learn in their native language, but Spanish-speaking children in Texas, for example, are required to speak English upon entering school. The resultant damage to generations of Spanish-speaking children in terms of academic achievement, self-concept, and social mobility is probably incalculable. Moreover, the inability or unwillingness of schools to deal with the problems of bilingualism continues to inflict hardship and prejudice on the Spanish-speaking child.

Spanish-speaking children have sometimes been labeled and placed in classes for the mentally handicapped because of their inability to pass intelligence tests written in English. Similarly, other children have frequently been classified as having speech impediments because they are not native speakers of English. Discrimination, however, need not be so blatant. In Los Angeles many schools apparently operate on the assumption that all Spanish-surnamed children work well with their hands. Consequently, many of these children are counseled into high school vocational training programs without consideration for their individual talents, needs, or interests. These practices are now being challenged by the Chicano community, but this stereotyping has caused considerable damage to many children.

In addition to the problems of language, the Chicano child also faces the problem of reconciling the demands and values of different cultures. As Louis Villareal points out so poignantly in his book *Pocho*, Chicano children are caught between the conflicting demands of two cultures: the dominant culture is strange to them, while the familiar culture is subordinate and considered inferior. The Chicano child is forced to choose between the two worlds, one culture over another, rather than being allowed to benefit from both. While the dominant culture offers the possibility of success in life for the Chicano child if assimilation is total, the child's family and friends belong to the subordinate culture. Even if the pocho tries not to make a choice, the dominant culture will label him or her as inferior, prove it so, and take the choice from his or her hands.

Historically, the thrust of most social science research on minorities has been to determine why minorities do not achieve well in school. Only recently has the emphasis been placed on how schools must change to accommodate the cultural and social-class values of minorities, rather than on how minorities must change to conform to the way schools do things.*

In my own Teacher Corps experience and the experience of the federal government in funding various programs, the most productive approach to improving education for minorities has been a school-community partnership. In this partnership, the community's contribution is to define the problem. The school, representing both the dominant culture and the education profession, then contributes its problem-solving abilities. The coequality of school and community can strengthen school-community relationships and can reveal problem areas which have escaped previous identification, and consequently impeded progress. Where school and community have not functioned as coequals, research tends to fault people rather than the institutions which are supposed to serve the community, and programs prove almost uniformly unsuccessful in achieving their objectives. Success with the school-community partnership at a number of levels suggests that further exploitation of this approach could be quite profitable.

The Partnership Approach: Some Proposals

Recent federal programs and various community efforts have demonstrated productivity of a school-community partnership. While federal programs in the war on poverty were controlled by the school without significant community input, later programs have shown the success of the school-community partnership. For example, when the Chicano community began articulating its demands, bilingual-bicultural education emerged as a possible solution to the cultural and value clash with the dominant society. Though the concept is still being refined and developed, Title VII programs demonstrate significant success when compared to earlier federal efforts. Moreover, such programs are indisputably needed. A recent court case, Lau v. Nichols, established the right

---

* Recent emphasis on new fields such as bilingual/cross-cultural education, multicultural education, and linguistics (e.g., spoken black dialect) suggests that the burden of remediation is on the school, rather than on its clientele. In other words, schools must adapt to the needs of their clientele rather than the other way around.

of all children who do not speak English in the home to bilingual education. As a result, the San Francisco public schools, and by implication all public schools, must now provide bilingual education for children reared in a different language. Bilingual-bicultural education programs developed with Title VII money now serve as models for an established nationwide need. However, in spite of the gains made in recent years, needed improvements still can be identified.

First, a commitment to staff development as a professional norm is needed if federal programs are to have a significant impact on the quality of education. To this end, various professional organizations must stress the obligation toward continuous development for the professional. Professional development should speed the diffusion of innovation in the educational system, and also should overcome the patchwork effect of federal programs that do not have any significant impact beyond the expiration of funding. Moreover, training teachers rather than specialists should insure the survival of various innovations during economic crises. Second, there is room for considerable development of bilingual-bicultural materials. Although we now possess the knowledge, we do not have the necessary materials to best use our knowledge. For example, bilingual textbooks that print even-numbered pages in Spanish and odd-numbered pages in English could prove useful in all subjects. Publishers will produce such books if the demand is sufficient. The same approach can be taken for individualized instructional systems; for example, the Individualized Math System (IMS) published by Ginn or any of the large number of aptitude and achievement tests could be duplicated in Spanish. Similarly, transitional materials such as those used to teach Spanish as a foreign language can be developed to teach English as a foreign language. Such transitional materials usually consist of short stories or paragraphs in which two languages are mixed together in a way that facilitates an understanding of the foreign language. There may be other promising approaches to bilingual-bicultural education not yet tested on a large scale.

Paulo Freire's* adult basic literacy program proved successful in Brazil and is being implemented by the United Farmworkers as an educational program for migrant workers. Several

---

* Paulo Freire, *Pedagogy of the Oppressed* (New York: Herder & Herder, 1970).

of Freire's principles might be implemented in the public schools at any level; however, they await a full-fledged test. Similarly, more effective migrant education programs are badly needed, yet little work seems to be done in this area.

Our point here is that a partnership between school and community seems mandatory if a program is to achieve fully its goals. Conversely, a school-community partnership will not guarantee success for a program; it will merely make success fully possible when the program is well planned and capably administered. Success with this approach in curriculum development and federal programs suggests certain strategies which might prove profitable in the area of budget and personnel.

Community Involvement in Budgeting

One of the most productive procedures for involvement of the community in school budgeting occurred in Vallejo, California, where the central office made extensive efforts to decentralize budgeting for Elementary and Secondary Education Act (ESEA) funds. An assistant superintendent went to all schools receiving ESEA funding with that school's ESEA budget for the forthcoming year to present both the amount of funding and the cost breakdown of various instructional aids available to the school. The teaching staff and community people worked together to allocate the school's funds, determining jointly the number of school aides to be hired and how the remaining funds would be spent. In this case, the value to both school and community was considerable. Not only did the teachers and staff feel more professional and more able to develop adequate systems of instruction, but the community people felt themselves to be a genuine and valuable part of the education system.

The tactic of decentralizing the budget was valuable primarily because it diminished the barriers created by hierarchy and made the central office, school staff, and community coequal partners in structuring the educational process. The self-esteem of both faculty and community was raised, thereby increasing the positive attitudes of all parties toward education, improving the school, and school-community relationships.

Though it is unlikely that boards of education would share

accurate, complete budgets with communities in general (as teacher organizations often have great difficulty in determining just how much money a board has at its disposal), the concept of a community partnership to determine the allocation of funds in individual schools appears to be quite feasible, provided that a sufficient discretionary budget is available to the individual school. Further, it seems likely that many community resources could be tapped through joint decentralized budgeting. For example, community people in Vallejo, California suggested the use of General Services Administration surplus materials in order to free more funds for another aide. Moreover, a retired member of the community repaired a number of items which the GSA considered worthless because of high repair costs. The retired handyman eventually began working at the school and taught several children some carpentry, and explained the workings of typewriters. In other words, joint decentralized budgeting resulted in several productive spinoffs which strengthened the relationship between the school and the community.

School Personnel

When an alternative school was set up in Stockton, California, parents played a major role in staff selection. Conflict quickly emerged when teachers were unable to meet parent expectations, and the teachers countered with charges that there was insufficient parent support and involvement. The showdown came at a special parent-teacher meeting. Though the meeting started out somewhat bitterly on both sides, each side proved willing to recognize its deficiencies and moved to correct them. As a result, parent involvement increased considerably to a more than acceptable level, and two teachers decided to seek transfers because they preferred traditional to open classroom instructional systems. The parents, in turn, developed specific ideas and questions for the new teachers and chose far better replacements. They now have specific ideas of what qualities they demand from a teacher. Though a confrontation was needed to establish a school-community partnership, the partnership has proved productive for all involved.

Another example of a positive program of community involvement in personnel selection is the community's role in choosing principals in Chicago. Before a principal can be appointed to a school, he or she must be approved by the community. Though the experience has been mixed so far, informants indicate that a process of leadership development appears to occur there. In the first stage, those who claim greatest militancy often control the selection committee, which has the power to specify certain characteristics, such as race and experience, of a new principal. This stage appears to be transitional. As more community people are attracted to power, militant leadership gives way to a more representative committee to develop its criteria (often identical to those developed by the first leaders) and manage its selections, in terms of a partnership with the school district rather than a confrontation. The various communities begin to come to grips with the responsibilities inherent in the power of their committees. Again, the community becomes increasingly sophisticated as it learns to organize and manage itself in partnership with the central office.

The examples cited here indicate that a productive three-way partnership between the community, local school, and central office can, over time, achieve a variety of desirable objectives and strengthen the whole educational process. Though the personnel issue is highly sensitive to everyone, community involvement has demonstrated considerable potential in this area.

Curriculum Development

Training community people as Community Resource Advisors (CRAs) to work with Teacher Corps teams at various schools has proved productive in a number of ways. The most effective teaching strategy in working with community people was a partnership approach with the CRAs defining problems, with the teachers working individually or jointly toward a solution. The basic component of this teaching strategy was, simply, listening. Listening to both opinion and fact raised CRAs' self-esteem and comprehension. Everyone learned easier, faster, and more effectively when this strategy was employed. Skills developed by the CRAs were put to use. One CRA wrote a proposal and obtained funds to pay parents to be trained as tutors and aides. Discussions with uninvolved community personnel revealed that many local people would like work in the schools if they could be paid for their time while they were being trained. Judging by the results, paying local personnel for their training would appear to be an effective tactic to strengthen community involvement in education.

In another case, one team's efforts to develop home instruction by training parents (without pay) was fairly successful, though more parents would have been willing to participate if some compensation for their time had been available. In terms of working with teacher aides, the most successful experiences are those in which the teacher works with the aide as an equal and attempts to diminish the barrier created by the authority inherent in the teacher's role compared to that in the aide's role. Avoiding the further development of hierarchical structure in the classroom appears to be productive. In this situation, it might help if teachers were trained to work with aides, especially since unhappy aides have been observed to increase the level of tension in the classroom and to affect learning negatively rather than positively.

The Partnership Approach in the University of the Pacific–Stockton Unified School District Teacher Corps Project

The partnership approach between the community and profession is demonstrated in this project in several ways. For example, all role groups are involved at every step of the process of developing a proposal for a new cycle. All groups work on project identification, proposal writing, budgeting, and evaluation; further, all groups, including the community group, have the power of approval. All changes are resubmitted to each group because everyone must approve every aspect of the final proposal. The steering committee also functions as a training vehicle for community participants, to develop skills related to evaluation, proposal development, and budgeting.

The project's summer program in 1974 illustrates fully the value of the partnership approach. Within the project guidelines to provide training for students and community people, all groups brainstormed at the beginning of the summer. The staff's role, in addition to submitting its own ideas, was to crystallize and synthesize the variety of ideas developed at our conference. We developed a series of weekend retreats in which parents were trained in the use of various community services and in working with children in informal instructional settings. The children were taught health practices and were exposed to a variety of new environments. At every stage of the project, all ideas were re-submitted to all groups for further critiquing and approval. Though the interns were charged with the responsibilities of developing their own materials and budgeting, all groups passed on their plans. The program was evaluated as completely successful by both the participants and an independent evaluator.

Other examples of successful partnerships with the community include a parent training conference in 1972 and a highly successful theater group operated primarily by an intern as his community-based education project. In all cases, the total partnership among all role groups, and the requirement that skill training and development be incorporated into any project, resulted in successful programs. The weakest part of these programs was the inability to pay community members for their participation and work. All groups except the community receive tangible financial benefits for their input and receive experience and training for their efforts. The community's role is no less important than that of any other group, and their input provides us with as much valuable training as we provide for them. On this basis alone, the community deserves financial support. But in addition, participation can be increased, indeed maximized, with financial support for the input of community people. Experience has demonstrated both sides of this question—paying the community members increases participation and not paying them limits participation. Overall, not paying for community participation is not only illogical and unfair but constitutes a major deficiency, which can be corrected only by the federal government because of increasingly limited local funds.

Summary

Wherever tried, the concept of a school-community partnership has demonstrated considerable potential for improving education. Though attempts at equalizing the power of the community with that of the school have occasionally involved considerable conflict, these attempts to involve communities in a meaningful way will result in a more productive educational environment.

Community involvement in education appears to be maximized by two specific but unsurprising factors—the distribution of money and power to the community. Along with this, the most productive involvement emerges from situations in which hierarchical relationships are minimized and genuine partnership is maximized. This situation arises even in initial stages of partnership development, such as the training of community personnel, when the tactic of listening is employed extensively by both role groups. Community involvement is most productive when handled as a joint exercise in communication and redistribution of power, responsibility, and money.

Community Participation in Education

A Minority Viewpoint

Edison Uno

California State University
San Francisco, California

As a parent, resident, taxpayer, and concerned citizen, I have been
involved with the San Francisco educational system for many
years. When the San Francisco Unified School District was under
court order to desegregate and integrate its schools, I was selected
to participate in the Citizen Advisory Committee for Desegregation and Integration. I also have made frequent appeals before
the San Francisco Board of Education, the District's Superintendent, and other officials of the school district on behalf of an
aggressive affirmative action policy, a multi-cultural curriculum,
teacher training in cultural pluralism, bilingual-bicultural educational programs, integration, quality education, and other local
issues.

I speak from a perspective of over twenty-seven years of
community involvement in my ethnic community and in the larger
urban communities of Los Angeles and San Francisco, California.
I speak as a member of a racial minority and as a critic of our
educational system. My viewpoint is a personal one and may not
be representative of the majority of Japanese Americans.

"Community participation in education," as a theme, may
give an illusion that there is a willingness or an eagerness to have
a community participate in decisions that affect the education of
its children. This would be the ideal theory in a democratic
society, whereby the principles of participatory democracy assume
that citizens have the right to self-determination or, at a minimum, to some influence in the decision-making process of governance. However, the theory is far from reality. I have seen
well-meaning, dedicated, and responsible individuals try to make
community participation a productive effort for the best interests

163

of students. But what started out to be a cooperative effort soon deteriorated into an adversary proceeding. Those who had a vested interest in maintaining the "status quo," namely the school board, superintendent, administrators, tenured teachers, and conservative elements of the school community, were called "we" and those who opposed their interests were called "they." The we-they language soon became a political designation in terms of social and economic definitions. "They" referred to the community and although it was not spelled out in certain terms, the community was often viewed in a derogatory way.

As a person of Japanese ancestry, I frequently was conditionally accepted by the "we" group and vicariously shared a superior attitude in the deliberation of educational policies. I shocked some of my white middle-class friends when I attempted to identify with minorities, especially when I injected the Third World identification to all people of color. It has been my experience that Asian Americans, especially educated Chinese Americans and Japanese Americans, are not considered minorities by the established power structure of education. For example, in many Educational Opportunity Programs and minority student programs, Asian Americans are not included because the guidelines are distinctly inclusive of blacks, Chicanos, and native Americans. Any inclusion of Asian Americans usually is an attempt to give a program the surface appearance of multi-ethnic representation. This form of tokenism is difficult to detect unless the individual has the ability and courage to articulate a perspective that is not divisive in relationship to other minorities.

One of the first steps in the process to seek community involvement would be to insure adequate funding in any budget. School superintendents, boards of education, and other school officials often hire consultants or experts, such as structural engineers, computer analysts, clinical psychologists, and investment advisors, to solve special technical problems. These consultants usually are paid handsomely for their advice and for special reports and evaluations. In the area of human relations and community relations, many well-qualified representatives of minority communities are also experts in their own right. They have much to contribute, but too often they are expected to give of their time and knowledge without remuneration.

This difference usually is explained by the fact that the

budget does not include funds for this kind of community input; therefore, if community input and involvement are desired, they must be attained at the expense of those who are willing to volunteer their time, effort and energies into the educational program.

I do not know if the San Francisco school district would be a typical example, but some statistics for the year 1975–76 include:

- Approximately 70,777 students were enrolled in San Francisco.
- There were 5,582 people employed by the school district.
- Approximately 89 percent of the budget paid salaries and benefits.[1]
- It cost $160,811,359 to run the school system.
- The per-pupil expenditure was $2,327.87.[2]
- Approximately 76 percent of the school population was non-white.[3]

The per-pupil cost is one of the highest in California, and the lack of leadership and quality education has been under constant attack by community groups.

Budget priorities set by the Board of Education are insignificant when 89 percent of the budget is committed to salaries and 7 percent for buildings and improvements, thus leaving less than 4 percent for supplies, materials, equipment, and furniture. Very little can be budgeted for innovative curriculum, community resources, teacher training, human relations, and other programs desired by ethnic communities to improve the quality of education for all students.

Many school districts are finding it increasingly difficult to obtain voter approval of school bond issues. This problem may be interpreted as a rejection of or lack of confidence in those charged with the responsibility of educating our young. "White flight" to the suburbs is another phenomenon which contributes to the lack of confidence in urban public schools. Originally, the term was used to define decreasing white enrollment; however, in recent years it not only explains the movement of whites out of urban areas, but it also has implications in terms of "economic flight." As minorities progress up the economic ladder, many middle-class minorities move to the suburbs. There seems to be no guarantee that this movement can be reversed or stabilized in the near future.

Under these circumstances, how realistic is it to expect community participation in the formulation of budget priorities? Approximately 98 percent of the school budget comes from local and state taxes. The remaining funds come from federal sources, which leaves a very small portion to be used for community interests. In times of tight school budgets, declining enrollment, increasing salaries and fringe benefits, and public apathy, the function of community participation usually is a defensive one, a rallying of community representatives before a board to preserve an existing or pilot program from budget cuts. Programs originally initiated by community interest groups are usually the first to be eliminated in the name of economy. Community activists charge that these programs are sabotaged from the beginning because they are "programmed for failure" by those who make decisions to pacify community interests. This method of school administration contributes to the frustration level of community representatives and increases the distrust and lack of confidence in decision makers in the public educational system.

Budget priorities also are used to control a variety of competing community interests. Often various communities find themselves competing against each other for the same dollar for their respective programs. Dissension caused by budget priorities has created serious disagreements among community groups who have common problems and yet find themselves at odds with each other regarding the necessity of a particular program. One group may be supporting a program for remedial needs, whereas another group may be lobbying for an enrichment program.

At this point, I think it is important to compare community needs with those needs articulated by professional educators. My reference is to the testimony made before the Select Committee on Equal Educational Opportunity of the United States Senate, 92nd Congress, transcript of the hearings held on March 3, 4, 5, and 6, 1971, in San Francisco and Berkeley, California. The following quote is from the preamble which represents a consensus position of professional educators from Santa Clara County.

The attainment of goals for community development—environmental, economic, social, and political—clearly affects, and is affected by, the attainment of educational goals.

A sound, attractive physical *environment in the commu-*

nity as a whole helps to support the functioning of the schools, and the schools themselves are an important element in a wholesome community environment.

A healthy economy in the community provides the tax base needed to support the schools, and the educational system in turn helps to attract economic growth and provides trained employees for commerce and industry.

The community's social structure greatly affects the schools. In an area where people of different backgrounds and income levels reside, where these differences are respected, and where there are effective means for resolving conflicts, the schools can best fulfill their responsibility of educating children for a heterogeneous world. However, where conflict and hostility prevail, where racial and ethnic polarization is increasing, and where residential segregation produces the psychology of the black, white, or brown ghetto, the schools find it difficult or impossible to do their job.

The public school districts, although maintained separately from other local government functions, are part of the overall State and municipal political structure. The schools must compete with other public service needs for State and local funds. To the extent that the political structure is efficient and responsive, the schools' effectiveness will be enhanced. Conversely, the schools are a vital means of encouraging and providing for informed citizen participation in political processes.

Neither community development goals nor educational goals are being attained in this county and other urban parts of the United States at anywhere near the pace needed to cope with rapid growth and change. The physical environment is rapidly becoming polluted. Adequate and truly moderately priced housing is in short supply, and urban centers are faced with deteriorating structures and neighborhoods. The public is reluctant to pay for school improvements as local property taxes reach maximum levels. Racial and ethnic polarization and hostility, aided by minimal housing and economic and social segregation, are increasing. It is not coincidental that many Americans have become alienated from the traditional political process as corruption, influence peddling, conflicts-of-interest, graft, and other forms of political abuse have become commonplace.

Amidst this confusing milieu of rising expectations, increasing problems, and scarce resources, community participation is expected to contribute toward the solution of these serious problems. However, the educational crisis is but a reflection of the greater problems in our society. We are beginning to pay for our past sins and to realize that the pretense of freedom, justice, equality, and liberty has not been part of the "American dream" for many in our communities.

Compare the goals and objectives of the professional educator with the concerns of a minority community as stated before the Select Committee on Equal Educational Opportunity by blacks from the Berkeley community. The overall purpose of the program is:

1. To develop values in human life, and responsibilities to each other.
2. To develop the belief in every student that he is intelligent, essential, and has unlimited capacity to learn.
3. To build mutual respect between students and teachers based on instruction geared to the student's cultural and personal needs.
4. To stimulate each student to think creatively, and to develop skills of concentration and analysis.
5. To teach basic skills of reading comprehension, writing, and debating.
6. To involve students in actually determining programs to combat and neutralize racism in America.
7. To analyze, study, and evaluate events of the past and present.
8. To develop social skills which will enable youth to develop humanistically oriented communities.

This list of goals and objectives was developed to support the need for black studies in the Berkeley school system. The community's request for this special program was part of the basic concept of quality education. If these goals and objectives were implemented decades ago, I believe many of our major problems today could have been effectively eliminated or at least minimized.

The lofty objectives of any program will remain utopian ideals unless there is an adequate delivery system to implement them. In the area of school personnel, community participation has had little influence in changing school administrations. Some exceptions to my indictment of the effectiveness of community participation probably exist because certain districts have hired well-qualified minority superintendents and other school officials. But, I believe that other school districts are still struggling with administrators who do not know how to solve problems, or who continue to blame society for problems that can be attributed to our educational system.

In principle, the goals of an aggressive affirmative action policy should reconcile the long history of exclusion and discrimination of minorities in education. However, often when an attempt to implement affirmative action is made, the charge of "reverse discrimination" can be heard. This reaction is totally unacceptable to me and others in minority communities. It is predicated on the assumption that all things being equal, a white person is being discriminated against because a minority person is given a priority. Indeed, if all things were equal it would be a prima facie case of discrimination, but that is not the case. Many school districts have a notorious record of personnel practices when it comes to hiring minorities. Even with the advent of affirmative action, one must carefully analyze statistical data. We have seen examples of an increase in minority personnel hiring, but on closer examination the personnel are at the lowest levels, are the lowest paid, and in many instances are found in dead end jobs where advancement opportunities do not exist.

Members of minority communities have to respond to public outcries of reverse discrimination when this charge plays on public sympathies that preferential treatment is totally wrong. Advocates of reverse discrimination charge that it is unfair to give an advantage to someone equally qualified for a position on the basis of his or her race or sex. This concept of "an unfair advantage" is not new. Many civil service agencies give veterans a percentage point advantage over non-veterans in civil service examinations. I understand this policy rewards those who served our country in military service, in an attempt to equalize the time lost while non-veterans may have been on the job or working in a similar classification to obtain valuable experience. Likewise, I believe minority candidates should be given some preference over non-minority candidates because past racist policies must be paid for, much as old indebtedness must be repaid with interest.

Some progress has been made in affirmative action; however, I believe we have seen signs of tokenism at various levels. In San Francisco we constantly urged our board and district to upgrade, promote, and recruit qualified minorities for some of the top administrative positions. For a district which had a 76 percent minority school population in 1975–1976, the percentage of minority administrators and teachers in the district was and is grossly imbalanced. Minority personnel recently hired by the district are the last to be hired and the first to be fired when budget economies cut salaries and programs.

Minorities have been hired in nonprofessional positions such as teachers' aides, bilingual-bicultural assistants, school monitors, bus guards, cafeteria helpers, and other paraprofessional categories, using Federal or state funds. These positions are often temporary and contingent upon the availability of funds. In many instances they provide no job security nor include any retirement or other fringe benefits afforded to other school personnel. Community participation has played an important role in obtaining these positions; nevertheless, these jobs do not provide the same type of security, benefits, status, and pay as those positions held predominately by non-minorities. Advocates of community participation fight to sustain these jobs and speak on behalf of minorities who regularly face the uncertainty of unemployment because a program has been eliminated or funds have been exhausted.

Organizations of minority teachers and administrators have formed to increase the opportunities for minorities within the system. Many minority teachers and administrators are underemployed. Given their experience, training, skill, and education, they have little opportunity toward upward mobility, especially if they have an assertive minority perspective or will not compromise their personal integrity to conform to the established policy of tokenism. Little tolerance exists for these minority teachers or administrators, who are willing to risk their professional careers for the benefit of all minorities.

Wide community participation should be encouraged in the selection of all top administrators, from the superintendent to department heads. Community advisory committees should have input in the initial screening of candidates and in the final recommendation for selection or appointment. The quality of community participation is extremely important. It is essential to obtain input from those who represent the vital concerns of a community rather than the self-interest of the individual. This may be a difficult task, but it is not an impossible one. Most representatives of minority communities who can articulate their collective interests are recognized because of their accomplishments in civil and human rights. In most cases, involving a variety of community individuals will insure that the best qualified individual will make judgments and decisions on behalf of the community. There is no single spokesperson for an ethnic community, nor is there any single perspective that all will agree to. Like other communities, ethnic minorities are diverse and cover a wide spectrum of political views; the best one can hope for is an individual who has the respect and integrity of the group. It is important to set up a procedure that will insure community participation by a network of community contacts.

San Francisco recently passed a law whereby members of the Board of Education are no longer appointed by the mayor, but instead are elected by the voters. This change has increased the opportunity for community participation via the electoral process. Heretofore, appointments made by the mayor were usually made without consultation with the community, and often reflected the educational philosophy of the mayor. Minority board members were generally conservative, nonthreatening, conformist, and easily manipulated by the power structure.

My personal community perspective of token minority representation on a school board is that it is more detrimental than beneficial. When a minority school board member falsely gives the illusion that he or she is representing a community perspective, I strongly believe that such an individual is an obstacle toward progressive change. My experience confirms my belief that we can put more faith and confidence in a non-minority board member who is willing to take some courageous stands on behalf of the community.

There are other realities one must face in dealing with personnel in school administration. One must acknowledge the existence and practice of nepotism, political patronage, and pre-selection. I have witnessed the charade of community involvement in the selection process for various school officials. The hidden agenda of pre-selection became obvious after several interview sessions when the best qualified person was not selected.

Community participation in curriculum development, textbook selection, teacher training, and other aspects of multicultural education has been relatively ineffective. Attempts have been made to involve community participation in these areas; however, the results have been minimal, mainly because the system is not designed to have input at the school level. Curriculum development usually takes place at the university and college levels, where specialists design what they think is best for our children. Schools of education and state departments of education make very little effort to incorporate the expertise of the community. I believe educators and curriculum specialists feel that it is below their dignity to seek advice from ethnic communities because their educational philosophy is that of the missionary mentality, "we know what is best for you." Textbooks often reinforce this concept and some classroom teachers reflect an insensitivity to cultural differences, lifestyles, values, language, and other virtues.

In California our legislature passed an amendment to the Educational Code commonly known as Article 3.3 which requires all school districts which have a 25 percent or more minority student population to provide minimum exposure to ethnic awareness, multicultural curriculum, cultural pluralism, and human relations. The intent of this new law is to make teachers sensitive to cultural differences. I have some reservations as to its effectiveness; surely it must be helpful to some who become aware, but I wonder how much attitudes of teachers and administrators really change.

Article 3.3 is a noble effort and I would support the continuation of the training it calls for. However, I believe a more effective method of accomplishing the same goal would be to require schools of education to mandate a series of ethnic studies courses as part of the curriculum of future educators and administrators.

Perhaps community participation least affects the classroom textbook. The national distribution of books makes it difficult for community participation to reflect a certain regional perspective without the jeopardy of controversy in another region. Consequently, some publishers prepare books for the South and other editions for the North. This is the domain of the professional— the writers, the artists, the graphic designers, the educational psychologists, the language specialists, and others. If there is any community participation at all, I suspect it comes as the end product is developed and minority consultants are asked to review the final drafts, with the admonition that drastic changes may be too expensive. Textbooks have made some superficial improvements over the years, especially in areas such as design, color, typography, photography, and graphics. Content has also improved, but not at the same rate as outward appearances would suggest.

Many would disagree with my opinions about community participation in education. I regret that I must paint such a dim picture, but I believe my viewpoint is close to reality. Community participation in education is a very middle-class activity. I would go one step further and state that it is also very elitist because it excludes the great majority of those at the grassroots level of the community. How often are school board meetings announced in languages other than English? Are interpreters provided for those parents who may not speak English? Does school curriculum provide for the development of healthy self-esteem of minority students?

I am reminded of an example of the frustration and despair concerning community participation felt by a group of dedicated community advocates for bilingual education in San Francisco. The famous Lau v. Nichols case was filed by parents who believed in community participation and who patiently lobbied for their cause. Hundreds of hours were spent in meetings, discussions, conferences, and personal contact to support their program. When all else failed, they filed suit and fought their case to the Supreme Court of the United States where their efforts were rewarded by a favorable adjudication. But their victory was empty. They had worked within the system, using all of the legal apparatus available to them, and yet when the decision was won, the district responded with indifference and apathy.

Community participation demands motivation, determination, perseverance, discipline, and confidence that one can influence school policy. Change is often painfully slow, frustrating, and difficult to accomplish. Unfortunately, many school districts are crisis-oriented and react only to acute situations.

I do not suggest abandoning the concept of community participation, but the future for this involvement is not particularly bright. If the citizenry fails to address substantive problems of education, it may well be impossible to salvage a system that in many ways seems to be programmed for self-destruction.

NOTES

1. San Francisco Unified School District, "General Fund Trends in Enrollment, Teacher/Pupil Ratio, per Pupil Expenditures, Staffing, Facilities Utilization, and Total School Tax Rates." This document provided by the Office of the Superintendent, 1976.

2. San Francisco Public Schools Commission Report and Recommendations; "Fiscal Future, Part 1, Revenues and Expenditures," 1976.

3. San Francisco Unified School District. Ethnic school population data, 1976.

Curricular History
and Social Control

Michael W. Apple
The University of Wisconsin, Madison

Barry M. Franklin
The University of South Carolina, Spartanburg

Introduction

Imagine yourself as living in one of the larger ghettos of an American city. Another community member comes up to you and says, "You know, schools work." You look at him somewhat incredulously. After all, your children are doing relatively poorly on intelligence and achievement tests. Most of the community's young go on to lower paying jobs than their white counterparts. Many are rather disheartened about their futures. The school has increasing violence and vandalism. The curriculum seems out of touch with the reality and the history of your people. The community, rightly, feels it has little say in what goes on in the institution that is supposed to educate its young.

You lay this all out for him, explaining each of these issues and trying to show him that he is either just plain wrong or one of the least perceptive people you have seen in a long time. Then he says, "I agree with all you have told me. All these things you have just mentioned occur, not only here but throughout the United States in communities where people live who are poor, politically and culturally disenfranchised, or oppressed." Yet he goes on and insists that schools do work, especially these schools. Then he begins documenting an important set of facts. Carefully, yet somehow passionately, he shows that these "community" schools are doing what they were in fact historically built to do. They were not built to give you control; quite the opposite is the case. As he talks, it slowly begins to make sense to you. A few more pieces of a larger picture begin to come together. What if he is correct? What if schools and the curriculum within them evolved

in such a way that the interests of my community were to be sub-
sumed under the interests of more powerful people? What if existing social and economic arrangements *require* that some people
are relatively poor and unskilled and others are not? Then you
begin to get an understanding of how schools help to maintain
this set of institutional arrangements. You begin to agree, and you
add something important he forgot to verbalize. You say, "Yes,
schools work . . . for them." And you both nod.

Now this little vignette was meant to be more than simply
an exercise in imagining. Rather, it was meant to point out both
that schools have a history and that they are linked to other powerful institutions in ways that are often hidden and complex. This
history and these linkages need to be understood if we are to know
the real possibilities for our own action on schools in that hypothetical community.

The curriculum field has played a major part in the relationship between school and community. Because of this, it can
also serve as an excellent exemplar for an analysis of the linkages
schools have had with other institutions. By focusing on some of
the past moments of the curriculum field here, we hope to show
that the conclusions of the people in the imaginary story we
started out with are not that imaginary at all. They provide, unfortunately, quite an accurate description of the hopes, plans, and
conservative vision of community held by a significant portion of a
group of educators who had a large impact on what was taught in
schools, and how that subject matter was chosen.

In order to illuminate these things, there are a number of
questions we need to ask here. What did "community" mean for
the educators and intellectuals who first had a strong influence on
the curriculum field? What social and ideological interests guided
their work? These questions are critically important for a number
of reasons. The knowledge that got into schools in the past and
gets into schools now is not random. It is selected and organized
around sets of principles and values that come from somewhere,
that represent particular views of normality and deviance, of good
and bad, and of what "good people act like." Thus, if we are to
understand why the knowledge of only certain groups has been
primarily represented in schools, we need to see the social interests
which often guided curriculum selection and organization.

As we shall demonstrate here, the social and economic interests that served as the foundation upon which the most influential curriculum workers acted were not neutral, nor were they random. They embodied commitments to specific economic structures and educational policies, which, when put into practice, contributed to inequality. The educational and cultural policies, and the vision of how communities should operate and who should have power in them, served as mechanisms of social control. These mechanisms did little to increase the relative economic or cultural efficacy of those groups of people who still have little power today. But before examining the roots the curriculum field has in the soil of social control, let us look briefly at the general perspective which underpins this chapter's critical analysis.

Power and Culture

Discipline—the rules and routines to keep order, the hidden curriculum that reinforces norms of obedience, punctuality, and so on—is not the only means schools use to exercise social and economic control. Control is exercised as well through the forms of meaning the school distributes. That is, the "formal corpus of school knowledge" can become a form of social and economic control.[1]

Schools do not only control people; they also help control meaning. They preserve and distribute what is perceived to be "legitimate knowledge"—the knowledge that "we all must have." Thus schools confer cultural legitimacy on the knowledge of specific groups.[2] The very fact that certain groups' knowledge becomes school knowledge is prima facie evidence of its perceived legitimacy. But this is not all, for the ability of a group to make its knowledge into "knowledge for all" is related to that group's power in the larger political and economic arena. Power and culture, then, need to be seen, not as static entities with no connection to each other, but as attributes of existing economic relations in a society. They are dialectically interwoven so that economic power and control is interconnected with cultural power and control. Thus, as Antonio Gramsci perceptively argued, the control of the knowledge-preserving and knowledge-producing institutions (such as schools) in a society is a critical element in enhancing the ideological and economic dominance of certain classes and groups. This very sense of the connectedness between knowledge or cultural control and economic power serves as the basis for our analysis here.

Two things are central to this approach. First, it sees schools as caught up in a nexus of other institutions—political, economic, and cultural—that are basically unequal. That is, schools exist through their relations to other more powerful institutions, institutions that are combined in such a way as to generate structural inequalities of power and access to resources. Second, these inequalities are reinforced and reproduced by schools (though not by them alone, of course). Through their curricular, pedagogical, and evaluative activities in day to day life in classrooms, schools play a significant role in preserving if not generating these inequalities. Along with other mechanisms for cultural preservation and distribution, schools contribute to what has elsewhere been called the *cultural reproduction of class relations* in advanced industrial societies.[3]

Accepting these two central concerns—the entrapment of schools in a powerful set of institutions and the role of the school in reproducing inequalities—means that one interprets schools in a different way from most educators. Rather than interpreting them as "the great engines of democracy" (though there is an element of truth in that), one looks at schools as institutions which are not necessarily progressive forces. They may perform economic and cultural functions and embody ideological rules that both preserve and enhance an existing set of societal relations. These relations operate at a fundamental level to help some groups and serve as a barrier to others.

This is not to imply that all school people are racist (though some may in fact be) or that they are part of a conscious conspiracy to "keep the lower classes in their place." In fact, many of the arguments for "community" put forth by some of the early educators, curriculum workers, and intellectuals whom we shall examine were based on the best intentions of "helping people." Rather, the argument being presented here is that "naturally" generated out of many of education's commonsense assumptions and practices about teaching and learning, normal and abnormal behavior, important and unimportant knowledge, and so forth, are conditions and forms of interaction that have latent functions. And these latent functions include some things that many educators are not usually aware of.

As has been pointed out elsewhere, for example, one important tacit function of schooling seems to be the teaching of different dispositions and values to different school populations. If a set of students is seen as being prospective members of a professional and managerial class of people, then their schools and curriculum seem to be organized around qualities such as flexibility, choice, and inquiry. If, on the other hand, educators see students' probable destinations as semi-skilled or unskilled workers, the school experience tends to stress punctuality, neatness, habit formation, and so on. These expectations are reinforced by the kinds of curricula and tests schools give, and by the labels affixed to different kinds of students.[4] Thus, the formal and informal knowledge that is taught in schools, the evaluative procedures, and so forth, need to be looked at in connection with their social significance or we shall miss much of their real significance. These everyday school practices are linked to economic, social, and ideological structures outside of the school building. These linkages need to be uncovered both today and in the past. It will be just this past that will concern us here.

Urbanization and the Historical Function of Schooling

Any serious attempt at understanding whose knowledge gets into schools must, by its very nature, be historical. It must begin by seeing current arguments about curriculum, pedagogy, and institutional control as outgrowths of specific historical conditions, as arguments that were and are generated out of the role schools have played in our social order. Thus, if we can comprehend the economic and ideological purposes schools have served in the past, we can see the reasons why progressive social movements which aim at certain kinds of school reforms—such as community participation and control of institutions—are often less successful than their proponents would like them to be.

To make this clear, we shall briefly focus on some historical purposes of urban schooling in general, on what its community role was seen to be, and how it functioned. Then we shall turn to a more extensive historical examination of the part of schooling that dealt with the knowledge students would receive in schools— the curriculum field.

Because of the ahistorical nature of education, we are in danger of forgetting many of the origins of city schools in the United States. This is unfortunate, for these roots might help explain why many black, Latino, and other communities find little of their own culture and language in schools. Recent investigations of the growth of education in the urban centers of the East are quite helpful in this regard. In New York City in the 1850s, for example, when the public school system became increasingly solidified, schools were seen as institutions that could preserve the cultural hegemony of an embattled "native" population. Education was the way in which the community life, values, norms, and economic advantages of the powerful were to be protected. Schools could be the great engines of a moral crusade to make the children of the immigrants and the blacks like "us." Thus, for many people who were important in the growth of schooling as we know it, cultural differences were not at all legitimate. Instead, these differences were seen as the tip of an iceberg made up of waters containing mostly impurities and immorality. The urban historian Carl Kaestle catches this attitude exceptionally well when he quotes from a New York State Assembly report which warned that, "Like the vast Atlantic, we must decompose and cleanse the impurities which rush into our midst, or like the inland lake, we shall receive their poison into our whole national system." [5]

Kaestle goes on to note that:

> Putnam's Monthly *used the same metaphor and indicated the same solution to the pollution problem: "Our readers will agree with us that for the effectual defecation of the stream of life in a great city, there is but one rectifying agent—one infallible filter—the SCHOOL."*
>
> *... Most schoolmen were probably not adverse to the success of limited numbers of the poor through education, but the schools' mission—and most promoters were quite frank about it— was to inculcate cooperative attitudes among the city's children whatever the vicissitudes of urban life might bring them. Acculturation is thus a more accurate term for the school's intention than assimilation, although the terms are often used synonymously. The schools reflected the attitude of the general native public, who wished to Americanize the habits, not the status, of the immigrant.* [6]

This moral mission of the school had a major impact on the kinds of curricular selections made and on general school policy. But this was not all. The crusade to eliminate diversity was heightened by another set of factors. The scale of city problems increased as the population increased. Something had to be done about the rapid growth in the numbers upon numbers of "different" children to be acculturated. The answer was bureaucratization—the seemingly commonsensical consolidation of schools and standardization of procedures and curriculum, both of which would promote economy and efficiency. Thus, the emphasis on acculturation and standardization, issues community members still confront today, were intimately intertwined. In essence, "the bureaucratic ethic and the moral mission of the schoolmen arose from the same problem—the rapid expansion and diversification of the population—and they tended toward the same result—a vigorously conformist system." [7]

This moral mission with its emphasis on cultural conformity was not simply found in New York; nor was it limited to the early and middle parts of the nineteenth century. The moral values became increasingly coupled with economic ideologies and purposes as the country expanded its industrial base. Schools in New York, Massachusetts, and elsewhere were looked at more and more as a set of institutions that would "produce" people who would have the traditional values of community life (a life that may never really have existed in this ideal form) and, as well, the norms and dispositions required of industrious, thrifty, and efficient workers for the industrial base. Not just in 1850, but even more between 1870–1920, the school was pronounced as the fundamental institution that would solve the problems of the city, the impoverishment and moral decay of the masses, and, increasingly, would adjust individuals to their respective places in an industrial economy. [8]

Marvin Lazerson's portrayal of the growth of schooling in the urban centers of Massachusetts makes these points in a rather telling fashion.

By 1915 two central themes have thus become apparent in Massachusetts' city schools. One drew upon the reform ferments of the decades between 1870 and 1900 and saw education as the basis of social amelioration. The school would reach out and uplift the poor, particularly through new techniques to teach traditional moral values. *The second theme, increasingly promi-nent after 1900, involved acceptance of the industrial order and a concern that schools mirror that order. It made the school's major function the fitting of the individual into the economy. By the teaching of specific skills and behavior patterns, schools would produce better and more efficient workers and citizens, and they would do this through a process of selection, [testing], and guidance. These developments would transform the idea of equality of educational opportunity in America* for they made segregation—by curriculum, social class, projected vocational role—fundamental to the workings of the school.[9]

Thus, at the base of schooling was a set of concerns which, when put together, embodied a conservative ideology. "We" must pre-serve "our" community by teaching the immigrants our values and adjusting them to existing economic roles.

This account gives us a general picture of the ideological climate of the times, particularly in the urban areas of the East, when the curriculum field began to define itself. It was a climate that pervaded the perceptions of more than just the public at large. It also affected many articulate intellectuals and educators, even those whose own roots were outside of the urban centers. As we shall see, neither the members of the rising intelligentsia nor the early leaders in the curriculum field were immune from these perceptions. Both the school's role in the moral crusade and in economic adjustment and stratification were things with which they felt more comfortable than not. In fact, the notion of im-munity is something of an inaccurate one. A large portion of the early leaders of the movement to make curriculum selection and determination into a field of professional specialization whole-heartedly embraced both the moral crusade and the ethic of eco-nomic adjustment as overt functions of schooling. They saw the standardized procedures for selecting and organizing school knowl-edge as contributing to both of these purposes.

By examining the work of some of the most forceful and influential of these intellectuals and curriculum workers, we can see the ideological commitments that have guided a good deal of curriculum decision making in the past. For just as the vision of schooling as an institution of acculturation was slowly combined with the vision of schooling for economic adjustment in the minds of the public, so too did a generation of educators and social scientists begin to combine the two. We can also understand, hence, how an economically and culturally conservative curricular model took shape and became the paradigm that still dominates the field today. It will be clear that, historically, curriculum theory and development has been strongly connected to and influenced by economic needs and changes, and, as we shall see, by a rather interesting notion of what the ideal community should be.

The Social Function of the Curriculum

The curriculum field's most important early members—Franklin Bobbitt, W. W. Charters, Edward L. Thorndike, Ross L. Finney, Charles C. Peters, and David Snedden—defined the relationship between curriculum construction and community control and power that continues to influence the contemporary curriculum field.[10]

In delimiting the basic social role of the school curriculum, the critical social and economic issue that concerned these formative theorists was that of industrialization and its accompanying division of labor. Such a division, according to Bobbitt, had replaced the craftsman with the specialized worker. The small shop was replaced by the large corporation. In this situation the individual was no longer responsible for the design and production of a single product. Instead he or she was responsible for the production of only a portion of a product, the nature and specifications of which were provided to him or her by a supervisor. Beyond this narrow task in the production of a larger product, the individual worker was also dependent on other individuals, particularly the supervisor, for direction and guidance in his or her work. Furthermore, the individual was now almost totally dependent on other lines of work for food, shelter, and all the additional requirements needed for physical survival. Such a situation brought forth new needs, needs unknown in nineteenth century rural, agrarian America. On the one hand, this new corporate working class, which Bobbitt referred to as "group or associated workers," needed to be able to perform their specialized function in the hierarchical mode of organization that dominated the corporation.[11] And on

185

the other hand, they needed enough knowledge of their economic and social tasks to allow them to work together toward the completion of a product which they had little role in designing.[12]

Bobbitt and Charters responded to this new economic need for specialized training by adopting the procedures of job analysis. They borrowed from the scientific management movement and built a theory of curriculum construction that was based on the differentiation of educational objectives in terms of the particular and narrow functions of adult life.[13] This is of no small moment, for it was the need in adult life for unity, cooperation, and an accepting attitude among these specialized workers that led the formative theorists of the field to define one of the major roles of the curriculum as developing "community." The curriculum would be used to foster "social integration." [14] Bobbitt, for instance, saw the curriculum as one means to develop what he called "large group consciousness," his term for the individual's feeling of belonging to his social and economic group or community and his commitment to its ends, values, and standards of behavior.[15] Yet it was the very definition of a person's community that made this model of curriculum selection and determination an exceptionally conservative one.

Social Homogeneity and the Problem of Community

Two features of the social function that people such as Bobbitt and Charters gave to the curriculum are important here. First, oddly, in defining the purpose of the curriculum these educators were concerned to identify that function with the needs of the community. Bobbitt in fact made a special point of stating that the task of the curriculum worker was to be determined by the local community in which the school resided.[16] This does sound progressive. However, the second feature may make us a bit more cautious, for these theorists also viewed the social role of the curriculum as that of developing a high degree of normative and cognitive consensus among the elements of society. It was this that Bobbitt referred to as "large group consciousness:"

> *How does one develop a genuine feeling of membership in a social group, whether large or small? There seems to be but one method and that is,* To think and feel and ACT with the group

as a part of it as it performs its activities and strives to attain its ends. *Individuals are fused into coherent small groups, discordant small groups are fused into the large internally-cooperating group, when they* act together *for common ends, with common vision, and with united judgment. (Bobbitt's emphasis)*[17]

These two aspects of the social task of the curriculum are rather significant. Both issues, community and "like-mindedness," were common themes in American social thought, particularly in the newly emerging fields of sociology, psychology, and education, during the late nineteenth and early twentieth centuries. Looking at these themes and how they were employed during this period will go a long way in telling us about the nature of the curriculum field and its past and present response to the relationship between school and community.

Like the author of the *Putnam's Monthly* piece we quoted earlier, the formative members of the curriculum field, as well as most of the early leaders in sociology, psychology, and education, were by birth and upbringing members of a native and rural middle class, Protestant in religion and Anglo-Saxon in descent. In defining the nature, boundaries and interests of their fields of study, these intellectual leaders, along with other social scientists, reflected and spoke to the concerns of the middle class. Specifically, they reflected what they believed was the declining power and influence of the middle class in the wake of America's transition in the late nineteenth and early twentieth centuries from a rural, agrarian society to an urban, industrialized one.[18] They defined the issues in a particular way—as a problem of the *loss* of community.

As we saw, in the discussion of the growth of urban education, the period during which these future leaders came to maturity, 1865 to 1900, was a time of doubt and fear for the small farmers, merchants, and professionals who made up the nation's middle class. They felt their social order, which they viewed as being rooted in the small rural town with its deep, face-to-face personal relationships, was endangered. They were afraid of the emerging dominance of a new economic unit, the corporation. They also felt that a new economic and social class of great wealth and power, composed of the owners of these corporations and their financial backers, would threaten the economic security and political influence of the small town, thus harming its economic base in agriculture and small scale manufacturing. The growth of a corporate economy also was tied to the growth of urban centers. The cities were increasingly being populated by immigrants from eastern and southern Europe and blacks from the rural South. These diverse people were seen as a threat to a homogeneous American culture, a culture centered in the small town and rooted in beliefs and attitudes of the middle class. The "community" that the English and Protestant forebearers of this class had "carved from a wilderness" seemed to be crumbling before an expanding urban and industrial society.

Of these two concerns, the early spokespeople of the new social sciences focused most of their attention on the problem of immigration. They suspected that these immigrants, whom they believed to have a higher birthrate than the native population, would soon outnumber the "native well-bred population." Increasing numbers of immigrants, with their urban enclaves and different political, cultural, and religious traditions, were a threat to a homogeneous culture. This unitary culture was not only the source of America's stability and a key to progress, but was synonymous for these members of the intelligentsia with the idea of democracy itself.[19]

At first these intellectuals talked of the issue of community in terms of a threat to the existence of the rural town. For Edward A. Ross, one of the first American sociologists, the deep, intimate, face-to-face relationships of the small town provided a natural and spontaneous mechanism of social control.[20] For Ross and other early social scientists, the small town assumed almost mystical proportions as the guarantor of social order and stability. The small town, its politics, its religion, its values, came to be seen, as the sociologist Robert Nisbet puts it, as the very essence of the American community.[21]

Later and more importantly, the members of this new group of intellectuals (who in actuality owed the emergence of their professions and the opportunities it offered them to both urbanization and industrialization) took a different tack in defining the problem of community, one that did not require them to defend the small town as a physical entity.[22] Instead, they took what they thought constituted the basis of the small town's ability to provide for stability, its like-mindedness in beliefs, values, and standards of behavior, and idealized this feature of small town life as the basis of the order necessary for an emerging urban and industrialized society. The notion of community became synonymous with the idea of homogeneity and cultural consensus. If their upbringing in the rural town taught these individuals anything, it taught them that order and progress was dependent on the degree to which beliefs and behavior were common and shared. Applying this view to the increasingly urban society in which they lived, they argued for the maintenance of a unitary culture (what they meant by a "sense of community") rooted in the values, beliefs, and behavior of the middle class. When it seemed to them that cultural homogeneity was dissolving because of urbanization, industrialization, and immigration, and that their sense of community was being eclipsed, they acted by ". . . striking out at whatever enemies their view of the world allowed them to see." [23]

Social Control and the Problem of Community

In the name of cultural conformity, these early social scientists struck out with a particular passion at the eastern and southern European immigrant. Adopting for the most part an hereditarian perspective, they viewed the immigrants as being inferior to the native population. Given their supposedly high birthrate, they were concerned that these immigrants would come to threaten the existence of the more economically advantaged classes with what Ross called "race suicide." [24] More immediately, however, these immigrants were perceived as a threat to the existence of democracy itself. Charles A. Ellwood, another early American sociologist, argued that genetically, immigrants did not seem to have ". . . the capacity for self government and free institutions which the peoples of Northern and Western Europe have shown." [25]

To deal with this supposed threat, the intellectuals joined the growing movement during the late nineteenth and early twentieth centuries for immigration restriction.[26] However, to ensure cultural homogeneity in the face of the immigration that had already occurred, they saw a need for a second line of defense. In essence, they perceived that the imposition of meaning could be an instrument of social control. The immigrant could be increasingly acculturated into middle class values, beliefs and standards of behavior. One such instrument, according to Ross, was the school. Ross argues in a manner strikingly similar to those seen in our treatment of the ideological climate surrounding the growth of urban schools.

> . . . *to nationalize a multitudinous people calls for institutions to disseminate certain ideas and ideals. The Tsars relied on the blue-domed Orthodox church in every peasant village to Russify their heterogeneous subjects, while we Americans rely for unity on the "little red school house."* [27]

It was in this vein that Bobbitt and his colleagues would use the curriculum to serve the cause of community. The *curriculum* could restore what was being lost.

The Curriculum Field and the Problem of Community

The most influential early leaders in the curriculum field seemed for the most part to share these views about the declining position of the middle class and the threat posed by immigrants and other diverse peoples. Ross L. Finney, an early curriculum theorist and one of the first educational sociologists, like earlier social scientists and educators viewed the middle class as being threatened from above by a class of corporate capitalists and from below by an immigrant working class, who were entering the population in growing numbers to meet the demands for a cheap labor supply. Writing in the post-World War I period, he reflected the national paranoia known as the Red Scare. He argued that the eastern and southern European immigrants, whom he believed had carried with them to America a Bolshevik ideology, would attempt to overthrow the nation and with it the middle class, in a revolution similar to the Russian Revolution of 1917.[28]

In making his defense of the middle class, Finney bemoaned the loss of community. He spoke longingly of what he viewed as a more serene time in the history of the nation, a time when industrialization had not taken the ownership of the nation's wealth out of the hands of those who produced it and thereby created conflicting economic and social classes and interests.[29]

Finney's solution to this problem was familiar. The nation must instill the immigrants with specific values and standards of behavior. The immigrant working class had to hold the same firm commitments to their work which he attributed to people from his own class. It was this commitment, he believed, that would reduce their potential revolutionary threat by making them happy performing the "humbler" economic functions that he saw as the future lot of the mass of the American population in an industrialized society.[30] Along with the other intellectuals of his day, he argued that "... if a democratic people's conduct is to be dependable and harmonious, they must think and feel alike." [31]

Other major curriculum workers had a similar commitment to likemindedness. Charles C. Peters, who like Finney was both an influential curriculum theorist and educational sociologist, viewed the immigrants as a threat to American civilization until they came "... to think about, and act on, political, social, economic, sanitary, and other matters in the approved American way." [32] Just as importantly, Edward L. Thorndike, who did more than any other individual to articulate the behavioristic psychology that has dominated the curriculum field since its earliest times, viewed blacks in the same way as these other educators viewed the immigrant. He not only doubted their ability to adjust to democratic institutions, but he saw them as an undesirable element within the population of most American cities.[33] But how were we to cope with these undesirable elements? Since the people were already here, how could we make them to be like us? How could we restore community?

Just as in earlier periods, these individuals looked to the schools. The school curriculum could create the consensus on values that was the goal of their economic and social policies. Finney in this respect argued that "a far wiser propaganda for the workers is one that will ally and amalgamate them with the middle class. And such an alliance and amalgamation should be forced upon the lower classes, whether their agitators like it or not by compulsory attendance laws that make high school graduation practically universal.[34]

But when these social scientists and educators actually came to deal with the practicalities of the nature and design of the curriculum, an important change in their argument occurred, a change which proved important for both the future development of the field and those people whom these developments would affect. Instead of talking about the need for homogeneity in terms of ethnic and racial differences, they began to talk about the question in terms of differences in intelligence. "Science" became the rhetorical, though often unconscious, cloak to cover conservative social and educational decisions.

Finney, for example, seemed to alter his view about what constituted the principal problem facing American society. The primary threat to the middle class was no longer the growing, immigrant, working class. More important was the fact ". . . that half the people have brains of just average quality or less, of whom a very considerable percentage have very poor brains indeed." [35] Joining him in this view of the problem was Thorndike, who argued that individuals of low intelligence within the population constituted a threat to the very existence of "civilization." [36] Bobbitt and others increasingly codified their arguments in scientific terms. In fact, they even warned against extreme nationalism and the hatred of European peoples which it engendered. [37] When these individuals came to deal directly with the issue of curriculum construction, it does appear that they altered their view of the problem of community. The problem was no longer that of maintaining the hegemony of the more advantaged members of the community, but that of maintaining the hegemony of those of high intelligence in a society in which the mass of the population was believed to be at best of average intelligence. As we shall see, this is less of a change than one might think.

Curriculum Differentiation and the Issue of Community

The theory that the curriculum needed to be differentiated to prepare individuals of differing intelligence and ability for a variety of different but specific adult life functions dominated the thinking of these early educators, and still dominates the thinking of contemporary curriculum theorists. [38] This is a critical point. These varying adult functions were seen to involve *unequal* social responsibilities yielding unequal social power and privilege. These educators believed that individuals of high intelligence were more moral, more dedicated to their work, and more willing to apply their talents to the benefit of the larger society than were the majority of the population. As a consequence, Thorndike and others argued that the views of these individuals were of more social import than those of the majority. Therefore, these individuals deserved a position of social and political preeminence.[39]

This view of the unequal distribution of responsibility and power was reflected when they talked about how curriculum differentiation would fulfill two social purposes—education for leadership and education for what they called "followership." Those of high intelligence were to be educated to lead the nation by being taught to understand the needs of the society. They would also learn to define appropriate beliefs and standards of behavior to meet those needs. The mass of the population was to be taught to accept these beliefs and standards whether or not they understood them or agreed with them.[40] As Finney argued, "instead of trying to teach dullards to think for themselves, the intellectual leaders must think for them, and drill the results, memoriter, into their synapses."[41] In this way, curriculum differentiation based on "intelligence" would create cultural homogeneity and thereby stability within American society.[42]

In short, what these early curriculum workers were concerned about was the preservation of cultural consensus while at the same time allocating individuals to their "proper" place in an interdependent industrialized society. Bobbitt alluded to this concern in his identification of the two principal functions of modern, industrial life. There was the "specialist" worker mentioned earlier, whose function was to be skilled in one narrow task within a given organization. Beyond that, the worker needed a limited knowledge of the total organization to understand the importance of one narrow function within the larger process of production and distribution, to provide for "willing and intelligent acquiescence" in the purposes of the organization.[43] The "specialist" worker only needed a thorough understanding of a particular task. Outside of that task, according to Thorndike, he or she only needed to "... know when not to think and where to buy the thinking he needs."[44] And there was the "generalist," Bobbitt's term for the manager or supervisor. The manager did not need to be skilled in any one task, but rather needed a complete understanding of and commitment to the purposes of the organization to allow him or her to direct the activities of the "specialists" and to gain their acquiescence.[45] Thus, some people of greater wisdom would direct others. What could be wrong with that? It is who these people would be that makes this vision less than neutral.

Ethnicity, Intelligence, and Community

As we just saw, in defining the function of the curriculum many of the most influential members of the field, although they seemed to fear and dislike the immigrants, increasingly talked of the issue of maintaiinng community as a problem of widespread low intelligence within the population. But there is evidence to suggest that this redefinition was not indicative of a change from the viewpoint they shared with the earlier leaders in the social sciences. Although they talked about differentiating the curriculum in terms of intelligence, both Bobbitt and David Snedden, another individual who was both a curriculist and an educational sociologist, suggested that the differentiation should also be made in terms of differences in social class and ethnic background respectively.[46] When Thorndike identified those within American society whom he believed possessed greater natural capacity and high intelligence, he pointed to the businessman, scientist, and lawyer.[47] These were occupations that during his day were almost totally monopolized by members of the native middle class. The highly intelligent, hence, were to be predominantly found within this class and not the lower ones. The unintelligent masses were the elements of diversity within the population, primarily the eastern and southern European immigrant and to a lesser degree the black population. Thus, what was originally seen by American intellectuals as a cultural problem of ethnic differences was redefined in the seemingly neutral language of science as a problem of differences in intelligence, in this way divesting the problem of its economic and social content. Social control therefore became covered by the language of science. By controlling and differentiating school curricula, so could people and classes be controlled and differentiated as well.[48]

But why did they do this? The formative theorists of the curriculum field, despite their identification with the middle class, increasingly viewed industrialization and the emergence of the corporation with favor. They were particularly enamored of the seeming efficiency and productivity of industrial processes and thus incorporated into their conception of curriculum construction the principles of scientific management that were thought to be responsible for it.[49] But beyond this faith in corporate procedures, they were committed to its hierarchical mode of organization as *a model for society itself.* We can see this most clearly in Finney's vision for American society:

> ... *This conception of leadership and followership—leads us again to the notion of a graduated hierarchy of intelligence and enlightenment ... At the apex of such a system must be the experts, who are pushing forward research in highly specialized sectors of the front. Behind them are such men and women as the colleges should produce, who are familiar with the findings of the experts and are able to relate part with part. By these relatively independent leaders of thought, progressive change and constant readjustment will be provided for. Back of these are the high school graduates, who are somewhat familiar with the vocabulary of those above them, have some feeling of acquaintance with the various fields, and a respect for expert knowledge. Finally, there are the duller masses, who mouth the catchwords of those in front of them, imagine that they understand, and follow by imitation.*[50]

Notice that this view of social organization does not attempt to eliminate all diversity but rather to control it by narrowing its scope and channeling it toward areas that do not seem to threaten the imperatives of social stability and economic growth. Industrialists, for example, from the 1880s to the early 1920s, the period in which these formative theorists grew to maturity and carried on their work, resisted the growing national movement for immigration restriction. Instead they attempted to diminish the immigrants' supposed threat to American society by instilling them with middle class attitudes, beliefs, and standards of behavior. At the same time, they employed their "willingness" to work for low wages to meet demands of industrialization for a cheap source of labor.[51] Here, the formative members of the curriculum field, unlike some of the early social scientists, seemed to share this view held by the industrialists.[52] They may have believed that, given the growing nativistic sentiments of the post–World War I period, they would be more successful in promoting the integration of diverse elements of the population into a hierarchically organized society if they conceptualized that diversity in terms of intelligence and not ethnicity. In the context of the time, they no doubt believed that American society was more willing to deal with diversity in intelligence than diversity in ethnicity or race.[53] But they undoubtedly felt secure in their belief that a "real" community could be built through education, one with "natural" leaders and "natural" followers, and one in which people like "us" could define what "they" should be like.

It is this commitment to maintaining a sense of community, one based on cultural homogeneity and valuative consensus, that has been one of the primary, though tacit, legacies of the early workers in the curriculum field. It is a function that is embedded in the historic reliance of the field on procedures and techniques borrowed from corporate enterprises. Oddly (though perhaps not, given what we have seen of the field's past) this reliance remains as strong today (with the dominance within the field of things, for example, like systems management procedures) as it did almost sixty years ago when the leaders of the field turned to the scientific management movement for direction in articulating the nature of curriculum construction.[54] Since the historic tendency of this commitment is to build a community that reflects the values of those with economic and cultural power, it is one that may pose the same threat to contemporary blacks, Latinos, and American Indians as it did to early twentieth century blacks and immigrants from eastern and southern Europe. Given the historic tendency of many curriculum theorists to articulate their rather conservative commitments in the scientific and seemingly neutral language of intelligence and ability, it is also a threat that historically has remained unrecognized. Only by seeing how the curriculum field often served the interests of homogeneity and social control can we begin to see how it functions today. We may still find, unfortunately, that the rhetoric of science and neutrality covers more than it reveals. At the very least, though it may be unfortunate, we should not expect the curriculum field to totally overthrow its past. After all, as in our imaginary vignette at the beginnings of this analysis, schools do work . . . for "them." In education, as in the unequal distribution of economic goods and services, "them" that has, gets.[55] If we are indeed serious about making our institutions responsive to communities in ways they are not now, the first step is in recognizing the historical connections between groups that have had power and the culture that is preserved and distributed by our schools. This recognition may do something else. It may cause us to ask similar questions today. Perhaps we could start by returning to our initial vignette and asking again, "For *whom* do schools work?" Some educators may be quite discomfited by the answer. But who ever said that an awareness of one's tacit political stance was supposed to make one comfortable?

NOTES

1. Here we are using Dawe's notion that control involves the imposition of meaning on a dominated group by a dominant group. See Michael F. D. Young, ed., *Knowledge and Control* (London: Collier Macmillan, 1971), p. 4.

2. Pierre Bourdieu, "Intellectual Field and Creative Project," in Young, *Knowledge and Control*, pp. 161–188.

3. Michael W. Apple and Nancy R. King, "What Do Schools Teach?", in *Humanistic Education*, Richard Weller, ed. (Berkeley: McCutchan Publishing Corporation, 1977). See also, Samuel Bowles and Herbert Gintis, *Schooling in Capitalist America* (New York: Basic Books, 1976).

4. Cf., Michael W. Apple, "Power and School Knowledge," *The Review of Education* III (March/April, 1977) and Michael W. Apple, "Commonsense Categories and Curriculum Thought," in *Schools in Search of Meaning*, James B. Macdonald and Esther Zaret, eds. (Washington: Association for Supervision and Curriculum Development, 1975) pp. 116–148. See also, James E. Rosenbaum, *Making Inequality: The Hidden Curriculum of High School Tracking* (New York: John Wiley & Sons, 1976).

5. Carl F. Kaestle, *The Evolution of an Urban School System* (Cambridge: Harvard University Press, 1973), p. 141.

6. Ibid., pp. 141–142.

7. Ibid., p. 161.

8. Marvin Lazerson, *Origins of the Urban School* (Cambridge: Harvard University Press, 1971), p. xv. See also, Elizabeth Vallance, "Hiding The Hidden Curriculum," *Curriculum Theory Network* IV (Fall, 1973/74), pp. 5–21.

9. Lazerson, *Origins of the Urban School*, pp. x–xi, emphasis ours.

10. We have selected these individuals as the most important

formative members of the curriculum field because we believe that their identification with the social efficiency movement and a behavioristic psychology place them in the mainstream of the field. We are not including John Dewey and others identified with child-centered education and the child's needs/interest tradition. Although their ideas are interesting and important, they had little impact on either the curriculum field as it developed or on school practice. For a discussion of this position with reference to Thorndike see Clarence J. Karier, "Elite Views on American Education," in *Education and Social Structure in the Twentieth Century,* Walter Laquer and George L. Mosse, eds. (New York: Harper Torchbooks, 1967), pp. 149–151.

11. Franklin Bobbitt, *The Curriculum* (1918; reprint ed., New York: Arno Press, 1971), Chapter 9.

12. Ibid., p. 95.

13. Ibid., p. 42; Franklin Bobbitt, *How to Make A Curriculum* (Boston: Houghton Mifflin Company, 1924), pp. 29, 97; W. W. Charters, *Curriculum Construction* (1918; reprint ed., New York: Arno Press, 1971), chapters 4–5.

14. Harold Rugg et al., "The Foundations of Curriculum-Making," in *The Foundations of Curriculum-Making, The Twenty-Sixth Yearbook of the National Society for the Study of Education, Part II,* Guy Montrose Whipple, ed. (Bloomington, Indiana: Public School Publishing Company, 1926), p. 16.

15. Bobbitt, *The Curriculum,* Chapter 12.

16. Bobbitt, *How to Make A Curriculum,* p. 281.

17. Bobbitt, *The Curriculum,* p. 131.

18. Our analysis here does not reflect support for the late Richard Hofstadter's status anxiety thesis as an explanation for middle class support of the social reforms of the progressive movement. Rather, we are simply reflecting the views, which we do document throughout this paper, of the early leaders of sociology, psychology, and education. For a presentation of the status anxiety thesis, see Richard Hofstadter, *The Age of Reform* (New York: Vintage Books, 1956), Chapter 4. For an interesting analysis and critique of the status anxiety thesis see Robert W. Doherty, "Status Anxiety and American Reform: Some Alternatives," *American Quarterly* XIX (Summer, 1962), pp. 329–337.

19. These fears about industrialization and urbanization had important implications for the development of the curriculum field as well as for the social sciences generally. See Barry M. Franklin, "The Curriculum Field and the Problem of Social Control, 1918–1938: A Study in Critical Theory," unpublished Ph.D. dissertation, University of Wisconsin, 1974. For a similar analysis of the development of the field of educational sociology, see Philip Wexler, *The Sociology of*

Education: Beyond Equality (Indianapolis: Bobbs-Merrill Company, 1976).

20. Edward A. Ross, *Social Control* (New York: Macmillan Company, 1912), pp. 432–436; R. Jackson Wilson, *In Quest of Community: Social Philosophy in the United States, 1860–1920* (New York: Oxford University Press, 1968), pp. 89–99.

21. Robert A. Nisbet, *The Quest for Community* (New York: Oxford University Press, 1967), p. 54.

22. Robert H. Wiebe, *The Search for Order* (New York: Hill and Wang, 1967), Chapter 5.

23. Ibid., p. 44.

24. Edward A. Ross, *Foundations of Sociology*, 5th ed. (New York: Macmillan Company, 1919), pp. 382–385.

25. Charles A. Ellwood, *Sociology and Modern Social Problems* (New York: American Book Company, 1913), p. 220.

26. Ibid., pp. 217–221; Edward A. Ross, *Principles of Sociology* (New York: The Century Company, 1920), pp. 36–37.

27. Ross, *Principles of Sociology*, p. 409.

28. Ross L. Finney, *Causes and Cures for the Social Unrest: An Appeal to the Middle Class* (New York: Macmillan Company, 1922), pp. 167–172.

29. Ibid., p. 43.

30. Ross L. Finney, *A Sociological Philosophy of Education* (New York: Macmillan Company, 1928), pp. 382–383.

31. Ibid., p. 428.

32. Charles C. Peters, *Foundations of Educational Sociology* (New York: Macmillan Company, 1924), p. 25.

33. Thorndike seemingly accepted the views of the American anthropologist, R. H. Lowie, that "... the Negroes evince an inveterate proclivity for at least the forms of monarchical government." See Edward L. Thorndike, *Human Nature and the Social Order* (New York: Macmillan Company, 1940), p. 728; Edward L. Thorndike, *Your City* (New York: Harcourt, Brace and Company, 1939), pp. 77–80. For an examination of Thorndike's behaviorism and its impact on the curriculum field, see Barry M. Franklin, "Curriculum Thought and Social Meaning: Edward L. Thorndike and the Curriculum Field," *Educational Theory* XXVI (Summer, 1976), pp. 298–309.

34. Finney, *Causes of the Social Unrest*, p. 180.

35. Finney, *A Sociological Philosophy of Education*, p. 386.

36. Thorndike, *Human Nature and the Social Order*, p. 440.

37. Bobbitt, *The Curriculum*, p. 158; William Chandler Bagley, "Supplementary Statement," in Rugg, et al., *The Foundations of Curriculum-Making*, p. 38.

38. Bobbitt, *How to Make A Curriculum,* pp. 41–42, 61–62; Edward L. Thorndike, *Individuality* (Boston: Houghton Mifflin Company, 1911), p. 51; Edward L. Thorndike, *Education: A First Book* (New York: Macmillan Company, 1912), pp. 137–319; David Snedden, *Sociological Determination of Objectives in Education* (Philadelphia: J. B. Lippincott Co., 1921), p. 251; Finney, *Foundations of Educational Sociology,* p. vii. Finney took a somewhat different view of differentiation than the other formative theorists of the field. He advocated what appeared to be a common curriculum dominated by the emerging social science disciplines. But he made a critical distinction on how these subjects were to be taught to individuals of differing ability. Those of high intelligence would be taught their social heritage through a study of the social sciences. It would be a study that would teach them to understand not only their heritage but the social demands it would make on them. Those of low intelligence would only be taught to obey the demands of their social heritage. They would not study the social sciences themselves but would be conditioned to respond to appropriate slogans that reflected the content of these disciplines and the social demands embedded in them. See Finney, *A Sociological Philosophy of Education,* Chapter 15, pp. 393–396, 406, 410. For the importance of curriculum differentiation in the contemporary curriculum field see Herbert M. Kliebard, "Bureaucracy and Curriculum Theory," in *Freedom, Bureaucracy, and Schooling,* Vernon F. Haubrich, ed. (Washington: Association for Supervision and Curriculum Development, 1971), pp. 89–93.

39. Finney, *A Sociological Philosophy of Education,* pp. 388–389; Thorndike, *Human Nature and the Social Order,* pp. 77–79, 792–794, 800–802; Edward L. Thorndike, "A Sociologist's Theory of Education," *The Bookman* XXIV (November, 1906), pp. 290–291; Edward L. Thorndike, *Selected Writings from a Connectionist's Psychology* (New York: Appleton-Century-Crofts, 1949), pp. 338–339.

40. Finney, *A Sociological Philosophy of Education,* pp. 386, 389; Edward L. Thorndike, "How May We Improve the Selection, Training, and Life Work of Leaders," in *How Should a Democratic People Provide for the Selection and Training of Leaders in the Various Walks of Life* (New York: Teachers College Press, 1938), p. 41; Walter H. Drost, *David Snedden and Education for Social Efficiency* (Madison: University of Wisconsin Press, 1967), pp. 165, 197.

41. Finney, *A Sociological Philosophy of Education,* p. 395.

42. Ibid., pp. 397–398.

43. Bobbitt, *The Curriculum,* pp. 78–81, 95.

44. Edward L. Thorndike, "The Psychology of the Half-Educated Man," *Harpers* CXL (April, 1920), p. 670.

45. Bobbitt, *The Curriculum,* pp. 78–86.

46. Ibid., p. 42; David Snedden, *Civic Education* (Yonkers on Hudson, New York: World Book Company, 1922), Chapter 14.

47. Thorndike, *Human Nature and the Social Order,* pp. 86–87, 783–785, 963.

48. For an examination of this tendency in social thought see Trent Schroyer, "Toward a Critical Theory for Advanced Industrial Society," in *Recent Sociology No. 2,* Hans Peter Dreitzel, ed. (New York: Macmillan Company, 1970), p. 212. For the appropriateness of this view in interpreting American education see Walter Feinberg, *Reason and Rhetoric* (New York: John Wiley & Sons, 1975), p. 40.

49. Kliebard, "Bureaucracy and Curriculum Theory," pp. 74–89; Raymond E. Callahan, *Education and the Cult of Efficiency* (Chicago: University of Chicago Press, 1962), Chapter 4.

50. Finney, *A Sociological Philosophy of Education.*

51. John Higham, *Strangers in the Land* (New Brunswick, New Jersey: Rutgers University Press, 1955), pp. 51, 187, 257, 303–310, Chapter 9.

52. Ross, in similar circumstances, lost his job at Stanford University because he angered Mrs. Leland Stanford, the wife of the founder of the university and its chief authority after his death. He attacked the business community for its support of unrestricted Chinese immigration. See Walter P. Metzger, *Academic Freedom in the Age of the University* (New York: Columbia University Press, 1955), pp. 164–171; and Bernard J. Stern, ed., "The Ward-Ross Correspondence II 1897–1901," *American Sociological Review,* VII (December, 1946), pp. 744–746.

53. Higham argues that in the decade of the 1920s, the period in which curriculum emerged as a field of study and in which the educators we are considering did their most important work, American nativist sentiments turned away from attempts at assimilation through Americanization programs and instead turned to support of immigration restriction. It was in 1924 that the Johnson-Reed Act was passed which firmly established the "national origins principle," with the restrictions it applied to eastern and southern European peoples, into American law. See Higham, *Strangers in the Land,* Chapter 11.

54. Michael W. Apple, "The Adequacy of Systems Management Procedures in Education," in *Regaining Educational Leadership,* Ralph Smith, ed. (New York: John Wiley & Sons, 1975), pp. 104–121.

55. For further explication of this relationship, see Michael W. Apple and Philip Wexler, "Cultural Capital and Educational Transmissions," *Educational Theory,* XXVIII (Winter, 1978).

Schools and the Symbolic Uses of Community Participation

Thomas S. Popkewitz
University of Wisconsin, Madison

"Community participation" is a powerful and pervasive slogan. Our political ideology places a high value on people's involvement in public affairs. We believe that people should actively participate in the political life of their community and that its institutions should be responsive to their policy. Yet there is an increasing bureaucratization and impersonalization in our public agencies. Schools, police, courts, and governmental service departments seem removed from those very communities they are to serve. Schools, in particular, are vulnerable to this charge. The organization of schools is often impervious to the culture, conflict, and aspiration of many of those it is to educate. Community participation, many believe, can provide an approach to eliminating the alienation people feel from schools. For the poor and minority groups, community participation offers a hope of gaining direct power over an institution which directs the lives of their children.

Like all symbolic forms, community participation has dual functions. It condenses our anxieties, frustrations, and hopes into a form that has strong meanings. Community participation also has concrete meanings. It legitimates programs that benefit particular groups and individuals. In understanding the significance and consequences of community participation, we cannot take for granted the relationship between its symbolic meanings and concrete institutional actions. Edelman warns us that symbols often function to provide a dramatic outline to events that are empty of realistic detail.[1] Instead of facilitating actual change, participation can be used as a vehicle to obtain quiescence and promote social adjustment.

The purpose of this chapter is to consider various symbolic

uses of "community participation." Specifically, it will focus on community involvement in school governance. It will be argued that participation can serve basically conflicting political purposes and be used to maintain as well as to change institutional practices. It is hoped that an examination of the possible latent interests of community participation can promote a critical dialogue that will better enable educators to transform ethical commitments into concrete programs. The analysis is undertaken with a commitment to make schools more responsive and just institutions.

Community Participation as a Political Problem

In order to adequately evaluate the function of community participation in school affairs, we must first locate the ethical and political roots of that participation. Too often, value commitments are obscured by procedural and technical questions of participation. "Parity" in governmental programs is a case in point. Prevailing arguments give attention to mechanisms for participation by various interest groups. Rarely does discussion go beyond establishing a mechanism, to questioning whether the existing arrangements actually support a just and equitable system. It is important, therefore, to reaffirm some underlying values of community participation before examining its actual uses.

Much of the argument for community participation in education is framed around an ideological commitment to democracy. There is a belief that individuals should assume responsibility for decision making in institutions that affect their lives on a day-to-day basis. This commitment has certain rites: elections are held to select community representatives; different role groups meet to discuss school policy; surveys are conducted to assess community feelings. In each of these activities, an effort is made to involve people in determining the events that shape and govern their community.

The reorganization of school governance structures to include community participation has two components prompted by ethical considerations. One, community participation can reallocate material goods and services. Various communities have used different means to do this. There may be an increase of minority group members in decision-making positions. For example, an early action of the New York experimental community schools was to assume professional hiring responsibilities. One result was to secure better paying jobs and opportunities for some members of that community. A different type of reallocation involves the inclusion of ethnic and cultural studies within the traditional content of schools. Community participation brings pressure on the school for instruction in black studies, native American languages, or Latin American cultures. In general, the community participation movement has focused upon obtaining a more equitable allocation of goods, services, and knowledge.

The second and less emphasized element of participation concerns the responsibility of individuals in public institutions. Classical democratic theorists argue that individual involvement in public affairs is essential to maintain the vitality and creativity of a society. Democracy provides concrete forms for individual growth and self-development. Bachrach argues, for example, that human development is closely tied to the ability of people to actively participate in their community life:

> *Classical theory, I emphasized at the outset of this essay, is based upon the supposition that man's dignity and development as a functioning and responsive individual in a free society is dependent upon an opportunity to participate actively in decisions that significantly affect him. The psychological soundness of this supposition has in recent years been supported by the well-known experiment contrasting the impact of authoritarian and democratic leaders on group behavior . . . . But surely one does not have to rely upon hard data to share in the belief of Rousseau, Kant, Mills, Lindsay, and others that man's development as a human being is closely dependent upon his opportunity to contribute to the solutions of problems relating to his own actions.* [2]

This second element of participation is often ignored in discussions of decentralization. Political theorists in this country often view participation as restricted to the elite. We seek groups of representative "leaders" to talk for and act upon the total community. Community participation is conceptually defined as activity to influence the few who are leaders.[3] The "gatekeeper" approach" in federal programs, for example, restricts participation to a few. Initially government agencies identify visible leaders for participation in a "representative council." [4] As these individuals develop expertise, small numbers of other less visible but interested people are trained as community leaders. Political involvement for the majority of people is reduced to receiving information from experts about school programs, voting for school board representatives, or being polled about preferences. Our approaches to participation tend to legitimate a few with power to make decisions for the many.

Classical democratic theorists, in contrast, are concerned with developing institutions that involve all individuals in all policy making. The Greek assembly and the New England town meeting, in which all citizens participated in community decisions, are the closest approximation to this. Acceptance of elite governancy contributes little, if any, to the classical purposes of self-development.

> *The crucial issue of democracy is not the composition of the elite—for the man on the bottom it makes little difference whether the command emanates from an elite of the rich and the well born or from an elite of workers and farmers. Instead the issue is whether democracy can diffuse power sufficiently throughout society to inculcate among people of all walks of life a justifiable feeling that they have the power to participate in decisions which affect themselves and the common life of the community, especially the immediate community in which they work and spend most of their working hours and energy.*[5]

Participation that provides individuals with access to power entails a radical reconsideration of institutional arrangements. To seek direct involvement of a school's constituency in school governance entails including both students and parents, thus altering the very power arrangements of school and the notion of teachers as professionals and experts. Educational thought must help to establish a social structure for students in which ideas are treated as humanly constructed and hence changeable.[6] One of the contradictions of schooling in a democracy is the determinism found in much curriculum and the use of human engineering techniques by some professionals to control definitions of knowledge. Direct involvement also requires attention to the social and economic conditions, especially of the poor, that limit parent involvement.[7] Our very notion of participation assumes characteristics not common of working-class communities. Often, the poor work long and arduous hours. A parent coming to a school conference may have to lose pay needed to support the family. At the end of the day, physical exhaustion and the immediate needs of the family make participation exceedingly difficult.

The relationship between economic structures and educational performance is one of the least examined findings of mass standardized testing. The accumulated data suggest that gross differences are related to social and economic stratification. Improving the family's economic position does more for achievement than reducing class size, providing remedial teachers, or arranging for community participation. While these latter efforts should be continued, they should be understood to occur within larger institutional contexts.

Finally, school rhetoric often glosses over the political nature of community participation by giving attention to supposed relationships between children's performance and parent involvement. This focus upon school outcomes is misplaced for two reasons. First, and practically, current research suggests achievement, reading scores, or student dropout rates are not significantly affected by community participation. The Coleman Report, for example, failed to reveal any association between the level of parental participation and achievement. Cohen, in summarizing the research, states:

> *The one thing my brief review of the educational evidence* does *mean is this: if one were guided solely by research on achievement and attitudes, one would not employ community control of decentralization as the device most likely to reduce racial disparities in achievement.*[8]

Second, the sole focus on student outcomes tends to eliminate consideration of substantive political dimensions of participation. Discussions tend to proceed upon a belief that there is a general consensus about what schools should do. Reforms are limited to such devices as forming parent advisory councils, organizing parent conferences, or hiring paraprofessionals to give remedial or secretarial help. Rather than considering how organizational beliefs and procedures prevent parent and student power, student-outcome arguments make the current assumptions and priorities of the institution unproblematic.

Whose Political Problem?

Upon establishing the call for community governance as a political idea, we must proceed by asking "Whose crisis does this movement for community participation reflect?" All crisis situations have a double-edged nature and impulse. The problem is often defined differently by those who rule and those who are ruled. What might seem from one perspective revolutionary may seem from another to reinforce the inequities of choice and possibilities.

For the rulers, decentralization may be viewed as an intervention process to maintain a social consensus. Katznelson argues that community participation is a response to the demise of machine politics.[9] With the old political machines, the ward leaders served as an insulating link between the elite and the citizenry. The ward politician provided services and goods to individuals in return for votes to maintain central control. The face-to-face contacts with ward politicians had a latent function of humanizing and personalizing assistance and providing social mobility.

As reform politics replaced the machine, a new integrating process developed. Political reformists sought to provide greater governmental efficiency by strengthening city bureaucracies. The new efficiency, some political scientists argue, tends to isolate governmental service agencies from their constituencies in the city. When Chicago machine politics are compared to the reform government of New York, the reform government is relatively unresponsive to political conflict.[10] The bureaucratic nature of New York's government allows each autonomous agency to shape important public policy. During the 1960s, the mayor of the city was unable to change work hours to put more patrol officers on beats during high crime times. Sanitation workers would not increase refuse pickups in high density, inner city areas. The outcome in New York was a mayor denuded of power.

One appeal of decentralization is that it holds out the possibility of re-creating linkage between the polity and citizenry. Community participation can serve as a way to defuse political conflict, restore trust in the political system, and conserve the essentials of the status quo. Altshuler, for example, suggests black demands for massive income redistributions, better jobs, and access to positions of economic and political power are difficult to achieve.[11] Participatory reform, he continues, is a more feasible goal since whites really have no stake in who governs the ghetto or reservation. The critical issue, according to Altshuler, is to persuade the disenfranchised that the system is fair. "Perhaps its most important positive potential, from the standpoint of city-wide elected officials, would be to divert much of the force of community dissatisfaction from them to neighborhood leaders." [12] From the perspective of those in power, community participation can be a social control technique used to maintain stability without conceding resources to the discontented.

The perspective of community participation as a supportive mechanism is clearly illustrated in certain educational programs. Much of the effort to decentralize schools in New York can be viewed as an attempt to make government seem benevolent without providing concrete changes in the actual control of schools.[13] Another example is parental involvement in federally funded Title I programs. Its intention is to produce greater support of existing institutions. The Office of Education considers participation as: (1) a motivational device to increase children's performance in school programs; (2) an approach for gaining parent acceptance of *school* goals and educational strategies; and (3) an administrative arrangement to make programs more efficient.

The partnership that would exist between home and school can have many facets—and many benefits. Traditionally such groups as Parent-Teacher Associations and Home and School Associations offered support, both financial and moral, to individual schools. *Today many parents are beginning to take a more active role in the school system. Some are employed as officeworkers or teacher aides. Others volunteer their services, to help in the classroom, correct papers, or supervise lunchroom or playground activities. Such help lowers the pupil-teacher ratio, thus providing for more individualized attention, and also* frees teachers for better planning. *Some parents take the cause of the schools to the public forum, campaigning for a seat on the local school board or urging support of a bond referendum. . . .*
The exchange of such information with trained professionals can help educators in planning a better, more relevant, school program. There is a subsidiary asset to parental involvement, one which deals with the age-old problem of motivation. As children see their own parents more involved in school affairs, they will be encouraged to take a more active interest in school. They will have less opportunity for playing home against school and vice versa.[14]

A different perspective is provided by the advocates of the poor or minority communities. For those who suffer from social inequities, decentralization promises not only efficient and responsive governance but a decision-making process they can control. James, for example, defines five potential gains from community participation.[15] It can help change the destructive self-image of being poor, provide increased visibility to the decision-making process, cause the "system" to be more representative to the poor's interest, provide substantive policy change, and give legitimacy to the poor's position in shaping public policy. For James and many others, the potential of decentralization lies in its redistribution of power.

The conflicting reasons for community participation require that we do not take its meanings for granted. Although it is desirable to include individuals and groups who have traditionally suffered from societal inequities, we must further inquire into the actual interests decentralization and participation serve.

Is Participation the Issue?

At this point one could still ask, "Should not the visible fact that changes occur in school warrant a conclusion that the institution is a more just and humane place?" "Should not the fact that Indian-controlled boards of education exist, that black history is being studied in schools, or that parents are participating in school programs prove that ethical commitments are being honored?"

These questions about intent and consequences are not easily answered. Many of our interests and wants are determined by the objective conditions of our institutions. In any organization, certain values and rules are taken for granted. These background assumptions orient participants toward definitions of problems and strategies of reform. Ivan Illich argues that the peculiar way we institutionalize social affairs structures the very approaches we take for solving problems.[16] In aiding developing nations, for example, Illich states we see medical care from our own point of view. We build multi-million dollar hospitals which can serve only a few. The real medical need in many third world nations is training for paramedics to clean water supplies and eliminate intestinal diseases, the major cause of death. In an analogous situation, our background assumptions about school direct many to see reform as making current programs more efficient through behavioral strategies of manipulation. In doing this, we ignore the historical and empirical evidence that these very programs we seek to make more efficient have failed. Our preferences must be seen as mediated and legitimized within a framework of the institutions in which we live.

Much of the public discussion of community participation does not consider the interplay of these objective institutional elements with our subjective interests.[17] Our feelings and beliefs are, in part, conditioned by our participation in communities. To say someone is satisfied, competent or has a "healthy self-concept" is meaningless without reference to the institutional context in which the feeling is expressed. Put differently, there is no psychology of individuals without a sociology of community. They are dialectically related.[18]

Subjective interests refer to a psychological state in which people express preference or opinion. The rituals of committee meetings and the use of surveys or elections ostensibly provide mechanisms for people to express their preferences, interests, and wants in school matters. "Needs assessment," a type of education survey, identifies subjective interests of community members.

When dealing solely with subjective interests, community participation is analogous to industrial efforts to achieve job satisfaction. It may or may not concern the basic nature of the work arrangements—what fragmentation of labor does to workers, or schoolwork does to children. Subjectively-oriented participation gives people a *feeling* that others are listening to their ideas, that they are contributing to the selection and shaping of policy and that the workplace is being improved. The meaning of subjective interests lies in the feelings and attitudes generated as people engage in institutional patterns of conduct.

When we place these subjective interests within an institutional context, we find they are related to shared rules which can favor certain groups and handicap others.[19] In some instances, organizational biases can prevent consideration of substantive issues while maintaining a symbolic illusion of meaningful participation. Researchers, for example, may cite the satisfaction gained or efficacy promoted by having minority groups participate in institutional policy-making. Yet the actual decision making may not touch the roots of discrimination or bias that produces inequitable treatment.

What types of organizational biases might produce this condition? The use of parliamentary procedure, for example, requires a verbal aggressiveness. This might be disadvantageous to native Americans whose cultural orientation rejects verbal competitiveness. The decision-making process may also create certain hierarchies of "images of self" that limit the involvement of certain groups. The school superintendent in *Small Town in a Mass Society*, for example, recognized the local town board's conservative beliefs and made subliminal assessments of his chances of succeeding before submitting items.[20] Often the superintendent chose not to publicly air issues because of the dominant beliefs on the board. The norms, beliefs, and patterns of behavior in institutions make certain types of decisions "permissible" for discussion and eliminate others from public discourse. Thus, while many groups may participate and express interests, certain issues may never be discussed publicly and the existing values of an institution never challenged.

The political problem of "community participation" therefore must go beyond overt acts of involvement or feeling of satisfaction. We must consider the relationship of subjective and objective interests and whom the organization of participation serves. To concretely examine how biases may be organized to prevent minorities from assuming actual control, we turn to the federal use of administrative reforms to produce community participation. Our concern in the following section is with conflicting meanings of reform and with certain organizational assumptions that work against the ethical purposes of redistributing power.

Biases of Federal Reform

Much of the federal reform movement is tied to an administrative concept of politics.[21] Politics is believed to be a network of associations which represent diverse ethnic, occupational, economic, and regional interests. These interest groups compete for support of policies. Government, within this context, supports and promotes an exchange between groups. Justice and fairness in our legal system, for example, is defined as consistency and neutrality in decision making rather than by advantages given or the inherent qualities of the decisions themselves. Labor relations boards, the Federal Food and Drug Administration, and the Interstate Commerce Commission are designed to provide methods of "due process" among competing interest groups. Consumer interest is merely another competing interest group. Government in these cases provides mechanisms to insure impartiality among groups in decision-making processes.

The notion of "parity" or "shared responsibility" used in many community involvement programs reflects this interest-group philosophy. The role of government is to bring together various role groups and establish clear and precise rules for reaching a consensus. The 1970 Teacher Corps Guidelines for Projects, for example, required school, university, intern, and local community people to participate in program policy making.[22] The development of the programs was organized around objective management systems. "Detailed time sequenced" plans with prescribed "objectives," specification of program "components" interrelationships, and "mechanism for feedback and evaluation" were to provide rational and orderly decision-making processes. Through systematic management design, it was believed various groups would develop programs that would be mutually beneficial.

For our discussion of the political uses of community participation, certain salient points about interest-group politics should be considered. First, the problem of community participation is defined as a matter of organizing the poor into viable interest groups. These interest groups compete in existing social structures and thus may do little to break down the anonymity of modern institutional life and the powerlessness of most individuals. Second, organization is often concerned with competition for power, based upon subjective interpretations. The objective conditions of institutions which produce racism, inequities, and injustices are ignored. Third, interest-group politics assumes decision making is essentially rational and altruistic. Planning is conceived as primarily technical and is thought to bring needed resources to bear on identifiable social needs. A belief exists that *one* best course of action exists and that it can be technically or scientifically derived. These three assumptions are found in systems analysis, Planning Programming Budget Systems (PPBS), and other management criteria used to control federal reform programs.

The emphasis on rationalism poses a paradox for educational planning. "Due process" as a legal concept has served to protect the poor and marginal individuals, as well as the wealthy, from some abuses. Further, a belief in just procedures does help to reduce tension and unproductive conflict among groups. However, any change in powerful social institutions posits a different complex of social phenomena and consequences than the mechanisms designed for law. A central question in federal reform is whether a rational administrative approach to change is warranted.

The efficacy of rationality in political issues is problematic. There is considerable evidence from the "War on Poverty" and educational reform programs such as the Teacher Corps that existing institutions are not altruistic, that "neutral procedures" hide forms of social control, and that community participation can produce policy and demands solely compatible with the existing institutional arrangements.[23] By seeking to avoid deep value conflicts, management approaches tend to replace political and ethical dialogue with an interest in technique. Politics, as Mannheim argues, is an irrational process and to make politics rational is to impose someone's control on those events.[24] The empirical problem is not are there procedures, but *who* controls them.

The community action program of the "War on Poverty" started with an orientation toward objective institutional change.[25] Federal officials who worked on the initial phases sought to define community programs as "fervently anti-establishment." The psychological and social difficulties encountered by the poor were thought to arise from imposed contradictions between culturally-prescribed aspirations and socially-structured access routes. Schools, which were to provide movement within the socio-economic structure, for example, actually restricted the poor's mobility. Schools, employment services, welfare agencies, and city halls were viewed as dysfunctional, and there was a need for alternative structures. Haryou (Harlem Youth Program), Mobilization for Youth, or the Community Youth Worker Program were to organize local communities into coherent voices that would challenge existing social, economic, political, and educational patterns. "Maximum feasible participation" was a stipulation that the poor would be part of a process of major social change.

The actual poverty programs were constructed from an administrative concept which was not derived from the planners' commitment. Reform was interpreted as administration of welfare policy through a more logical integration of relevant institutions. In each community, local boards were created to provide mechanisms to facilitate communication among the various groups. Planning boards included representatives of communities and existing public and private agencies. These local boards were to develop cooperatively and administer social action programs directed at the participating agencies. Administrative organization was thought to be a technique for social action.

The administrative approach unintentionally gave power to the local educational and service agencies.[26] Policy shifted from an emphasis on institutional change to traditional social service. Over 92 percent of the monies allocated to community action programs were used by professionals to modify and expand the existing programs. Often these programs were designed to change cultural and individual patterns of life among the poor. An assumption was that the poor have a distinct subculture of deviant behavior, values, and concerns which determines the socioeconomic position of a group. "Social action" meant eliminating the pathologies and deviances of poor communities. Self-help had a therapeutic sense of remediation, counseling, and guidance. In the few situations where a dysfunctional social structure policy was supported, parity did not exist and decision-making processes were dominated by the poor themselves.

A major consequence of the adopted service strategy may lie in the consciousness of the poor. The rituals of community involvement may give a new plausibility and reasonableness to the existing definitions of school failure and its strategies for solution to all participants. Meetings, discussions, and voting symbolically call attention to the joint interests and relatedness of the various groups.[27] The involvement creates an impression of a political system designed to translate individual wants into public policy. The acting out of decision making is a psychologically effective mode for instilling convictions and fixing patterns of future behavior. One could suspect, therefore, that the actual function of community involvement in a majority of programs was to maximize compliance and cooperation with existing dispositions toward schools.

How the administrative concept of community participation functions can be understood more specifically from a case study of a project to change the institutional character of three rural schools that were failing large numbers of native Americans.[28] Here, as in community action programs, the planners were deeply concerned about social inequalities. The project design called for community members to share responsibility for providing direction to its activities. Native Americans, school and university staffs jointly participated in local and project-wide steering committees. In addition, native Americans were hired as school paraprofessionals, a post of Native American Home-School Coordinator was created for each school, and community people were paid to develop after-school educational programs related to Indian needs.

The significance of the administrative perspective in the project can be found in three factors. First, Washington emphasized the problem of planning and implementing as central and distinct from the moral and political issues inherent in Indian education. Evaluation of funding proposals and of the on-going project gave attention to administrative questions: Were competencies written for program objectives? Were meetings held? A second and related factor was the vesting of financial control in school administrators. Third, the guidelines stipulated all proposed changes had to be accepted and part of the regular school program. The last two provisions gave power to schools because reform was tied to what schools considered permissible, and school officials had veto power over any new proposals.

The administrative focus had two functions in the program. First, it prevented articulation or conscious consideration of the premises and patterns that existed in school. Administrative matters became the focus of discussion. While the public purpose of shared governance was to give native Americans significant power, the actual meetings were forums in which information was disseminated and procedures clarified. Discussion focused upon difficulties of obtaining supplies, intern leaves of absence, payment of secretaries, and so on.

Second, the seeming neutrality of the organizational procedures actually created hierarchies which further legitimatized the status, privileges, and initiative of those who already had power. To some extent, the use of highly technical jargon tended to set apart those who had been initiated (teachers, university professors, interns) from those who were outsiders. Discussions about "competencies," "modules," "cycles," "sites," replaced common-sense language and made Indians dependent upon experts for interpretation of school experience. Further group differentiation was made by calling professionals "Mr." or "Professor," while using the first names of the Indian representatives. Status was also given to those who could speak for power sources like Washington and boards of education. Indians had no control over money and could only speak for themselves. In these interactions, conditions were established which favored the schools and handicapped American Indians in assuming responsibility.

"Shared responsibility" in the project sustained the school's background assumptions of Indian failure as related to a pathological community life. Teachers tended to view Indians as lazy, lacking in ability and initiative, and having poor social habits. The function of school was to enforce morality. Administrators and teachers hoped to promote Indian adjustment and blending into white society. School labeling of "discipline problems," "remedial," "slow learner," and "culturally disadvantaged" tended to support the school ideology. By focusing upon implementing procedures at community participation meetings, the ethical implications of school experience were effectively screened out from the dialogue between school and community. The objective interests in the institutional arrangements were taken for granted.

The meaning of educational change is given direction by the objective school interests. Differentiated staffing, intern volunteer community work programs, Pow-Wows, and arts and crafts classes had particular meaning to school personnel. These activities, teachers thought, would help uplift the moral and intellectual fiber of Indian life and move Indians out of the pronounced poverty syndrome. Indian culture curriculum, many thought, would counteract the psychologically debilitating conditions of community life and would provide a solution to Indian educational failure.

In both the community action programs and the native American projects, the meaning of reform reflected the policies of those who already had power. In subtle ways, community involvement served as an expressive and reassuring symbol without actually altering the arrangements of school. Credence was given to the school's assumptions of community pathology and therapeutic strategies. The various groups and meetings created an illusion that schools were changing and becoming better. The poor were encouraged that they had a protected status, that policies were based upon objective standards, and the school was seen as a benevolent institution. The major beneficiaries were the existing institutions. Participation as a technical rather than political issue served as a form of social control.

Conclusions

Community participation is first and foremost an ethical commitment involving political activity. We argue for it because we believe more just and humane institutions can be developed. Our attempts to implement participation require a form of social action. Institutional arrangements are challenged. The distribution of power is questioned. While at this point it might seem a belaboring of the political nature of this issue, the empirical evidence suggests that educational arguments often obscure the fundamental conflict inherent in redefining who actually participates in society.

Participation can have two functions. It can maintain the status quo or fundamentally alter social conditions. We have to consider proposals for educational reform, therefore, beyond overt actions and public declarations. Increasing minority leadership or including cultural programs in school, while important, takes place in objective institutional contexts. It is within the norms, beliefs, and patterns of behavior of an organization that participation takes on concrete meanings and political overtones.

Much of the federal effort toward institutional change has ignored the fundamental relationship between subjective and objective interests. Planners have focused upon the expression of subjective interests through defining reform as an administrative problem. The effect has been to blunt conflict and depoliticize the issues. Techniques no longer emerge from social discourse, but are treated as separate from moral issues and social norms. Neutral experts perform system analysis, budget planning, or management by objectives. It is assumed that socially complex problems can be reduced to logical and rational procedures. The sociological consequence of this stance is to dissociate methods from human purposes and goals. The political consequence is to serve those who have power and already receive benefits.

The assumption of federal planners that schools will voluntarily became part of a program which seeks to change its basic functions may be naive. The capacity of existing institutions to legislate and plan for their own change seems to belie experience. The primary function of bureaucracies, such as schools, is to preserve their power. Becker argues that the organization of a school is a system of defense that systematically prevents outsiders (students and parents) from exerting any authority.[29] Looking beyond community participation, one can view much of the current educational reform as serving to repair and maintain the existing institution. Behavior modification, educational competencies, and standardized or criteria-referenced tests help to maintain a stable and predictable work setting, and, in turn, legitimatize the status position of professional experts.[30] Educators must begin to consider the institutional structure of schools as a system of control if community participation is to have any objective meaning.

While many government reform programs seek to establish miniature versions of federal bureaucracies, this pressure poses an irony. Indigenous leaders learn to talk and act in the manner demanded in formal organizations. But these styles of action isolate them from the rest of the community. Wax and Wax, for example, argue that the Bureau of Indian Affairs' creation of tribal councils produced bodies alien and extraneous to the traditional system of band organization.[31] These attempts to centralize authority do not fit traditional Indian patterns. The leaders are mistrusted and have no credibility except among bureaucrats.

Community participation as a viable concept should maintain a conception of critical scholarship. Part of the problem of participation is to engage in a dialogue. This conversation must proceed in a skeptical manner, a manner that considers things as possibly having meanings different from what they appear to be. A function of participation is to focus upon the myths, customs, traditions, and procedures of institutions that may produce suffering. The importance of a critical stance is illustrated in the history of decolonization. Even where the native population gained positions of leadership, shedding colonial institutions and beliefs was difficult.[32]

Finally, and most importantly, we need to be cautious that community participation does not lead to new "packaging" of ideologies that handicap the poor. In a recent university "needs" assessment of an Indian community, for example, the community identified counseling and behavior modification as important to its children's education. Examining the latent assumptions of these recommendations, we find that the clinical and therapeutic approaches which seem liberating and altruistic, in fact hide arbitrary and speculative diagnosis and convert actions into mechanisms of social control.[33] As we question further, we find that the community "needs" were, in fact, defined and articulated as the problem by local educational leaders and internalized as appropriate by community members.

NOTES

1. Murray Edelman, *The Symbolic Uses of Politics* (Chicago: University of Illinois Press, 1964).

2. Peter Bachrach, *The Theory of Democratic Elitism: A Critique* (Boston: Little, Brown & Company, 1967), p. 99.

3. In some instances in a modern society, there is a need for quick decisions by political leaders. National defense might be one example. Our concern in this paper is with institutions such as schools where centralized decision making is not a necessary criterion.

4. "Community Parity in Federally Funded Programs." A position paper presented by the Leadership and Training Institute on Recruitment, Center for the Improvement of Educational Systems, Office of Education, June 1972 (mimeograph).

5. Bachrach, *Theory of Democratic Elitism*, p. 92.

6. This issue is explored further in Thomas Popkewitz, "Myths of Social Science in Curriculum," *Educational Forum* 40 (March, 1976), pp. 317–328.

7. E. Schattschneider, *The Semi-Sovereign People: A Realist's View of Democracy in America* (New York: Holt, Rinehart and Winston, 1960).

8. D. Cohen, "The Price of Community Control," in *The*

Solution As Part of the Problem, ed. C. Greer (New York: Perennial Library, 1973), p. 53.

9. Ira Katznelson, "Urban Counterrevolution," in *1984 Revisited, Prospects for American Politics,* ed. R. Wolff (New York: W. W. Norton & Company, 1969).

10. Theodore Lowi, *The End of Liberalism: Ideology, Policy and the Crisis of Public Authority* (New York: W. W. Norton & Company, 1969).

11. Alan Altshuler, *Community Control: The Black Demand for Participation in Large American Cities* (New York: Pegasus, 1970).

12. Ibid.

13. Annie Stein, "Strategies of Failure," *Harvard Educational Review* 42 (May, 1971), pp. 158–204.

14. *Parental Involvement in Title I ESEA, Why? What? How?* Pamphlet, U.S. Department of Health, Education and Welfare, Office of Education, HE 5237: 37094, Washington, 1972, p. 1. My emphasis.

15. D. James, "The Limits of Liberal Reform," *Politics and Society* 2 (Spring, 1972), pp. 309–323.

16. Ivan Illich, "Outwitting the Developed Nations." (Mimeograph, n.d.)

17. See Isaac Balbus, "The Concept of Interest in Pluralist and Marxian Analysis," *Politics and Society,* 1 (February, 1971), pp. 151–179.

18. See Peter Berger and Thomas Luchmann, *The Social Construction of Reality: A Treatise on the Sociology of Knowledge* (Garden City, N.Y.: Anchor Books, 1967).

19. Peter Bachrach and Morton Baratz, *Power and Poverty* (New York: Oxford University Press, 1970).

20. Arthur Vidich and J. Bensman, *Small Town in a Mass Society: Class, Power and Religion in a Rural Community* (Princeton, N.J.: Princeton University Press, 1958).

21. Theodore Lowi and Robert Wolff, *The Poverty of Liberalism* (Boston: Beacon Press, 1968).

22. Teacher Corps, "Teacher Corps Guidelines Information and Guidance for Preparation and Submission of Proposals for 1971–1973 Teacher Corps Projects." Final draft, Office of Education, U.S. Department of Health, Education and Welfare, 1970.

23. G. Thomas Fox, Jr., "Who Is Being Evaluated?" *Journal of Teacher Education* (Summer, 1975), pp. 141–142.

24. Karl Mannheim, *Ideology and Utopia* (New York: Harcourt, Brace and World, 1936).

25. J. Donovan, *The Politics of Poverty* (New York: Pegasus, 1967).

26. Stephen Rose, *The Betrayal of the Poor, The Transformation of Community Action* (Urbana, Ill.: Schenkman Publishing Company, 1972).

27. Edelman, *Symbolic Uses of Politics.*

28. Thomas Popkewitz, "Reform as Political Discourse: A Case Study," *School Review* 84 (November, 1975), pp. 43–69.

29. Howard S. Becker, *Sociological Work: Method and Substance* (Chicago: Aldine Publishing Company, 1970).

30. Thomas Popkewitz and Gary Wehlage, "Accountability: Critique and Alternative Perspective," *Interchange* 4 (1973), pp. 48–62.

31. Murray Wax and Rosalie Wax, "The Enemies of the People," in *Native Americans Today: Sociological Perspectives*, eds. H. Bahr, B. Chadwick and R. Day (New York: Harper and Row, 1972), pp. 177–192.

32. For a discussion of this problem, see R. Thomas, "Colonialism: Classic and Internal," *New University Thought* 4 (Winter, 1966–1967), pp. 37–45.

33. Murray Edelman, "The Political Language of the Helping Professions," *Politics and Society* 4 (1974), pp. 295–310.

Community Education

A Means for Developing Micro-Political Processes for School Governance

Donald Tobias
Syracuse University

Donna Hager
State University College at Potsdam

The school as a political institution is a reality to a few and a frightening prospect to many. The few who most often understand the reality are those intimately involved, those in charge, and those already disenfranchised. For the rest of society, the school serves a variety of functions from babysitting to socialization, none of them necessarily political. With such divergence of views on the political factors of education, what role will schools be assigned in the future? What will be the nature of community involvement in schools?

Rather than accepting the timid, narrow, traditional approach, schools should organize communities into a series of micro-political systems to face the wide variety of issues confronting each neighborhood or community. These political systems would be linked together by structural beliefs, grass roots involvement and a commitment to the effects of cooperation and change. Such a system would be fluid, depending on high levels of communication to facilitate the restructuring of alliances as institutions and neighborhoods change. Each small unit would be strengthened by the high degree of involvement of members and the resulting personalization of the goals and values of individuals and units. This involvement would satisfy personal needs rather than organizational expectations.

The question is not if the community be involved, but rather, how? Professional educators and school boards continue to determine how best to involve community. In recent years decisions have been made during periods of rapid social fluctuation and changing educational climate. Policies that reflected limited involvement in decision making for parent groups confronted complaints about shrinking student populations and increased tax burdens for non-parents. Policies that relied on representative school boards faced changing and growing communities whose members' values were too diverse to be represented by a few board members. Social factors, political considerations, and educational change continue to challenge the validity of traditional strategies for community involvement. New issues require new definitions of community and create new pressures on decision makers.

Concurrently, some educators, including Reimer (1971), are challenging the traditional ideas of schooling and education, and the nature of their relationship. If we are to believe that education takes place outside the school, then it follows that schools need to consider what form of involvement they should have with that learning activity. Furthermore, if we accept professional educators' thoughts on the community's impact on the child, shouldn't we question the school's impact on the community? Can the school's activity in community matters facilitate improvement in school-based activities?

These questions have often been addressed by proponents of community education, but typically in the context of past relationships of school and community. The concept of community education is seldom examined in view of existing differences between educators and citizens, schools and communities. Our intention is to examine the concept of community education in light of today's society and to suggest a new basis for uniting school and community.

In this chapter we will examine the evolution of the community education concept and will discuss questions applicable to community involvement and democratic principles in relation to the concept of community education. Our assumption is that the community education concept lends itself to the establishment of activities that lead to the organization and growth of community at the neighborhood level—a micro-political process which takes advantage of local resources and commitment for problem solving. This chapter will not deal with the considerable literature on developing community education programs, but rather with the plausibility of such programs as a means to integrate school and community goals.

Changing Focus of Community Education

Community education, like many emerging concepts, is open to a variety of interpretations, but three common characteristics can serve as a definition. These characteristics are (1) concern for the individual's ability for self-determination; (2) identification of community needs and resources; and (3) development of the leadership potential of the community. Minzey and LeTarte (1970) describe the mission of community education as development of a process that encourages community members to unite in order to identify and solve problems. Any variance in defining community education comes in the application of this concept. While some researchers (Minzey, 1972) are committed to the school-based vehicle, others (Nance and Pond, 1974) have suggested different approaches. These models are often located in various institutions or departments under the broad title of local government. For example, the Tulsa Project manifests itself through the Municipal Recreation Department, and the Independence, Missouri, Project first developed through the offices of City Hall.

The early history of community education is closely linked to Frank Manley and C. S. Mott; their mutual friendship and personal beliefs created an educational philosophy that outlives both of them. Frank Manley had been associated with recreation programs long before there was a community education program in Flint, Michigan. Young and Quinn (1963) suggest that Manley's strong belief in the "social value of sound recreation" provided the impetus for the programs developed in Flint. Manley's concept of community education was program development based on needs identified by trained professionals working within neighborhood communities. Such programs usually had a self-help or socialization thrust and emphasized recreation, homemaking, or remedial skills. This brand of community education philosophy has often been viewed as a "Flint" or "Mott" export; consequently, during Manley's life, the emulation of that model highlighted those program concepts that he valued. Equally true for the community school directors who left Flint to develop other school districts, this philosophy led to the belief that community education was the development of programs both recreational and educational on school sites at times other than the traditional school day program. Weaver (1972) suggests that this led to a dichotomy between beliefs and practices of community school directors. As they administered similar programs, community school directors questioned whether these activities were responsive to the unique advantages and problems of their communities.

Community school directors were encouraged by school districts to develop activities that would be highly visible demonstrations of community enrollment. Successful programs were passed from community to community with little regard for the communities' different needs; examples include sewing programs for people without machines or materials or vocational programs with no regard for existing labor needs.

Kerensky and Melby (1970), as well as Minzey and LeTarte (1970), challenged what had been a singular philosophical approach (programming) and suggested that community education had a responsibility to deal with both program and process with vigor, if not resources. In a few years, "process" had become a popular topic and an integral part of the community education philosophy. Process came to mean leadership development in the community and the opening of decision-making channels for community influence. These activities, such as citizen-oriented groups, advising councils, task forces, and steering committees have influence but are not viewed as having community control. Traditional policy makers and supervisors will allow themselves to be influenced by the public for a variety of reasons, from self-preservation to improved choices, to covert manipulations of the public. Sugar and Nance (1974) have developed operational models that boast of a high concentration of resources on process development with little or no concern for program development.

Such models place primary emphasis on high involvement and tend to be oriented toward problem solving. This activity tends to increase involvement as diverse groups come together to plan their collective future. Additionally, opportunities for influencing decisions are increased as organizations and people interact on a humanistic level. Interestingly, these process models are receiving much attention after some thirty years of programming.

The process models may well deserve new attention as community residents become frustrated from attempting to influence educational decisions or policy without an adequate understanding of the political influences and governance issues which may block their efforts. Some institutions or organizations (such as the PTA), may teach the mechanics of the small group process, but an organization that attempts to influence the school locally is seldom aware of the web of formal and informal systems that interact to govern education.

To those writers concerned with the dichotomy between philosophy and practice in community education, this shift would indicate potential for the development of new intervention strategies. Baillie (1974) described the dichotomy between theory and practice, using Warren's learning paradigms. She stated that community school directors emphasized the development of programs to deal with specific problems, i.e. learning deficiencies. Baillie suggested that the literature on community education indicates a need for an interactional paradigm. Such a paradigm would necessitate the development of strategies for uniting a community in a synergistic manner to solve problems. Baillie's (1974) concern for development of an interaction paradigm, rather than an individual paradigm, may be satisfied, at least momentarily, if the premise of community involvement through programming is accepted. On the other hand, Baillie by-passed the program stage to achieve this end in her Bowling Green Project (1975). This project created opportunities for involvement prior to program activities through community planning and education. This may be indicative of a shift from "paternal programming" for those perceived as disadvantaged, to meaningful involvement for all members of a community along with a realization that the combined thought and power of the community can benefit its members and its organizations. This realization can help to overcome other community problems, as well as educational ones. If schools teach the means for acquisition of resources, while society controls access to the resources, then affecting either institution could cause political conflict.

The Government and School Governance

Many community educators suggest that school-based vehicles for the delivery of the community education concept are appropriate for reasons of utility, including facilities and location, as well as a sense of ownership by the community in *their* school. In reality, the parameters governing facility usage, financing, and construction of schools, often limit the flexibility in community involvement. The question is one of where the greatest influence in the development of educational policy lies—at the local level or elsewhere, with traditional systems of governance or new systems?

The shift from local to state control of education, and federal influence on educational policy, is on the increase. Campbell (1975) cites four reasons for this change:

> *current federal disposition to emphasize state-level responsibility,*
> *increasing money demands for education, insistence on the part*
> *of teacher organizations for state bargaining laws and the estab-*
> *lishment of state professional practices boards, and the emergence*
> *of statewide accountability provisions often with the active sup-*
> *port of legislators and governors.*

Iannaccone (1975) couches his view in what he describes as "Constitutional Realities." He reminds us that ours is a federal system, implying shared responsibilities and powers, but "major policy decisions are ultimately determined at the state level." School systems may raise funds, but only in those manners prescribed by the state. Even federal aid to education is affected by the state's determination of acceptance and interpretation of federal guidelines (Berke and Kirst, 1972).

> *The people have delegated the primary control of education to*
> *state legislatures and state departments of education. Local*
> *boards have been delegated certain parallel and specific powers.*
> *But, the right to educate, certify teachers, and accredit teacher*
> *training institutions rests with the state government. It is impor-*
> *tant to remember here that local school boards are also the crea-*
> *tions of the state government.*

As states reject federal funds in an attempt to restrict overhead costs, local educational agencies, with the ability to absorb ancillary costs, will be denied the opportunity to receive those funds.

While the state is the central figure in the distribution of influence, the federal role is also important. Iannaccone (1975) points out the realistic imbalance:

Federal political symbols of policy direction have an indirect but, in the long run, potent effect on the political beliefs of Americans, particularly in the areas of race and economic inequalities and in a growing awareness of the need to accept pluralism in educational services for different people. It is here, in the long-term impact on the political ideology of Americans about education for all Americans, that the political conflicts and decisions at the federal level are likely to have their greatest impact.

Iannaccone also makes the point that while except for its financial considerations, this influence is often indirect, its longitudinal effect can be most important. He gives as examples White House statements, federal court decisions, and categorical aid; these avenues often are used to articulate new directions related to social and economic inequalities, as well as a multitude of educational services which take individual needs into account.

In summary, the question of governance at state and federal levels takes on several aspects. Constitutionally the federal government makes no provision for education; hence education becomes the province of the state. Practically, the federal government sets trends and asserts an influence disproportionate to its legal obligation. Financially, the pendulum seems to swing in rapid strokes with high federal funding being followed by strong positions for state financing, while the state maintains heavy influence in the administration and distribution of federal funds, or the negation of such funds.

Influence and School Governance

Beyond the problem of government intervention extends that of the growing pressure of interest groups on policy makers. While attempts to influence decisions are common in a democracy, the danger exists that not all segments of society have an equal opportunity to exert influence. To the degree that groups can determine common goals, the system works. In his study of Northeast states, Bailey (1962) explains that those states with a successful history of financial support for education also developed informal and formal coalitions to support education. These coalitions represented a variety of special interest groups, typically including administration, teachers, and institutional parent organizations. Their success was attributable to the impressive linkage of professional resources and numbers.

Typically, these groups are organized in a union or are supported by numbers large enough to affect legislative change. The high degree of involvement through commitment or professional obligation adds to the legitimacy of any recommendations for change presented by such a group. In addition, these coalitions were based on a broad knowledge or professional background which enabled them to utilize the political structure to their vested interest. These groups would include both ends of a continuum, including lay citizen groups with no "process" skills, and professionals with a high degree of "process" skill. A local parent or community group is unlikely to be aware of "matching" financial arrangements, departmental relationships in government, procedures to help a bill reach the floor for vote, lobbying, or other facets of the political arena which administers education.

However, this state of affairs no longer exists. Campbell (1975) refers to four reasons for the change: (1) fragmentation of the educational ranks, (2) general governance procedures for education, (3) increased state jurisdiction and (4) politicizing of educational governance. He suggests that the adversary model for negotiations and the strengthening of teachers' organizations have done irreparable damage. Additionally, in the past education has enjoyed a favorable position at the state level, being administered by educators outside of the usual political entanglements. Currently a number of states have replaced the chief state school officer with a secretary of education, thus increasing the impact of the political sector. This shift also has meant that educational objectives are evaluated in the larger framework of state objectives and are in direct competition with state programs for support. The absence of coalitions as educational advocates and the emergence of political functions related to teacher organizations have created a new leadership. With numbers and finances, as well as organization, teachers exert pressure on political figures and consequently on educational policy at the state level.

The teaching profession has long maintained that teacher accountability and quality education can only be achieved when teachers gain more control over education. The Bicentennial Commission on Education for the Profession of Teaching of the

American Association of Colleges for Teacher Education appears to support this option (Howsam, et al., 1976).

> *The Commission believes that teacher self-governance will move closer to becoming a reality only when the public is convinced that an increase in teacher rights will be accompanied by greater teacher responsiveness to the needs of the clients which the profession is dedicated to serve.*

Community Education's Impact on Governance

If the voter relies on forecasts of professional groups organizing to influence education, and of governmental control moving to regional or national levels, he or she has every reason for anger. The voter could assume that professional and governmental groups have the ability to determine means and goals for education, while the responsible citizen will pay for it. However, current consumer trends, and common sense, indicate that this assumption is unrealistic, and this view is often supported by reference to the *openness* of the current system.

Community education has moved toward acceptance of responsibility for process activities, such as mechanisms for developing participatory decision making, dissemination of information, and development of community leadership, in the context of traditional governance. The local school board develops educational policy first within state and federal parameters, and secondly by reflecting community norms. Iannaccone (1975) points out that such a system functions best in one-room school houses or small rural districts with minimal variance in population values. Unfortunately, the state has often sought to standardize and economize by encouraging consolidation. While the immediate effects—increased quality and reduced costs—are rewarding, the mingling of communities through consolidation has complicated the governance structure. An example of the problems facing school boards as representative policy-making groups is Dade County, Florida. Members of the school board have constituencies larger than some United States Senators, but fewer resources to serve them.

Urban settings often present an abundance of resources

and minimal physical constraints, but community education has grown most rapidly in rural areas. When attempting to deal with the larger populations and increased diversity of cultural norms in urban areas, local school boards are more likely to fail and, thereby generate political stress. This situation is most easily dismissed by professionals with axioms like "you can't satisfy everyone." Fortunately, such statements do not always remove such stress, and a certain degree of stress may be necessary to force new strategies for dealing with changing sociological factors.

This alienation of large segments of the population and the consequent advisory role of board members suggest an unattractive future. The inability to create meaningful relations with voters will discourage many qualified candidates from seeking school board positions, at a time when most observers see the position of board member becoming more complicated in matters of finance, law, and negotiations. Further, such divisiveness will undermine confidence in boards of education as majorities perceive interest groups becoming influential in board decisions.

The local school district is influenced by state and federal politics—"macro" politics—and by the school neighborhood values—"micro" politics. The resolution of the potential stress when these areas are not congruent has been investigated by McGivney and Moynihan (1972). There is a need for identification and development of micro-political systems to deal with governance as it moves away from the local area and as it affects the ability of educational systems to be responsive to local issues.

The process model for community education presents an opportunity to develop a micro-political system. First, this model assumes that schools confront the political realities of education; education represents economic advantage, social mobility, and personal power. The distribution of and access to education, and its policies, present an opportunity to change the structure of a community.

Secondly, community education presents an opportunity to gather community members informally prior to development of a decision-making system. Early program development facilitates trust and involvement which can lead to decisions through a system that emerges from the community. This in turn facilitates the development of community leadership for and confidence in such a system.

Lastly, the relationship with a common institution, such as the schools, encourages the linkages of communities on common issues and reinstates a balance of power between those professional, governmental, and voter influence groups at the local level. It further creates an opportunity for individuals and local institutions to deal in larger circles or macro-politics.

The power of this type of organization is illustrated by Alinsky's The Back of the Yards Council which was instrumental in implementing a free Hot Lunch and Penny Milk program for school children.

After some months, officials of the Back of the Yards Council were informed that unless the Congress renewed its appropriation for the Hot Lunch project, the entire national Hot Lunch program would be terminated, including that of Back of the Yards. The Back of the Yards Council prepared to battle for its Hot Lunch project. Its officials were fully aware of the significance of the Hot Lunches for the physical welfare of the neighborhood children, but the Back of the Yards Council recognized that the only way the Back of the Yards Council could continue to have a Hot Lunch project would be for the national Hot Lunch program also to be continued. In order to fight for their own Hot Lunch project they would have to fight for every Hot Lunch project in every part of the United States. (Alinsky, 1969).

In order to accomplish this, the Council did an in-depth study of "matching" financial arrangements, departmental relationships in government, how a bill reaches the floor to vote, etc. They gathered all the facts they could on government administration, went to Washington, and impressed members of the Senate. The Council thus played a significant role in the ultimate passage of the appropriation for continuation of the Hot Lunch project. This example illustrates one way to start at the "micro" level and proceed to the "macro" level. Alinsky supports Iannaccone's opinions that educators need to be trained in politics in order to hold their own in the political arena.

The importance of institutional support cannot be minimized. Current funding and policy practices may necessitate collaboration between schools and community. Past histories of atrocities committed toward each other will make such ventures "high risk" activities. Drummond (1975) envisions the following role for state governments:

> *In our educational system decisions about schooling should be made as close as possible to the clients of the system. Most of the decisions now being made at the school district level should be either decentralized and given to the staff and faculty of the individual building and their clients or centralized and coordinated by the state department of education. In addition, it must provide the financial resources and the technical assistance that the local schools need to do their job. The state must allow and encourage the local school professional staff and their clients to create and carry out their own educational program. If this is to be done, state departments of education must play very different roles from what they have in the past, especially in the areas of curriculum and personnel development.*

Most authors seem to agree that any change must result in more responsibility at the local level with less control at the state and federal levels. Local education authorities need to be cognizant of political and social influences and power structures, both informal and formal, in order to do active battle in the political arena. The trend has been to let trained politicians control the education profession.

If community education is to develop its process goals, then political conflict is necessary. The impact of opening new lines of communication for data dissemination both in and out of the system will create a new focus of attention and discussion. Additionally, the encouragement and development of community leadership are bound to be reflected in articulate statements regarding community priorities, and thus lead to community demands for a larger role in the decision-making process.

Conclusion

The future for community education seems clear: (1) it can continue to be identified as supplementing a fixed statement of public education procedures; (2) it can align itself with teachers' organizations or the political actors, thereby creating a role in policy making and rejecting its philosophy; or (3) community education can become the vehicle for development of a community political structure to maintain local influence in decision making and to make policies more representative of the community's needs.

A system of elitism and district regulations, which serves to block or contest those points not shared by decision makers, has allowed disregard for the public's expectations of schools. These veils of protection are being pulled back by a growing number of consumer protection, advocacy, and legislative investigations. Campbell's (1975) concern about the shift in influence to teachers' organizations does not consider the potential of community in resources and numbers. Administrators may be well advised to encourage community activity, if for no other reason than to maintain a balance of power. Educators should accept the political ramifications of their profession and realize their power is with the community.

Traditional institutions may not respond favorably to alternative education, economic reform, and social reform, but if programs are responsive at the local level, political influence will protect change. The development of those thought-structures and skills by community educators may be the next step in the evolution. As Bachrach (1967) indicated:

> The crucial issue of democracy is not the composition of the elite ... for the man on the bottom it makes little difference whether the command emanates from an elite of the rich and wellborn or from an elite of workers and farmers. Instead the issue is whether democracy can diffuse power sufficiently throughout all walks of life ... a justifiable feeling that they have the power to participate in decisions which affect themselves and the common life of the community, especially the immediate community in which they work and spend most of their working hours and energy. (p. 92)

Community educators must accept the reality that education is political and that the support, as well as the knowledge, of community is required to address and solve children's needs. Community education is uniquely charged with a responsibility to link school and community and to examine this role in light of changing governance patterns. Such attitudes require a definition of community education that would include community development, community organization, needs identification, shared decision making, and the importance of the individual.

REFERENCES

Alinsky, Saul D. *Reveille for Radicals.* New York: Vintage Books, 1969, pp. 167–168.

Bachrach, P. *The Theory of Democratic Elitism.* Toronto, Canada: Little, Brown and Co., 1967.

Baillie, Susan. "Community Education and Adult Education: Prospect for the Future." Educational Policy Research Center, Syracuse University Research Corporation, Syracuse, New York, 1974.

Bailey, Stephen K. *Schoolmen and Politics.* Syracuse: Syracuse University Press, 1962.

Berke, J. S., and M. W. Kirst. *Federal Aid to Education.* Lexington, Mass.: D. C. Heath, 1972.

Campbell, Roland. "The State and the Professor." Walter D. Cocking Lecture, National Conference of Professors of Educational Administration, Montana State University, 1975.

Drummond, William H. "Role of State Department of Education." In *New Perspectives on Teacher Education,* ed. Donald J. McCarty. San Francisco: Jossey-Bass, 1973, p. 99.

Howsam, Robert B., et al. (Bicentennial Commission on Education for the Profession of Teaching of the American Association of Colleges for Teacher Education.) *Educating a Profession.* Washington, D.C.: AACTE, 1976, p. 134.

Iannaccone, L. *Politics in Education.* New York: Center for Applied Research in Education, 1967.

Iannaccone, L. "State Educational Departments: Their Role in Administering Federal Programs." *New York University Educational Quarterly,* Vol. V, No. 2, Winter, 1974.

Iannaccone, Laurence. "School Governance and Its Community Sociopolitical Environment." Unpublished paper. Teacher Corps Recruitment and Technical Resource Center, University of Nebraska, 1975.

Kerensky, V. M., and Ernest Melby. "Education II Revisited: The Social Imperative." Midland, Michigan: Pendel Publishing, 1970.

McGivney, Joseph H. and William Moynihan. "School and Community." *Teachers College Record,* December, 1972.

Minzey, Jack, and Clyde LeTarte. "Community Education:

From Program to Process." *Community Education Journal,* August, 1970.

Minzey, Jack. "Community Education: An Amalgam of Many Views." *Phi Delta Kappan,* Vol. LIV, No. 3 (November, 1972), pp. 150–153.

Minzey, Jack. "Community Education vs. Community Colleges: A Case of Role Definition." *Community Education Journal,* Vol. V, No. 1 (January/February, 1975), pp. 23–25.

Nance, Everette, and Donna Pond. "Community Education: Broad-Based Comprehensive Community Planning: The Tulsa Model," *Leisure Today,* April 1974, pp. 23–25.

Reimer, Everett. *School is Dead.* Garden City, New York: Doubleday & Co., 1971.

Sugar, Marilyn Susman, and Everette Nance. "Bridging the Gap: Community Councils and Government." *Community Education Journal,* Vol. IV, No. 3 (May/June, 1974), pp. 34–37.

Weaver, Donald. "The Emerging Model." Unpublished Paper. Western Michigan University, Kalamazoo, Michigan, 1972.

Young, Clarence, and William Quinn. *Foundations for Living.* New York: McGraw-Hill, 1963.

Progressive School–Community Alliances as a Basis for Changing School Practices

Alex Molnar
University of Wisconsin, Milwaukee

This essay attempts to explain the necessity for school-community alliances as a basis for identifying and changing educational practices that mirror the oppressive aspects of social relations in America.* It is based on three premises: (1) that curriculum is, as Macdonald contends, "the study of what should constitute, and how to make a world;" [1] (2) that school practices in contemporary America affirm existing economic, political, and cultural relationships; (3) that much of the research and writing of professional educators is not useful to those who want progressive changes made in school.†

One reason why it has been difficult to move schools in a progressive direction is the way in which educational problems have been defined. Historically the concerns of many professional educators have been separated from social issues. The analysis of teaching problems usually converges on the smallest unit of analysis. Teachers discuss individual student problems, the adequacy or inadequacy of the school principal, or a particular instructional strategy or curriculum unit as though these relationships, teaching techniques and curriculum materials are isolated from a structure of relationships that serves recognizable social interests.

Critical analysis is largely absent from the professional literature. Therefore, teachers could easily read this literature and

---

* The term "practices" here denotes all organized activities conducted in school and the planning for those activities. This essay will focus on school curriculum and those practices over which teachers have direct control.

† The term progressive is used here as used by leftist groups to identify those people allied in the struggle for human liberation. It can therefore also be applied to those actions which combat oppression.

not understand the genesis of the teaching problems discussed. Proposed solutions are generally not solutions at all. Teachers are encouraged to invest energy in this or that teaching technique or curricular innovation in the hope that "this one will be the answer." As a consequence of this fragmented, non-relational approach to the problems of classroom practice, education is often conceived, both popularly and professionally, as an idealistic enterprise. In describing his experience as a university professor struggling to engage with his students in the critical analysis of literary works, Brent Harold explains his most difficult problems emerged from the students' idealism. He writes:

> *By idealism I mean the tendency to experience ideas as abstracted from the concrete, social experiences of the people holding them, as well as to abstract the people themselves from their actual classroom and other social situations.*[2]

Not only does most eductional writing reflect an idealist bias in what it *proposes,* it also reflects an idealist bias in what it *opposes.* When a given strategy or set of curriculum materials fails to produce the desired results, critics both in and out of the education establishment stand ready to blame the "mindlessness" of individual teachers, rather than to look for a structural explanation for the repeated failure of educational innovation.

Stating teaching problems in idealistic and therefore static terms transforms their solutions into commodities which can be packaged and sold. Take, for example, the problems of motivation and discipline. Teachers flock to workshops and lectures, buy books and read countless articles designed to help them "motivate" students, or at least control them. It is as if motivation and discipline are glands, and the teacher's job is to diagnose the exact hormonal imbalance of individual students, administer the proper dosage of Teacher Effectiveness Training, Affective Education, or Reality Therapy, and thereby bring the student back to normality. Aside from conveying a view of "normal" that may serve to keep people rigidly in place, this format makes it difficult to analyze motivation and discipline as functions of people in relation to the world and themselves. It asks us to grasp at solutions before we genuinely recognize the problem.

Recently, critical theorists have begun to describe the structural relationship between school practices and American political and economic organization. These writers generally discuss the problems of schooling through an analysis of the interests our educational institutions serve, and how they are structured to serve those interests.[3] Their analysis is relational, not static, and I find it compelling. What these theorists have yet to do, however, is describe the meaning of their analysis at the level of classroom practice. Take again, for example, the problem of motivation. Wide-spread lack of motivation among high school students can be described as a symptom of the almost complete lack of meaningful work for high school students upon graduation. As such, apathy can be seen as a coping mechanism with its roots in social organization rather than individual malfunction. Accepting this view, one could argue that teachers can do all those things they have always done, with perhaps even more skill, and many students will still remain unmotivated in school. And further, that teachers will never motivate students by focusing on only one dimension of the problem, student behavior, rather than on the larger question of why more highly trained teachers seemingly produce less adequate results.

It is not enough, however, to say that school problems relate to the structure and function of our society. Nor is it enough to hypothesize this connection, e.g., apathy among high school students as a function of high unemployment. If our analysis stops at that level, teachers are likely to throw up their hands and say that they can do nothing about unemployment, but at least they can make their lessons more interesting.

Our work, as teachers and people who work with teachers, is twofold. First, we must continually strive to better learn how to recognize the relationship that classroom practices have to social organization. In this area, Rist's work is particularly useful. He has documented with chilling clarity the extent to which class bias was reflected in the day in, day out teaching routine of primary school teachers in one ghetto school.[4] He describes in detail the differential treatment given to students according to teachers' perceptions of their class and how this differential treatment resulted in a rigid caste system within the school, with school rewards and punishment distributed accordingly. His conclusion is:

It should be apparent, of course, that if one desires this society to retain its present social class configuration and the disproportional access to wealth, power, social and economic mobility, medical care, and choice of life styles, one should not disturb the methods of education as presented in this study. This contention is made because what develops a "caste" within the classrooms appears to emerge in the larger society as "class." The low income children segregated as a caste of "unclean and intellectually inferior" persons may very well be those who in their adult years become the car washers, dishwashers, welfare recipients, and participants in numerous other un- or underemployed roles within this society . . . It appears that the public school system not only mirrors the configurations of the larger society, but also significantly contributes to maintaining them.[5]

Second, we must use our analysis to develop alternative teaching techniques and curriculum materials. In this task, we must keep in mind the distinction between what Freire calls "systematic education" and "educational projects." In *Pedagogy of the Oppressed,* he writes:

. . . how then is it possible to carry out the pedagogy of the oppressed prior to the revolution? This is a question of the greatest importance . . . One aspect of the reply is to be found in the distinction between systematic education, *which can only be changed by political power, and* educational projects, *which should be carried out* with *the oppressed in the process of organizing them.[6]*

One way for a teacher to identify potential educational projects for his or her classroom or school is to check for a phenomenon I call convergence. After years of being in and out of classrooms, I have noticed that children in kindergarten ask many more unsolicited questions, and questions for which an adult is not likely to have a pat answer, than, say, fourth graders. Fourth graders ask more such questions than junior high school students, and this pattern of questioning continues through graduate studies at the university level. There are individual exceptions, but the generalization seems true enough and is easy to recognize. Schools and classrooms should be examined for convergence because it is a phenomenon which, I believe, illustrates that the process of schooling in America teaches the vast majority of our children: (1) that answers are more important than questions; (2) that all answers given in school represent not just the legitimate but also an unchanging and unchangeable truth and (3) that truth is given by a higher authority, not created out of social practice. Neither our children nor ourselves are likely to learn what should constitute or how to make a world if we cannot question the circumstances of our existence. Therefore, if children ask fewer questions that do not have yes/no answers as they move through the grades at your school, or if they ask fewer such questions at the end of a year in your classroom than at the beginning, it is important to ask yourself why. Your answers are likely to lead to other questions which will help illustrate problems in your practice, reference those problems within a larger social context, and hopefully provide a basis for developing educational projects that unite you with progressive members of your community.

Educators have often found it difficult to make alliances with community people. As a profession, we have told people that our job is to teach, as though education best occurs in a vacuum. In describing the attitudes of the faculty at a university serving working-class students, McDermott comments that the faculty:

> ... did not feel called upon to know the specific cultural history and experience of the students they taught. Neither they nor anyone in their academic profession consider it their task to use their own superior symbolic gifts and wider historical perspective to identify the specific historical culture of their students, to clarify its ambiguities, to criticize it, purging it of its moral (not geographical) provincialism, and thus assist the students to develop a culture which is at once personally ennobling and politically self-conscious.[7]

McDermott's comments concern university professors but characterize the entire profession. Our elementary, middle, and high schools are filled with teachers who have been taught, and who believe, that their job is to give their superior wisdom to the masses and who see no reason to link what goes on in their schools to students' lives outside of school. School-community linkages are necessary and must be used as the basis for conducting, with students and community people, a critical analysis of the circumstances of their lives. In the context of such an analysis, reading, mathematics, science, and history can become powerful and liberating tools, whose importance is self-evident. Without such an analysis the curriculum of our schools amounts to cultural warfare, not only against many minority children but against poor and middle-class white ethnic groups as well. An article on education in coal mining regions published in the *United Mine Workers Journal* reports:

> *The schools claimed to teach about the principles of democracy, using books which were filled with the names of all the governors and senators in the state's history, but didn't see fit to use as an example the miners' long fight for democracy in their own union and coal field communities.*

> *Basford has picked up a few stories about the union outside of school from relatives and people in the community, but basically this high school graduate says he came to his new position as a coal miner, union member, and adult citizen of a coal community with almost no understanding of the union and industry which are so important in his life.*[8]

The school curriculum in many coal mining communities apparently does not overtly attack the culture of the coal mining regions—it simply ignores it. The curriculum thus becomes something to be learned "for its own sake." Under these circumstances, the biggest problems teachers face become how to motivate children who see no value in what they are asked to do, and how to control them when they refuse to do it. Schooling in this manner helps alienate the young from their cultural heritage and establishes the school as an alien presence in the community. All of this has political significance, because people whose past has been taken from them and whose present has been mystified cannot construct an adequate vision of the future. Recognition of the manifestations of injustice and oppression is necessary in the struggle to create and maintain freedom. Curriculum that retards such recognition is politically reactionary and serves only the dominant culture.

If it is to be part of the community, the school has the responsibility to make cultural criticism the basis of its curriculum and its instructional program. Within schools, teachers can begin to ask themselves and to design activities which help students to ask such questions as: What elements of our national

246

culture serve the interests of my community or the interests of people like me? If my interests are served, what is the effect on other people? What social institutions touch my life every day? Whose interests do they serve? How can those institutions be influenced? Such probing goes well beyond the scope and purpose of such classic "community involvement" strategies as bringing in "neighborhood helpers" to talk to primary school children or sponsoring anti-litter campaigns in junior high or high school. The purpose is different. Such questions are designed to illuminate the real world and to allow children to draw conclusions in a democratic and scientific fashion, rather than present a static conception of the world where good and bad are clearly identified, labeled, and contained within carefully prescribed boundaries. A useful handbook for teachers who want their students to explore and question the world around them and the social relationships of that world, as evidenced in their community, is W. Ron Jones's *Finding Community*.[9] Although the content is now somewhat dated, Jones provides a handy format for students to actively participate in the examination of their communities.

Any proposal requires interested, talented, and dedicated people to carry it forward. However, to rely solely on individuals, struggling alone to foster change, is a bankrupt strategy. On the other extreme, to rely on changes mandated from some higher source of authority reveals an elitist's lack of faith in the peoples' ability to act in their own interests and to recognize those interests. For educators that implies that the best place to work for progressive goals is in individual schools. I agree with Goodlad that:

> *The single school is the largest and the proper unit for educational change. The single teacher is too small a unit to be a focus for significant change. Cultivation of teachers' necessary knowledge, skills and attitudes is no assurance that the culture of the school will support their use. The school system is too large a unit and it is structurally not organic. What is good for its maintenance frequently is a destructive pollutant for the school.*[10]

If students can critically examine society as they experience it, so too, teachers, students, and community members can examine school practices. This examination will require abandonment of the siege mentality which is exhibited by many school people. If school practices do, in fact, best serve the progressive interests of the school community and its children, they will be strengthened by criticism and inquiry. If they do not reflect those interests, teachers should become the allies of community members and students who seek to change them.

An examination of school practices provides many possibilities for curriculum development, if teachers learn to use those possibilities. To do so, however, we must move away from reliance on packaged curriculum materials developed by outsiders. Too often, to walk into one elementary school is to walk into every elementary school. Educational corporations, large and small, peddle their wares regionally and nationally—mainly old stuff in new packages. Any variance in school curriculum is frequently limited to a narrow range of technical modifications within a standard format. We are asked to believe such modifications are significant in much the same way Burger King would like us to believe that "having it our way" somehow makes their product significantly different from that offered by McDonald's who "do it all" for us.

Despite their slick attractiveness, many of these materials have the cumulative effect of mystifying the world the children experience and erecting a barrier between the school and community members. Molnar and Roy have illustrated how elementary teachers could, given the desire, involve children and parents in curriculum using readily available, inexpensive materials.[11] Skills can be taught, knowledge acquired, and understanding deepened when teachers, children, and parents work together on the school curriculum. Curricular content is then far more likely to be rooted in the genuine experiences of the children in the community than when it is fabricated in some curriculum factory across the continent.

Educators are open to the same criticism that Victor Papanek levels at industrial designers in *Design for the Real World*. He attacks industrial designers for not designing products that people need, products that are straight-forward, useful, and uncomplicated. In his preface, Papanek proposes that one thing industrial designers could do for humankind would be to stop working entirely. However, he goes on to say:

It seems to me that we can go beyond not working at all, and work positively. Design can and must become a way in which young people can participate in changing society.[12]

If we carry this analysis forward into the schools and their curricula, we see that curriculum can not only help students identify the nature of the social relationships in their communities, but can also help provide them with the necessary tools to transform those relationships, if they so choose.

The catch-all criticism leveled at proposed changes in the nature and content of school curriculum is that change probably represents some value position and that schools and their curricula must remain value neutral. However, schools and their curricula are not, nor are they ever likely to be, value-free. Contemporary analyses of curriculum materials used to teach such basic and supposedly neutral subjects as reading and math have found evidence of pervasive racism and sexism. Even if a purge of all curriculum materials for racist and sexist content were possible, schools would remain under intense pressure to reflect the interests of the dominant culture.

In *Cultural Action for Freedom*, Freire discusses two lessons presented in a reading book used in South America to teach illiterate adults to read. The book:

> ... *presents among its lessons the following two texts on consecutive pages without relating them. The first is about May 1st, the Labor Day holiday, on which workers commemorate their struggles. It does not say how or where these are commemorated, or what the nature of the historical conflict was. The main theme of the second lesson is holidays. It says that on these days people ought to go to the beach to swim and sunbathe.... Therefore, if May 1st is a holiday, and if on holidays people should go to the beach, the conclusion is that the workers should go swimming on Labor Day, instead of meeting with their unions in the public squares to discuss their problems.*[13]

It is not possible to apply Freire's experiences in South America directly to schools in the United States. However, the point he makes here is valuable because it illustrates how the seemingly neutral content used to teach people to read can convey a powerful, though implicit, political message: a message that strengthens the status quo. Though many of us are now more alert to racist and sexist messages in curriculum materials, we must move beyond that to examine the curriculum for cultural content as well. We must analyze the content of readers, word problems in math books, social studies units, and so forth, and ask ourselves what vision of the world they convey and whose interests that vision serves. We must learn how to work with progressive community people in conducting our analysis. The argument over professional control versus community participation in curriculum decisions serves the interests of the dominant culture because it establishes a false and unproductive conflict. The conflict appears to be between professional expertise (which is claimed to be "objective" and value-free) and the non-objective, value-laden interests of community members. Fundamentally, however, the conflict is between the interests of those who want social relationships to remain as they are and those who would see them altered. The curriculum is the battleground but not the issue.

In such battles, the interests of the status quo will always win if the problem or issue is not posed correctly and if the school and community stand apart from one another. If schools are to have a transformational role in society, progressive forces in their communities must unite. For teachers who are interested in seeing schools play such a role, the place to work is not among the privileged; it is among those who are not being served well by the system—and that does not rule out many places. The list of potential schools would include schools in white- and blue-collar bedroom communities, as well as schools in the inner city. Examining the social relationships in those communities will more likely than not reveal to teachers, students, and community members bases for alliances across racial and class lines which could be part of a larger process of social transformation. A forum that can be responsive to teachers is in professional groups. The inclusion of parents and students in professional activities, as well as the formation of political caucuses within professional organizations, cannot only help identify allies, but also magnify strength.

Practical-minded teachers will fairly ask, but what do I do differently tomorrow? The honest answer is that curriculum materials and instructional strategies do not emerge from theory alone. They are bounded by our intentions, but they can only emerge from our practice. As teachers attempt to translate some of the ideas in this essay into practice in their classrooms, ideas for activities will occur and the ideas presented here will be criticized, modified, and further developed, allowing for the creation of additional activities.

To proceed in the manner I have described, each of us as teachers needs to understand the nature of our commitments, both strategically and tactically. Each of us must continually assess situations to understand what action we can take. Too many of us have, in the past, been willing to put the responsibility for change outside of our own practice. We *can* take action; and though the actions we take may be small, if they are principled, they can help build a basis for larger changes. Each of us must understand why we are taking a particular action and whether or not we are willing to make the personal commitment the action calls for. If we can state our reasons for a particular action or series of actions in terms of the positive things we are working toward, rather than that which we oppose, we will be more likely to understand our personal commitments and will find a basis for unity with more people.

Along with the need to understand ourselves within our practice, we must find ways in which we can help each other—concrete things we can do together. Students and progressive community people are natural allies; we must struggle to make connections with them. Once we break out of our professional isolation, the human and material resources available to us will increase.

Finally, we cannot view our struggle as a struggle for a single final victory which will set good over evil for all time. That is a romantic and idealistic stance that has resulted in having too many good people engaged in struggles that lead nowhere, burning out, and becoming cynical. Our struggle should strengthen, not weaken us. We must work on changes in such a way that one change will cause a confrontation with something else that should be changed. A seemingly dramatic victory will result in nothing, if we stop our forward motion and tell ourselves we have "won."

It is difficult to write anything hopeful about changing education in America. It is difficult to think about changing American society and be hopeful. But we must do what needs to be done. The roots of our schools' problems are buried deeply within our culture, and we must never lose sight of that un-alterable fact. We must learn better the connections between what we do in schools and what must be done in society. Changing the schools will not in itself change society, but schools can become laboratories in which students and community people learn what changes can be made and how to make them. As Marcuse has said, "The joy of freedom and the need to be free must precede libera-tion." [14] At first our steps will be small, but if they are progressive, these steps can be significant.

NOTES

1. James B. Macdonald, "Value Based Curriculum." Paper presented at the Milwaukee Curriculum Theory Conference, November 1976.

2. Brent Harold, "Beyond Student-Centered Teaching: The Dialectical Materialist Form of a Literature Course," *College English*, Vol. 34, No. 2, November 1972, p. 201.

3. See for example: Stephan Michelson, "The Further Responsibility of Intellectuals," *Perspectives on Inequality*, Harvard Educational Review, Reprint Series No. 6, 1973; Michael Apple and Nancy King, "What Do Schools Teach?" Unpublished paper; John Mann, "On Contradictions in Schools," in James B. Macdonald and Esther Zaret, eds., *Schools in Search of Meaning*, Yearbook of The Association for Supervision and Curriculum Development, 1975; Herb Gintis, "Towards a Political Economy of Education: A Radical Critique of Ivan Illich's *Deschooling Society*," in *Education, Participation and Power*, Harvard Educational Review, Reprint Series No. 10, 1976.

4. Ray C. Rist, "Student Social Class and Teacher Expectations: The Self-Fulfilling Prophecy in Ghetto Education," in *Challenging the Myths: the Schools, the Blacks, and the Poor*, Harvard Educational Review, Reprint Series No. 5, 1975.

5. Ibid., pp. 107–108.

6. Paulo Freire, *Pedagogy of the Oppressed* (New York: The Seabury Press, 1974), pp. 39–40.

7. John McDermott, "The Laying On of Culture," *The Nation*, March 10, 1969.

8. Matt Witt, "Coal Field Education: Do Our Children Learn Their Labor Heritage in School?" *United Mine Workers Journal*, March 16–31, 1975.

9. W. Ron Jones, *Finding Community* (Palo Alto, Calif.: James E. Freel and Associates, 1971).

10. John I. Goodlad, "Schools Can Make a Difference," *Educational Leadership,* November 1975.

11. Alex Molnar and Will Roy, *The Shoebox Curriculum: Practical Ideas for Active Learning* (Encino, Calif.: International Center for Educational Development, 1975).

12. Victor Papanek, *Design For the Real World* (New York: Pantheon Books, 1971).

13. Paulo Freire, *Cultural Action for Freedom* (Cambridge, Mass.: Center for the Study of Development and Social Change, 1970), p. 9.

14. Herbert Marcuse, *Essay on Liberation* (Boston: Beacon Press, 1969).

Subject Index

Reverse discrimination, 169

Schools:
  dissatisfaction of poor and minorities with, 26
  functions of, 126, 177–178, 180–181, 181–185, 225
  historical perspective of, 5–12, 68–69
  middle-class involvement in, 67, 126, 151
  mission of, 93, 183, 193
  outcomes of, 207
  as political institutions, 225
  role of, 180, 246, 250
Schools without walls, 90
Staff selection. *See* Personnel

Teacher Corps, 213, 214. *See also* Partnership approach
Teacher educators, responsibilities of, 106–108, 111, 243–245
Teachers:
  role in curriculum, 90–91, 250–251
  role in change, 70–71, 251–252
  responsibilities of, 243–245
  self-governance of, 233

United Federation of Teachers. *See* Ocean Hill-Brownsville
United States v. *Kagama*, 139–140

War on Poverty, 23, 153, 214, 215
White flight, 165

Author Index